PETE ELLIS

PUBLISHED WITH THE MARINE CORPS HERITAGE ASSOCIATION

PETE ELLIS

An Amphibious
Warfare Prophet, 1880-1923

DIRK ANTHONY BALLENDORF AND
MERRILL LEWIS BARTLETT

Naval Institute Press
Annapolis, Maryland

Naval Institute Press
291 Wood Road
Annapolis, MD 21402

First Naval Institute Press Leatherneck Classics edition published 2010
ISBN-13: 978-1-59114-026-9

Library of Congress Cataloging-in-Publication Data

Ballendorf, Dirk Anthony, 1939–
    Pete Ellis: an amphibious warfare prophet, 1880-1923 / Dirk Anthony
Ballendorf and Merrill Lewis Bartlett.
        p.   cm.
    Includes bibliographical references and index.
    ISBN 1-55750-060-6 (acid free)
    1. Ellis, Earl H., d. 1923. 2. United States. Marine Corps—Biography.
    3. Amphibious warfare. I. Bartlett, Merrill L. II. Title.
    VE25.E4B35   1997
    359.9'6'092—dc21
    [B]   96-43522

Printed in the United States of America on acid-free paper

17 16 15 14 13 12 11 10   9 8 7 6 5 4 3 2
First printing

To Lieutenant Colonel John J. Reber, 1916–1991
Because he never gave up the search for the mercurial Pete Ellis

∾ Contents

～ Foreword

Earl H. "Pete" Ellis could have lived in no time but his own, in no place but the United States, and served in no military organization except the Marine Corps. Pete Ellis represented the quintessence of the spirit of the American Century: a love of adventure, patriotism, and a firm belief that diligence reaps rewards. He entered the smaller of the naval services at a time when either better-educated young men or those with political connections appeared to be garnering commissions and promotion. On his own merits, Ellis progressed through the ranks, all the while attracting the support of senior officers who championed his career. He needed a niche of his own, however, and after a decade found it.

By the turn of the century, the Marine Corps appeared increasingly as an anachronism remaining from the Age of Sail. Senior Navy officers, although supportive of Marines when it appeared as if it required a wall of leatherneck bayonets to keep a motley enlisted force of sailors in check, thought the requirement no longer necessary. Most Marines took umbrage with arguments to remove them from the ships of the fleet, and bridled at suggestions that the service required a massive overhaul and a strong infusion of intellectual substance. But farsighted officers realized that either changes must be made, or the small armed force would wither into extinction. Ellis accepted his commission at a seemingly propitious moment.

After a decade of routine assignments, Ellis appeared to have found his destiny. A chance assignment to the Naval War College exposed him to the intellectual currents sweeping the Navy. Naval theorists recognized the requirement for advance bases in support of the fleet, and argued that the Marine Corps defend them. Ellis emerged as the most articulate spokesman for the idea following the first test of the concept at Culebra in 1913–1914 and after studying the role of an advanced base force in the defense of Guam a few months later. The mission seemed ideal for the Marine Corps as it sought to establish permanence within the Department of the Navy. World War I provided only a brief and glorious interlude in the evolution of the concept, but one which provided important succor for the next generation. Ellis played an important part in the deployment of the Marines to France as the adjutant of the 4th Brigade (Marine), AEF; during this era, the officer holding this position functioned as a combination S1 (personnel), S2 (intelligence), and S3 (operations) officer as well as the most important confidant of the brigade commander. Ellis held this consequential position through three of the brigade's five wartime campaigns: St. Mihiel, Mont Blanc, and Meuse Argonne.

Following the armistice and his return home, Ellis became an influential member of the coterie of intellectual and farsighted officers that surrounded the new Commandant of the Marine Corps. Maj. Gen. John A. Lejeune realized the fragility of the Marine Corps in the face of postwar retrenchment. The potential of a naval war in the Pacific and a simmering estrangement with the Empire of Japan meshed nicely with new-found beliefs that the leathernecks constitute the amphibious assault force of the fleet.

From his own perspective, Ellis likely concluded that his failure to command a battalion of infantry in the war meant that his career had stalled. Beginning in 1920, he began studies of the potential for amphibious operations in the event of another war. What followed has made him legend to a generation of Marines and students of military history.

This biography answers the nagging questions that have lingered for more than half a century. Believers in the inherent duplicity of the Japanese should now be willing to discard the notion that the *Kempeitai* poisoned the troublesome Marine. But almost unasked, and certainly never answered, is the complicity of officials beyond Ellis's Marine Corps chain of command. In the following pages, the authors portray a Department of the Navy increasingly worried over certain provisions of the Washington Naval Arms Limitation Treaties. At the same time, this biography of Ellis depicts the Marine Corps of the first two decades of this century through the career and life of a junior naval officer. Set against the panorama of new U.S. imperialism and emergence as a world power, Ellis and his peers appeared as archetypical harbingers of the emerging American character. The initiatives and imperatives of interservice and intraservice politics played no small part as Ellis's Marine Corps transversed an uneasy passage from duties as shipboard policemen to defenders of advance bases, and finally as the spearhead of an amphibious assault force in support of the fleet. The professionalism and intellectual foresight of the senior leadership of Ellis's era waxed and waned at times and often appeared beset with a variety of irksome problems involving alcohol abuse, interfering political influences, lapses in professional conduct, and predilection toward careerism on the part of its officers. This biography lays bare these infelicities without apology.

It gives a venerable professor no small amount of pleasure to witness the superb scholarship of two of his students. Merrill Bartlett earned his M.A. under my supervision in 1971–1974 and Dirk

Anthony Ballendorf spent a summer with me at the Japanese Studies Institute in 1995. Together, they have combined forces through a thorough mining of archival materials and a relentless series of oral histories to answer the nagging questions surrounding one of the Marine Corps's most enigmatic characters.

Alvin D. Coox
Director, Japanese Studies Institute
San Diego State University

∼ Acknowledgments

The authors' interest in the mercurial Pete Ellis took divergent paths. Dirk A. Ballendorf first became interested in the elusive and mysterious Ellis in 1966 when he was assigned as director of the Peace Corps in Palau. At that time, many of the eye witnesses in the Ellis adventure were still alive, and Ballendorf managed to interview and photograph all of them. He took on the investigation of the Ellis mystery as a hobby. While traveling through the islands from the Western Carolines all the way to the far-flung Marshalls, Ballendorf conducted oral histories with all of the Micronesian principals in the case.

For his part in the quest for answers to the Ellis enigma, Merrill L. Bartlett followed up leads uncovered during earlier researches into George Barnett, John A. Lejeune, Wendell C. Neville, and Ben H. Fuller. Studies of the turn-of-the-century Marine Corps through the World War I era fairly bristled with clues germane to Ellis. The placement of one of the Marine Corps's most puzzling characters into the life and times of that era stimulated Bartlett's detective-as-historian nature. Inconsistencies in printed materials, hagiographic accounts that faithfully repeated one another, and conflicting statements in a variety of personal and professional correspondence became the grist for his mill.

The authors owe a debt to those who knew Pete Ellis and his contemporaries and who consented to oral histories. These gracious folks, most of whom are now dead, are cited in the end notes. Dorothy Ellis Gatz welcomed Dirk Ballendorf into her home on two occasions, and shared many of her brother's mementos, uniforms, decorations, artifacts, and photographs. Tom Butler likewise welcomed Merrill Bartlett into the Butler family home, and allowed research into the private correspondence of his father, Smedley D. Butler. The late Lelia Gordon Lucas spent the better part of a day enchanting Bartlett with vignettes about her mother, Lelia Montague Barnett, the colorful and vivacious socialite wife of Maj. Gen. Commandant George Barnett.

At the various repositories cited in the bibliography, archivists and librarians alike assisted in the unraveling of the elusive Pete Ellis. Brig. Gen. Edwin H. Simmons, then the director, Marine Corps History and Museums, offered the full resources of his staff. Evelyn A. Englander located out-of-print volumes for the authors. First Benis M. Frank and then Richard A. Long provided transcripts of oral histories; Amy J. Cantin located numerous collections of personal papers; and Danny J. Crawford and Robert V. Aquilino of the reference section identified a variety of written materials to assist in the chase. Nearby, the staff of the Naval Historical Center contributed to this biography with materials on Ellis's contemporaries, and on witnesses to his mission to Micronesia.

Support for this historical effort ranged from grants provided to Merrill Bartlett from the Naval Academy Research Council while he served on the faculty in Annapolis, to stipends from the Marine Corps Historical Foundation for tangential efforts. At the National

Archives and Records Administration, Timothy K. Nenninger assisted immeasurably in the identification and location of elusive documents; he deserves special mention for finding the long-missing officer fitness reports of the Marine Corps of Pete Ellis's era.

The patience and professionalism of our publisher, the Naval Institute Press, have kept this project on task. Both Mark Gatlin and Paul Wilderson encouraged our work, and predicted that it could make a contribution to naval literature. First Mary Lou Kenney, and then J. Randall Baldini supervised the production effort while Matt Brook performed the chores incumbent to seeing the manuscript appear both scholarly and attractive. Jonathan Lawrence edited our work painstakingly and painlessly (for the authors, at least). If our work becomes a run-a-way bestseller, then it is the result of yeoman efforts by Susan Artigiani, publicity/copy manager.

Finally, Francesca Remengesau Ballendorf and Blythe Wright Bartlett endured far too much distraction from their husbands as they sought the capricious Ellis and the somewhat-quaint Marine Corps of that era. Their forbearance cannot be taken lightly. From the outset, however, it was the late John J. Reber who sparked a renewed interest in unraveling the mysteries surrounding the Marine Corps's most enigmatic character; to his memory, this monograph is dedicated. Semper Fidelis!

Dirk A. Ballendorf
Guam

Merrill L. Bartlett
Vashon Island, Washington

PETE ELLIS

∼ Introduction

Early on the morning of 21 May 1923, the cipher clerk on duty at the U.S. State Department in Washington read a message from the American embassy in Tokyo. On the surface, at least, it appeared to be nothing more than a routine report of the death of a U.S. citizen:

> Informed by Governor General of Japanese South Sea Islands that
> E. H. Ellis, representative of Hughes Trading Company, no. 2
> Rector St., New York City, holder of Department passport no.
> 4249, died at Palau, Caroline Islands on May 12th. Remains and
> effects in possession of government awaiting instructions.

Unconcerned, the official merely routed the cablegram to its office in New York City. The following Monday, the State Department representative in Manhattan called at the Hughes Trading Company. Its owner and director, John A. Hughes, appeared uneasy upon learning of Ellis's death. Pressed for further information about why his employee had been in the Central Pacific, in an area routinely denied to Western visitors by Japanese authorities, Hughes startled his visitor by blurting out that Ellis had never been his employee. Ellis was in fact an active-duty Marine Corps officer, and, most ominously, his association with the Hughes Trading Company had been merely a subterfuge furnished at the request of the Marine Corps to provide a cover for an intelligence-gathering mission.[1]

When the astonishing revelation disclosed in New York City appeared in a telegraphic report back to the State Department, officials remained confused and nonplussed. The widely scattered, tiny islands in the Western Pacific—the Carolines, Marshalls, and Northern Marianas—had been taken from Germany by the Japanese Imperial Navy in three weeks during October 1914. These islands—except for Guam, which had been an American territory since the Spanish-American War—were ceded to Japan following World War I according to the terms of the Treaty of Versailles. The Americans, however, insisted that Japan administer these Micronesian islands under the terms of the League of Nations's mandates system. This Japan did willingly, while also taking steps to isolate its newly obtained possessions.

Foreign ships were allowed passage through the islands but were only allowed to make port at Yap. Westerners applying for passage at the offices of the Nippon Yusen Kaisha Line were usually dissuaded with exaggerated tales of an arduous journey and the lack of suitable accommodations in the region. Thus the Japanese restrictions over the islands fueled Western speculation that Tokyo had begun to fortify these holdings. Few Americans had visited the region, and they for the most part consisted of missionaries, disenfranchised sailors, and sociopolitical dropouts. Officials at the State Department, however, were not the only people expressing concern about the mercurial Ellis.

Not too far from the State Department, Betty Allen Rogers arrived at the "Book and Gown" on 17th Street, N.W., punctually at 9 A.M. Scooping up the morning's mail from inside the door, she searched anxiously for a letter in Ellis's familiar handwriting. But as with each fretful day stretching back to the previous summer, today there was nothing. She was disappointed again. The estranged wife of another Marine Corps officer, Betty Allen Rogers had grown fond of the morose Ellis since his assignment in Washington. She and Ellis had developed a romantic attachment that dated to his posting to Head-quarters Marine Corps (HQMC) near the end of 1920. Ellis had taken her to dinner and the Knickerbocker Theater one last time, and he told her of an important mission to the Pacific. Ellis planned to stop briefly for a visit with his family in Kansas and then obtain steamship passage in San Francisco. Betty Allen Rogers never saw Pete Ellis again.[2]

By the next morning, an inquiry from the State Department—attached to the cablegram from Tokyo and a report of the unsettling disclosure obtained in New York City—had made its way to the offices of the Navy Department in the Bond Building on Constitution Avenue. The Director of Naval Intelligence, Capt. Luke McNamee, shared the puzzlement expressed by officials at the State Department. Naval intelligence-gathering activities were the exclusive preserve of the Navy, and the Marine Corps had never played any role in such efforts. Even if this was a new effort on the part of HQMC to expand leatherneck activities, McNamee's office would surely have known of it. Claiming to be perplexed, he sent the report on to the Comman-dant of the Marine Corps.

Despite the early-spring drizzle, Maj. Gen. John A. Lejeune had begun his day in the usual fashion. Promptly at 7 A.M., his aides-de-camp met him at the traditional home of the Commandants, "Eighth and Eye," in southeast Washington with fresh horses saddled and ready for a jaunt to Haines Point before reporting to work. As he settled into his desk chair after the brisk exercise, Lejeune found the original Ellis file on top of the documents in his "incoming" tray; by now, however, it had become several inches thick with addenda and inquiries as it passed from desk to desk throughout Washington.

Supposedly, Ellis had left Lejeune with a near-perfect explanation should his mission go awry. But Lejeune chose to burn Ellis's undated letter of resignation rather than betray a professional friendship that had lasted for almost two decades. He remained silent for as long as possible. As the shrill crescendos of the newspapers increased in volume, Adm. Robert E. Coontz, Chief of Naval Operations, and Edwin H. Denby, Secretary of the Navy, urged him to release a statement to the media. Lejeune issued only a single press release on Ellis and his ill-fated mission, one that created more questions than it answered: "Ellis was absent without leave. He had been a patient in the naval hospital in Yokohama, Japan, suffering from a kidney ailment, and was last seen on 6 October 1923. He was on leave touring the Orient. That leave had been revoked before Ellis vanished from the hospital."[3]

That terse, cold statement was clearly intended to protect the Marine Corps and the Department of the Navy. Lejeune had known Ellis since they served together in the Philippines in 1908 and 1909. When Lejeune became the assistant to the Commandant in 1914, he detailed Ellis to his personal staff as part of an embryo war-planning unit. Then, when Lejeune received orders to France in May 1918, Ellis accompanied him. For the remainder of the war, Ellis served on the western front: first, in the important post as adjutant of the 4th Brigade (Marine), American Expeditionary Forces; then, after the cease-fire, as executive officer of the 5th Marines, one of the infantry regiments in the leatherneck brigade. A persistent myth surrounded Ellis, suggesting that he was the "brains" behind the brigade and, indeed, had even devised the daring operation order for the entire 2nd Division in its successful assault on Blanc Mont.

A dark side of Ellis's character emerged, however—that of his heavy drinking. An acquaintance reported Ellis ending a rather boring dinner with the post chaplain during a tour in the Philippines by shooting the dishes off the table with his service revolver. But his superiors chose to overlook this flaw in his personal and professional character, and no one mentioned it in Ellis's fitness reports. On the eve of the assault to seize Blanc Mont during the war, Lejeune report-edly muttered—upon being told that "Colonel Ellis was indisposed" —that "Ellis drunk is better than anyone else around here sober."[4]

The furtive Ellis and the equally circumspect Lejeune left few clues in the wake of the surreptitious spy mission. Nothing in writing sent Ellis to Micronesia, only his oral request to investigate the area firsthand after spending a year pondering the possibilities of major amphibious operations in the region in the event of war with Japan. But when the Navy allotment officer reported Ellis's account overdrawn by more than fifteen hundred dollars, Lejeune instructed his paymaster to write off the debit because "Ellis, from 5 May 1921 until 20 September 1921, was in a status not that of leave, he being then engaged, under the authority of the Navy Department, on secret intelligence duty outside the limits of the United States."[5]

Meanwhile, an official inquiry into Ellis's death began. The U.S. naval attaché in Tokyo, Capt. Lyman A. Cotten, seized on the dilemma as an overt means to obtain information about the man-dated islands. Cotten conferred with Comdr. Ulysses R. Webb, the commanding officer of the U.S. Naval Hospital in Yokohama, and the two of them selected Chief Pharmacist Lawrence Zembsch for the task. In terse diplomatic language, Cotten informed the Japanese Naval Ministry: "I will send a representative to take charge of his [Ellis's] remains. This gentleman was an important personality in the United States, and we wish to bury him with the ceremony due his status."[6] The Japanese offered no objection, most likely because Zembsch was a medical officer and not reportedly involved in intelligence-gathering matters. Doubtless, the naval ministry con-ferred with the *Joho Kyoku* (Japanese intelligence apparatus), and neither agency could provide a reasonable objection to an official visit by a foreign official on what was clearly a humanitarian mission.

Zembsch boarded the SS *Tango Maru* of the Nanyo Boeki Kaisha Line at Yokohama on 4 June 1923 and sailed for Palau the following morning to retrieve Ellis's remains. On 3 August 1923, Japanese naval authorities notified the American naval attaché that Zembsch would arrive in Yokohama the next day. Lt. Comdr. Ellis M. Zacharias, a foreign-language trainee in Japan, led a party from both the embassy and the hospital to meet the steamer. After years of insatiate curiosity about the mysterious islands, Zacharias was especially eager for a firsthand report. After observing the passengers disembark with no sign of Zembsch, Zacharias came aboard and was greeted by an anxious captain. Escorted to the passenger cabins, they found Zembsch sitting on the edge of his bunk, unshaven, disheveled, and in filthy condition. He gave no sign of recognition and appeared to be in a catatonic trance. In his hands, he clutched the box containing Ellis's ashes.

Zembsch was taken to the naval hospital immediately, and Dr. Webb attempted to penetrate the wall between his chief pharmacist and the real world. By the end of the month, Captain Cotten had gleaned enough information from Zembsch to submit a secret report to the Director of Naval Intelligence. Zembsch provided no information on Ellis's death, except that the mysterious Marine had been drinking heavily and suffered from delirium tremens. In the opinion of Dr. Webb, Zembsch's condition could have been caused by prolonged exposure to the sun, a narcotic, or nervous strain. According to Cotten, Zembsch did convey the impression that Ellis's death was not natural, but he offered no specific reason for that conclusion. According to Zembsch, witnesses to Ellis's sojourn in the islands reported that the Japanese believed the erratic Marine to be an American spy and observed his movements closely. In his report, Captain Cotten added that since his return, Zembsch appeared violently anti-Japanese at times.[7]

Then the mystery of Pete Ellis took an even more bizarre twist. At 11:42 A.M. on 1 September 1923, a great earthquake shook the Kanto Plain, leveling much of the Yokohama area and destroying the naval hospital. Both Zembsch and his wife, Emma, perished in the ruins.

Decades later, an examination of Zembsch's medical records by modern medical personnel revealed nothing untoward, including the absence of any evidence that would support a drug-induced state or a history of physical or mental instability.

Those who knew Ellis persisted in their belief that something dreadful had befallen him, most likely at the hands of the Japanese. Evidence continued to be added to a growing file of unanswered questions. When Ellis's death became known, Maj. Howard W. Kipp told Maj. Gen. George Barnett that while serving in the Philippines in the 1920s, he had been informed by a Navy physician that Ellis was ill and confined to a hospital in Manila. Kipp then took steps to have Ellis transferred to the naval hospital in Cavite, where he remained for approximately two months. According to Kipp, Ellis returned to Manila briefly after his hospitalization and then took passage on a steamer for Japan.

Barnett reported that on 25 May 1923, Victor Hermann, a trader in the Caroline Islands, passed through San Francisco and read of Ellis's death in a local newspaper. Hermann recalled that Ellis accompanied him on the *Matsuyama Maru* to Palau, where they got off the ship. The time was mid-April 1923. Hermann related to Barnett that Ellis knew the Japanese were suspicious and watching him closely. Ellis told Hermann that the local police dogged his footsteps and had at one point threatened to jail him. Barnett, then serving as Commanding General, Department of the Pacific, dutifully reported both conversations to Lejeune.[8]

As far as Lejeune was concerned, or so it seemed, there was no mystery remaining. In a thoughtful letter to Ellis's brother, Lejeune acknowledged possession of the undated letter of resignation. Lejeune provided Ralph Ellis with a copy of Captain Cotten's secret report and notified him of the expected arrival of his brother's ashes. The Commandant of the Marine Corps and Ellis's friend of long standing then attempted to place a postscript on the affair: "I am personally of the opinion that Earl's death was due to disease, which probably was greatly aggravated by intemperance. Of course, there are rumors, but there is no evidence of any kind that these rumors are true."[9]

Curiously, Lejeune appears then to have reversed himself concerning the Ellis mission. When the Judge Advocate General of the Navy asked HQMC about Ellis's unpaid account, Lejeune reiterated his assertion that Ellis was in a duty status on a secret intelligence-gathering mission. But Lejeune claimed that Ellis's mission had ended on 20 September 1922, when he came under the control of the naval hospital in Yokohama. Most ominously, Lejeune acknowledged that on 7 October 1922 Ellis had apparently absented himself without leave. Thus, from that date until his death on 12 May 1923, he should be considered "an officer absent without leave."[10]

As the years slipped by, however, the mystery of Ellis's ill-fated mission and death in the Central Pacific refused to slide into the dustbin of history. His Marine Corps friends, especially, continued to believe that Ellis had run afoul of the Japanese secret police. Although the clouds of a second world war slowly enveloped the region and prevented further inquiry, researchers renewed their search for the details of his last days and death once Japan surrendered. Lieutenant Commander Zacharias wrote a memoir of his experiences as an overt intelligence-gatherer that fueled the speculations that Ellis had been murdered by the Japanese. In his published account, Zacharias devoted an entire chapter to the Ellis saga; inexplicably, however, the Japanese publication of the same memoir omits this chapter with a cryptic pronouncement: "Several chapters in the original which are not particularly related to Japan are omitted, partly in compliance with the author's request."[11]

From the Japanese perspective, the saga appeared fraught with ironies and replete with inconsistencies. In the 1920s no attempt had been made to fortify the mandated islands in the Central Pacific; not even the most clairvoyant strategist could have envisioned the massive amphibious campaign through the region. A study Ellis completed in 1921 regarding the potential employment of Marine Corps forces in the Central Pacific, while startling in its prophecy, never seized on the possibility of a multidivisional thrust in support of the greatest naval campaign in history.

Marines and those who admire them, however, are believers in lost causes and errant personalities. The image of Ellis as a straight-shooting loner, tormented by psychological problems—exacerbated by alcoholism—continues to attract admirers, deflect doubters, and encourage many to persist in believing that the Japanese authorities poisoned Ellis to prevent him from reporting on Japanese military activities in the Central Pacific. That no evidence exists to suggest that Japan had begun to fortify the mandates as early as the 1920s has not dissuaded Ellis's following.

The éminence gris of Marine Corps historians, Col. Robert Debs Heinl, Jr., pronounced solemnly that Ellis "died mysteriously at the hands of the Japanese," while noted Marine Corps historian Robert J. Moskin exclaims that "the Japanese said he became ill in the Palaus and died. It is believed that they murdered him." But a more seasoned historian, Allan R. Millett, has grasped the Ellis saga and placed it in perspective: "Ellis died under mysterious circumstances in the Palau Island Group. His disappearance made him a martyr in the eyes of World War II Marines and gave his studies the heroic glow of prophecy." More recently, Edward S. Miller, in his widely acclaimed study of War Plan Orange—the strategy developed in the interwar years in anticipation of war with Japan—appears also to disclaim any startling discovery by Ellis: "In the Palaus, he died from mysterious causes. Foul play by Japanese officials was rumored, but never proved. Ellis's notes were never found."[12]

Japanese researchers studying the Ellis saga, however, are not in agreement with Western accounts. A cablegram from the resident naval Japanese officer in the Central Pacific (South Sea Islands) to the Aide to the Minister of Marine and Navy General Staff announced Ellis's death. The message acknowledged Ellis's identity as "an officer in the [U.S.] naval service" and was sent three weeks after his demise. Ten days earlier, the South Sea Islands Government Office notified the Imperial Naval Ministry of his expiration: "He is said to be a commander on active service. If true, he is considered to have obtained [a] travel permit by falsifying his occupation. Is it all right to turn his effects over to American authorities?" But an unknown official penned a cryptic note in the margin of the cablegram, a comment that can either absolve the Japanese of any involvement in Ellis's death or merely add to the evidence suggesting foul play: "An improper action, but overlook it so we can use it as a countercharge, in case we are blamed for doing the same thing."[13]

Moreover, evidence from Japanese primary sources disputes the American claim that Zembsch examined Ellis's body and discounted any allegations of foul play. In the cablegram from the islands to Tokyo announcing Zembsch's arrival and the current disposition of the case, the resident Japanese naval officer noted that "cremation scheduled for 27 July [1923] *without opening coffin to examine dead body*. It appears as if cause of death is fully understood." The Japanese account suggests that Zembsch merely accepted the explanation of Ellis's death from local authorities and Ellis's circle of acquaintances and native wife in the Palaus. In sum, Japanese researchers have discounted any plot to murder Ellis. Instead, they conclude that the entire cause célèbre was a fabrication to shield the U.S. government, Department of the Navy, and Marine Corps from embarrassment over the disclosure that Ellis was in the islands on a covert intelligence-gathering mission. Because Ellis's death occurred just three months after the Washington Naval Arms Limitation Treaties, to which both the United States and Japan were signatories, his presence in the region was a diplomatic embarrassment. Japan had agreed not to fortify the islands, and yet Washington had dispatched an American naval officer to determine Tokyo's compliance with the accord.[14]

Cornelius Vanderbilt III claimed to have spoken to Jesse Hoppin, a medical missionary in the Carolines, during a brief visit there in

November 1923. Mother Hoppin told Vanderbilt that Ellis had recuperated from a serious illness at her home in Jaluit. She recalled that Japanese authorities were furious when Ellis persisted in entering restricted areas, and heard threats against his life. In 1926 Mother Hoppin visited briefly with Ellis's sisters, but she offered no new information. In 1933, during another home-leave from the islands, Mother Hoppin declined to discuss the Ellis affair when a Marine Corps officer attempted to interview her. Following her final trip home, in 1939, Japanese authorities refused to allow Jesse Hoppin to return to the Central Pacific. By the late 1930s, after Japan withdrew from the League of Nations, Tokyo ordered all missionaries expelled from the islands in the region.

The uncertainty surrounding Pete Ellis's death refused to be put to rest, and many continued to suspect Japanese treachery. During World War II, a Kansas newspaper proclaimed that "mystery still surrounds death of Col. Earl Ellis in Pacific Isles." The journalist reported that Ellis's relatives hoped that with recapture of the Carolines by U.S. forces, "the facts about the Kansas colonel's strange death may be known." Speculation by the fourth estate reached dizzying heights with the publication of a piece entitled, prophetically, "The Marines' First Spy."[15]

Throughout the war years, the Department of the Navy promised to investigate the circumstances of Ellis's demise once the Pacific War had ended. In response to an official inquiry in 1948, the Japanese Foreign Office conducted a search of available records, including those of the *Kempeitai.* It reported to the General Headquarters of the Supreme Commander for the Allied Forces that nothing whatsoever had been found. The discovery more than three decades later of conflicting accounts in the records of the naval ministry only exacerbated the controversy and whetted appetites for further investigation.[16]

In March 1950 the Commandant of the Marine Corps sent Lt. Col. Waite W. Worden to Koror to gather information and interview natives who had known Ellis. Informants revealed that the Japanese commissioner of police ordered Ellis followed because he was thought to be a spy. Supposedly, no one knew that he was a Marine Corps officer, according to Worden's report. The Japanese assertion that Zembsch neglected to examine Ellis's body before it was cremated suggests, moreover, that official American reports may be suspect. Ominously, surviving witnesses to Ellis's death provided versions of Zembsch's investigation that differ sharply from that recorded by the Japanese.[17]

The Marine Corps, however, remains obdurate in perpetuating the Ellis myth and the shroud of mystery that surrounds his death. Several generations of officers have heard the oft-repeated saga of Pete Ellis and accepted it without question. Periodically, published reports suggest that Ellis's oracular report was ignored by his superiors within the Department of the Navy. Moreover, the mercurial leatherneck is thought to have fallen into disfavor with his seniors within the Marine Corps because of his dogged determination to prove Japanese duplicity following the Washington naval treaties.[18]

Ellis's legend survives in a military organization that has spawned more than its share of colorful and bizarre eccentrics. In 1952 the Marine Corps dedicated a building at Quantico in Ellis's honor; appropriately, the facility houses a site for the study of amphibious warfare. Thus, Earl Hancock Ellis is honored by his country and the Marine Corps. He was a tragic figure; the events surrounding his final mission and death are filled with inconsistencies and paradoxes begging explanation and resolution.[19]

1 ~ Growing Up
1880–1901

AN OLD COAL-FIRED LOCOMOTIVE rolled onto the railway siding Sunday morning. A hot wind blew across the small Kansas town of Pratt that day, 27 August 1900. Gritty dust found its way into every nook and crevice, bedeviling homemakers as they went about their morning chores. Husbands, mostly farmers, took a welcome day of respite from the toil of earning a living from the hard-scrabble land. Located in south-central Kansas, Pratt County differed little from other rural agricultural towns, and did not offer much in the way of work except backbreaking toil in the fields. Usually the sons of these hardy rural folk followed their fathers into agriculture or found employment in retail establishments in the small towns that dotted the barren landscape. Young men who imagined broader vistas were rare, and few of them opted to strike out for the unknown. The railway station in this sleepy prairie town witnessed just such an event.

Catherine Axline Ellis and Augustus Ellis had accompanied their son, Earl Hancock Ellis, to the tiny railway station from their farm outside town. A strapping young man, reaching a shade less than six feet and weighing some lean 145 pounds, "Pete" Ellis had made an important decision: he was leaving home to enlist in the Marine Corps. Like many young men of his era, the excitement of first the Spanish-American War and then the Boxer Rebellion had captured his imagination. Seizing on the momentum of the moment, the Brigadier General Commandant of the Marine Corps, Charles Heywood, ordered an expansion of recruiting efforts to include America's untapped hinterland. A recruiting officer and staff took up station in Chicago and, like their counterparts everywhere, trumpeted Marine successes. Moreover, recruiters promised an exciting life, probably service overseas in expeditionary battalions or in the warships of the fleet. Advertisements appeared in small-town newspapers such as the *Pratt Daily Tribune*. Recruiters harped on the constant deployment of the Marines and coined a recruiting slogan difficult to match for the other services: "First to Fight." The lure of a march to the sound of gunfire in exotic, foreign lands seduced youths like Pete Ellis in record numbers, especially after the turn of the century.[1]

The train pulled out of Pratt at 7:40 A.M., headed east through Davenport and Joliet, and arrived in Chicago late the next morning. Pete Ellis's adventure had begun, but nothing in his background suggested any reason to abandon the prairie for an uncertain future in the smaller of America's naval services. Ellis's ancestors had followed the lure of new lands to the West as tillers of the soil. His paternal grandfather, John Wesley Ellis, migrated from Virginia to Bloomfield, Iowa, as a young man. There he met and married Elizabeth Jane Putnam, the daughter of a farming family that had emigrated from Illinois; their son Augustus (born in 1853) was Pete Ellis's father. Andrew Axline, Pete Ellis's maternal grandfather, migrated from Virginia to Ohio, where he answered the call to become a Lutheran minister. Eventually moving west to Iowa, Andrew Axline converted to the Presbyterian faith, continued his ministry, and married Almira

Stever in 1857. Their daughter Catherine—Pete Ellis's mother—was born on 6 November 1859. On 25 July 1876, Augustus Ellis and Catherine Axline exchanged wedding vows in the Iowa farming community of Fairfield.

During the winter of 1876–77, the Ellis and Axline families and others from southeastern Iowa mulled over plans to migrate to Kansas. Recently-surveyed lands, originally part of the Osage Indian Reservation, had been made available to settlers under the Homestead and Preemption Act. According to reports reaching Iowa farmers, the "Turkey Red" wheat seed, smuggled out of Russia by Mennonite immigrants to the American prairies, flourished in the dry soil farther to the west. While the lure of cheap and bountiful land drew settlers west, both the Axline and Ellis families sought a haven where they could raise their families free from the unsavory influences of Iowa's open saloons. Following the wagon trains west, both families filed claims for land and built homes. By 1876, Iuka, Kansas, was a thriving prairie town. John W. Ellis and his sons, Eugene and Augustus W., farmed nearby; Rev. Andrew Axline operated a small hotel along with ministering to his flock.[2]

There, in what became the Iuka farming community, Catherine Ellis gave birth to her first daughter, Nellie, on 5 April 1878. But during the following August, Nellie died of infantile cholera. That fall, Augustus Ellis filed proof of improvements to the land as required by the Homestead and Preemption Act and established ownership of 160 acres of land. On 27 July 1879 a second child, Ralph, was born to Augustus and Catherine Ellis. Seventeen months later, Ralph was followed by Earl Hancock Ellis, born on 19 December 1880 during the coldest Kansas winter anyone could remember. More than half the livestock in the county perished, and settlers found it difficult to keep warm. The Ellises, having already lost one child to sickness, feared for the health of the boys in the bitter cold. Moreover, after four years of great hardship, the family had little to show for their sweat and toil in carving out a bare existence on the prairie. Worse, blood had been shed in frequent gunplay over the fractious decision to locate a site for the county seat in Iuka. Just two years before, the notorious Masterson brothers had taken up residence in Dodge City, barely seventy-five miles west of Iuka.[3]

Word reached the Kansas prairie towns of bountiful green lands farther west, near the end of the Oregon Trail. Kansans who had migrated to the Willamette River Valley wrote of fertile lands, a milder climate, and ample trees for building homes. But then Augustus received a letter extolling the virtues of the wheat lands of Whitman County in the Territory of Washington. The writer described rolling hills and the tree-lined tributaries of the Palouse River that crossed the county every few miles. A local advertisement proclaimed that the area offered "no cyclones, no miasma, no hog cholera, no sunstroke, and no troublesome insects to damage grain." The brochure added that in the area, "crops never fail, big apples grow, the winters are mild, educational facilities are the best . . . good homes can be secured."[4]

Early in the spring of 1882, the Ellis family packed their belongings in a Conestoga wagon and joined a party of settlers moving west. Near Boise, Idaho, they left the Oregon Trail and headed northwest. On 28 April, Augustus Ellis had selected his homestead of 160 acres near present-day Colfax in Whitman County. By the end of the summer a small wooden-framed house and a barn dotted his land, and early the following year Augustus filed proof of his claim. By then he could report 150 acres fenced with barbed wire, 27 acres broken for tilling, and 10 to 12 acres planted in wheat.[5]

The promised prosperity proved illusory, however. While the bountiful land grew wheat and other seed grains aplenty, it took backbreaking labor to turn the soil. Winter winds blew just as cold as in Kansas, and much of the county became impassable during the heavy snows. The county seat offered little in the way of civilized amenities. Worse, the lawlessness that plagued rural Kansas pervaded Whitman County as well. During the few years that the Ellis family resided in the territory, cattle rustling and petty thievery resulted in the formation of vigilante gangs determined to bring law and order to the frontier. On occasion, outraged citizens even stormed the county jail, seized suspected felons, and lynched them.[6]

Augustus became discouraged and packed up the family to return to Kansas. The lawlessness he witnessed on the frontier only exacerbated his lack of material success. By then the Union Pacific Railroad had opened a branch line into Colfax, and the Ellis family returned to Iuka by train in 1887. Augustus purchased another farm, this one located between Iuka and Pratt, and farmed it until moving into Pratt in 1901 to take up a real estate business. The family had increased by then: Gwyune was born in Colfax on 23 October 1882, while Herbert (8 March 1889), Catherine (26 July 1891), John S. (25 December 1895), and Dorothy (5 May 1898) were all born in Kansas.[7]

Like many children in the district, Pete Ellis attended the Golden Valley Grade School. The tiny one-room school offered few comforts and little in the way of formal instruction. Teachers mostly allowed their small students to tutor each other. Like his classmates, Ellis came to school carrying his own lunch and even a bottle of drinking water. But whatever little the system offered, it was sufficient to encourage him to matriculate to Pratt High School; not every farm boy was so inclined. From 1896 through 1900, Pete Ellis studied a variety of academic subjects, earning marks in the 90s. An elderly spinster emphasized the rudiments of etiquette with a stern hand, and she expected Ellis and his chums to respect girls and ladies by tipping their hats. Religious and moral lessons prevailed in the classroom, and students sang such hymns as "Yield Not to Temptation" in shrill discord.[8]

His high school classmates recalled Pete Ellis's interest in baseball and noted that he was a good athlete. By then he had become an avid reader. He found P. G. Wodehouse's novels, O. Henry's short stories, and Rudyard Kipling's poems especially delightful. His sister remembered that when the Spanish-American War broke out during his

sophomore year, he followed the course of the war through newspapers and magazines with keen interest. While the massive contingent of American soldiers languished in a squalid camp at Key
West, Marines mounted out to Guantánamo Bay, Cuba, to establish an advanced base in support of the fleet. Other leathernecks
accompanied the fleet in actions in the Philippines. Newspapermen
reported favorably on the professionalism and élan of the Marines,
stories that apparently influenced the decision of a Kansas school-
boy to enlist.

Marine Corps successes at the turn of the century heralded the
capstone to almost two decades of attempts to improve its professional performance. The American Civil War marked a low ebb in
the military efficiency and public esteem for the Marines. Marine
Corps participation during the conflict contributed only superficially
to the success of the Union fleet. Following the upheaval, some
attempts surfaced in hopes of improving the performance of the
Marine Corps, but the efforts mostly floundered. Periodically, reform-
minded legislators initiated measures to either disband the antiquated force or transfer it to the Army or Navy and thus end its career
as a separate armed service. Many Navy officers viewed the Marines
and their role as shipboard policemen as an unnecessary anachronism
remaining from the age of sail. Even semiofficial military publica-
tions, such as the authoritative *Army-Navy Journal,* waxed critical—
if not sarcastic—when they described the Marines Corps as "the old-
est, the smallest, the best uniformed and equipped and most artist-
ically drilled branch of the fighting wing of the government."[9]

Although Brig. Gen. Jacob Zeilin made some gains in professionalism during his tenure as Commandant (1864–76), major reform
efforts eluded him and failed to reach fruition. His successor, Col.
Charles G. McCawley (1876–91), attempted initially to improve the
sorry lot of the enlisted force, a sometimes motley group plagued by
desertion and filled with immigrants or riffraff taken off the docks.
In 1880 muster rolls revealed that a fourth of the enlisted force were

foreign-born; in that year, the Commandant reported a shocking desertion rate of 25 percent. McCawley asked for an increase in appropriations to recruit additional men. He believed that a sharp reduction in the number of hours his Marines walked post as sentries would improve morale and might reduce the proclivity to desertion. The Commandant also sought a substantial augmentation to the daily ration in hopes of improving the dismal fare in the mess halls at the various barracks. Additional funding, McCawley pointed out, provided for such amenities as sheets, pillowcases, and mattresses to replace the straw-filled ticks. The naval services, especially, sought better-caliber recruits likely to serve out an enlistment; frustrated and vexed officers found all too often that many recruits simply lacked the rudimentary skills or intelligence levels with which to perform increasingly technical duties or to complete an initial period of service.[10]

As additional native-born Americans enlisted in increasing numbers and fewer illiterate or non-English-speaking recruits filled the ranks, officers experienced fewer difficulties with their men. By the end of the century and the inauguration of an age of neocolonialism, in which the Marine Corps played a major part, even the unrealized and disjointed portions of McCawley's program could be credited for the accolades enjoyed by the Marine Corps in the Spanish-American War. The hagiographic accounts of Marines in the conflict, penned by journalists disappointed in the performance of the U.S. Army at an early stage in the war and anxious to report military action, provided a luster to the Marine Corps's image that had escaped it for almost four decades. As a teenager, Ellis read of Huntington's Battalion at Guantánamo, the action at Cuzco Well, and Marine landing parties serving with Adm. George Dewey in the Philippines. Like other young men, the tales lured him to a life of adventure and into the clutches of Marine Corps recruiters.[11]

Pete Ellis checked into the River House, a budget establishment on Clark Street—his room cost only a dollar a day, he noted in his

diary. For some unexplained reason, Ellis spent the next week sight-
seeing rather than rushing to the recruiting offices. For a young man
from a prairie town, there was much to see. He observed a parade
honoring veterans of the Grand Army of the Republic, which Pres.
Theodore Roosevelt reviewed. Trips to parks, museums, commercial
houses, and the huge stockyards occupied his time until Monday, 3
September 1900. Ellis's diary entry on the following day notes that
"yesterday I enlisted in the Marines. That is what I came to Chicago
for, and it was only the carrying out of my plans. I passed the physical examination fairly easily, was sworn in, and by two P.M., Monday, 3 September 1900, I was a private in the U.S.M.C."[12]

Ellis warmed to the Marines who served in the recruiting office,
noting, as did countless other enlisted men who had been seduced
into military service by dubious promises of a better life or adventure, that "they were very nice fellows." For almost a week after, he
languished in Chicago armed with meal chits and hotel vouchers
provided by the Marine Corps while waiting for a draft of recruits to
be formed. At noon on 9 September, Ellis and the other new Marines
boarded the train, and it puffed into Washington's Union Station
two days later. An elderly sergeant, whose guttural speech revealed
his Central European origins, met the recruits and herded them
toward the old barracks in the Navy Yard where the Anacostia and
Potomac Rivers meet in the southwest corner of the nation's capital.
Ellis's career in the Marine Corps had begun.[13]

Whatever predestined Ellis to choose the life of a Marine is lost
to history. His outstanding high school record and solid family background must have made the young Kansan attractive to the Marine
recruiters, especially as young men of Ellis's station seldom, if ever,
flocked to the colors except in wartime. For most mothers, the image
of a son drawn up with a pack of tobacco-chewing, heavy-drinking,
and often obstreperous enlisted men was anathema. The coarse and
sometimes brutish manners displayed by many low-ranking men of
the armed forces underscored the undesirability of such a vocation.

In a letter to the Commandant, a senior Marine Corps officer complained that "rabble from the larger cities make very indifferent soldiers."[14]

Given his family's lower-middle-class status, it is unlikely that his parents' permission would have been granted for his enlistment without the enticement of a commission. For the first century following its establishment in 1798, the U.S. Marine Corps had commissioned officers directly from civil life. Most lacked formal education, and many did not demonstrate soldierly traits. Political patronage counted heavily in the selection process, apparently. A handful of young men who lacked redeeming social or intellectual virtues found a temporary niche in the Marine Corps as second lieutenants. Few performed satisfactorily or remained long in uniform.

As the ranks of junior officers declined, first Zeilin and then McCawley pleaded for legislative relief. Finally, in 1870, Congress authorized the commissioning of seven new second lieutenants, but directly from civilian life, as before. And, just as before, the new officers were the sons of wealthy and prominent families, and they lacked formal education. Only one young officer of the group, Littleton Waller Tazewell Waller, remained in uniform for a full-service career to make a substantial mark in the naval services. The remainder of the second lieutenants served briefly and without distinction, and then went on to whatever pursuits their influential families might provide. The sorry performance of the Corps's junior officers prompted one disappointed observer to observe sarcastically that "USMC meant 'useless-sons-made-comfortable.'"[15]

Periodically, successive Commandants of the Marine Corps complained to the Secretaries of the Navy and argued in vain for graduates of the Military Academy at West Point as a source for junior officers. But by 1882 an overabundance of graduates of the Naval Academy prompted Congress and the Department of the Navy to allow the surplus to provide the sole source of new second lieutenants for the Marine Corps. On 5 August of that year, Congress added a proviso to the annual naval appropriations bill stipulating that the number commissioned from the Naval Academy as line or engineer officers could be no greater than the sum of the vacancies in the fleet. Those for whom no space existed would receive a year's severance pay and discharge. But a minor addendum to the legislation allowed the Marine Corps access to the excess midshipmen. Of the Class of 1881, only ten received commissions in the Navy, while another ten became second lieutenants. A year later, another graduate from the Class of 1881 traded his Navy commission to become the eleventh Annapolitan in the group of new officers.[16]

While the new source of better-educated junior officers appeared promising, many second lieutenants performed not unlike their troublesome predecessors. An alarming number of the accessions from the Naval Academy Class of 1881 experienced severe problems with alcohol abuse. Charles A. Doyen's record of unauthorized absences from duty, caused by periodic episodes of binge drinking, resulted in a series of unflattering and unsatisfactory fitness reports. Repentant, at least by appearances, Doyen promised to follow the path of temperance for the remainder of his career; sadly, he did not. He and another classmate, James E. Mahoney, received courts-martial for drunkenness; however, Pres. Theodore Roosevelt pardoned both in response to political pressures. Another classmate, Lincoln Karmany, earned a reputation as a heavy drinker and inveterate womanizer. Despite these flaws in their professional character, all three officers advanced regularly in rank: Doyen died on active duty as a brigadier general, and both Mahoney and Karmany retired as colonels. A fourth classmate, Col. Henry Kidder White, was retired medically when he could no longer perform his duties because of severe bouts of delirium tremens.[17]

Whatever shortcomings the new source for junior officers displayed, it more than justified itself by raising the intellectual and professional status of the Marine Corps in the sometimes jaundiced view of Navy officers. Key members of Congress, especially those serving on the naval affairs committees, received fewer complaints about the Corps's junior officers, either from constituents or from the Commandant himself. This system of officer procurement continued until 1897, when the demands of Navy expansion required every Annapolis graduate to man the ships of the fleet. On 28 March 1898, Commandant Heywood submitted a request to the Secretary of the Navy that contained proposed solutions to several long-festering personnel problems. Heywood wanted higher ranks for his senior officers; additional officers, especially to fill vacancies within the junior ranks; and permission to commission those noncommissioned officers (NCOs) who had received their stripes because of meritorious service. By the turn of the century, Heywood's appeal had become written into law. Thus, it seems likely that Ellis and his family had been told by recruiters that a commission was a reasonable possibility.[18]

Ellis's avenue to commissioning came about through the Naval Personnel Act of 1900. Approved on 3 March 1899, it provided for a total of 140 officers for the Marine Corps—a sizable increase. As of 30 September 1900, eighteen vacancies existed among the ranks of second lieutenants. According to the stipulations of the legislation, only eight of these positions could be offered to civilian applicants; the remaining ten had to be accessed from either the ranks of meritorious NCOs or graduates of the Naval Academy. All of the graduates of the Class of 1900 went into the Navy. A year later, Heywood reported that four NCOs had been commissioned and eight others remained on a waiting list. Between 9 October and the end of the year 1900, six officers had been commissioned directly from civil life, along with two meritorious NCOs.[19]

For the next fifteen months, while the Commandant and his senior officers wrestled with the pesky problem of commissioning suitable junior officers, Ellis learned the rudiments of soldiering at the Washington barracks from the aged veterans of the Corps. Some had even served in the Civil War. Antiquated notions of warfare remained, perhaps typified by the sage advice on marksmanship appearing in the *Marine Manual:* "Take the best position for holding the rifle. Aim it correctly, hold it steady, and pull the trigger without deranging the aim." Ellis kept his personal behavior within the bounds of the strict discipline required, and his intellect soon garnered the attention of superiors. On 20 February 1901 he received the coveted stripes of a corporal, based on meritorious performance.[20]

By fits and spurts, the Marine Corps that Ellis had joined careened into the twentieth century. The previous half century had not been good for the leathernecks. Despite almost a decade of uneven reforms, many of the problems that plagued McCawley and his senior officers in 1880 remained. In 1890 only 948 young men enlisted in the Marine Corps, while out of only 2,000 men, 520 deserted and only 85 reenlisted. A year before, the *Army-Navy Journal* reprinted a story from the *New York Times* which noted that the "Marine Corps is credited with being a reliable body of men, but it has been asleep for the past 50 years."[21]

Meanwhile, however, Ellis's parents left nothing to chance concerning their son's future. They sought the assistance of Rep. Chester I. Long of Kansas's Seventh Congressional District, a neighbor from nearby Medicine Lodge. Congressman Long inquired on Pete Ellis's behalf with Secretary of the Navy John D. Long, who then passed the matter on to Commandant Heywood. No political fool, Heywood took his cue accordingly and ordered young Ellis examined for possible commissioning. Recommending an intelligent and meritorious NCO with a political connection—albeit minor—more than met the Commandant's criteria. During the interim, Ellis called on Congressman Long at his Washington home. Apparently, he received assurances that the way had been paved for his commission.

More formal steps to commissioning had been set in motion by the Commandant in 1898. Candidates first garnered the permission of the Commandant himself based on rather loose criteria of education and family. A written examination followed, consisting of tests in English, geography, history, constitutional law, surveying, general mathematics, trigonometry, and logarithms. Although confident, Ellis secured the services of a retired Army colonel to tutor him, and he earned a satisfactory grade on the test in the first attempt. The Commandant then reported to Congressman Long that Ellis had been found acceptable in all respects. The ambitious Ellis considered service in the ranks worthwhile only if it led to something better, such as a commission, but he found military life to his liking nonetheless, a sentiment he shared with his mother: "I will stay in this service [Marine Corps] 'til I am fired out and then I will go into some other country's employ."[22]

On 21 December 1901, Earl Hancock "Pete" Ellis took the oath of office of a second lieutenant; his commission had been signed two weeks prior: "Having been appointed a second lieutenant in the U.S. Marine Corps . . . you will procure the necessary uniforms and report to the Brigadier General, Commandant of the Marine Corps." By lineal precedent, Ellis appeared as fifty-first out of the fifty-seven second lieutenants. After outfitting himself in an officer's uniform, he reported to the Brigadier General Commandant for the pro forma personal audience. There he learned that his first posting as an officer would be to the Marine Barracks, Boston, for instruction in his new duties. Three other NCOs also became second lieutenants on the same day: Sgt. John A. Hughes, Corp. Arthur McAllister, and Corp. Walter A. Noa.[23]

Apparently satisfied with the outcome of his first year in the Marine Corps, Ellis shared his pride in a letter home and revealed that esprit de corps and professionalism, hallmarks of a sometimes antiquated naval service, had taken hold. Noting the high cost of maintaining his uniforms—nine hundred to a thousand dollars thus far—Ellis remarked sagely that "it was expected that [an officer] maintain the same high standards that he expected from his *men*."[24]

Meanwhile, the initiatives and imperatives of inter- and intraservice politics impinged full force on the Marine Corps. As 2nd Lt.

Pete Ellis took up his new profession in earnest, the General Board of the Navy met to determine the requirements of the fleet in wartime. The role of Marines in support of the fleet weighed heavily on the minds of Navy planners. Almost two-thirds of the Marine Corps had been deployed to East Asia in the halcyon days between the occupation of the Philippines and the Boxer Rebellion. Forces of Marines, in organizations of battalions and perhaps even brigades, appeared likely to be permanent fixtures overseas. In the course of its deliberations, the board assigned to the Marine Corps the mission of defending advanced bases for the fleet. On 22 November 1900, Commandant Heywood accepted the assignment with the understanding that it consisted only of providing a four-hundred-man battalion trained in field fortifications and coastal defense activities.[25]

Five years before, a promising young officer from among the first Naval Academy graduates to enter the Marine Corps displayed the temerity to suggest that the Corps's traditional mission had become an anachronism. In a thoughtful letter to Commandant Heywood, Capt. George Barnett demonstrated the effrontery to suggest that "on shore and at sea, the Marine Corps must be considered as an expeditionary force for use in any part of the world and not merely as a collection of watchmen." But even a year before, Lt. William F. Fullam articulated the feelings of many of his fellow Navy officers in arguing for the outright removal of Marines from the ships of the fleet. Fullam and the Navy reformers also envisioned a new role for the Marine Corps—that of manning advanced bases in support of the fleet. The political repercussions of the article and the rhetoric inflamed Marine officers and their supporters: "The name 'Marine' alone has been a synonym for idleness, worthlessness, and vacuity of intellect," Fullam fumed.[26]

Despite the stimuli for institutional reforms, most senior Marine Corps officers focused their attentions and frustrations on the stagnation of promotions—especially the inability for most to achieve field-grade rank before reaching the mandatory age for retirement.

Intramural politics on such subjects as desertions, administrative matters, and line versus staff controversies dominated most service debates. A newspaper waxed critical of the Marine Corps officers, laying bare the professional inadequacies that had brought the smaller of the naval services to such a dismal state: "The Marine officer wears corsets and parts his hair in the middle. He also has a pedigree and a sword. He carves out his career with his pedigree."[27]

Pete Ellis lacked the formal credentials of a university degree or a diploma from the Naval Academy. His family, while respectable, did not possess the political leverage that others might employ to further their kinsmen's careers. Moreover, he had yet to demonstrate a flash of brilliance or eccentricity, and his mettle had not been tested under fire. But in the next two decades, Pete Ellis would advance to field-grade rank, serve in wartime with distinction, become a confidant of the Corps's most distinguished general officers, establish a legacy as a prophetic strategist, and find an early grave on a remote island in the Western Pacific.

2 ~ The Junior Officer

1902–1911

THE NEWLY COMMISSIONED SECOND LIEUTENANTS, all from among the meritorious noncommissioned officers (NCOs), received orders to Marine Barracks, Boston, for their initial training. Walter A. Noa, Arthur McAllister, John A. Hughes, and Earl H. Ellis rode the Colonial Express train together from Washington to the northeast. On 11 January 1902 they reported to Col. Percival C. Pope, a veteran campaigner recently returned from the Philippines, who now commanded the barracks. Commissioned in 1861, the venerable Pope was expected to teach the young officers the rudiments of their new profession. Little formal instruction appeared in the daily routine. Mostly, Ellis and the others learned by observing. Each of them stood tours of duty as officer of the day and inspected the sentries once before and once after midnight. The older officers taught the new officers how to inspect the men, their weapons, and equipment each morning, and Ellis and the others learned what they could from Pope and his officers. Informal discussions in the officers' mess constituted much of the instruction.

Many of the officers had already seen service in the Spanish-American War, the Philippine Insurrection, and the Boxer Rebellion. Residents of the Legation Quarter of Peiping had unanimously praised the gallant Marines for their professionalism and rectitude in lifting the siege. Tales of their heroism and suffering filled the newspapers. For Ellis, Hughes, McAllister, and Noa, their association—however casual—with such seasoned veterans apparently produced the effect Headquarters Marine Corps (HQMC) desired in influencing the professional demeanor of the young officers. From 11 January until 1 March 1902 the new second lieutenants continued their instruction at the Boston barracks until they all received orders to report to Marine Barracks, Washington, to fill out a troop draft for the Philippines.[1]

The informal instruction that Ellis and the other new officers received in 1902 represented an untoward interlude in the recently established program of officer instruction for the Marine Corps. Beginning in 1891, the Colonel Commandant had directed that all new officers report to the Washington barracks for an eight-month period at the School of Application. There the second lieutenants studied infantry and artillery drills, administration, torpedoes, and minelaying. Trumpeting the program a success, Col. Charles G. McCawley ordered a second course of instruction for the 1892–93 academic year and inaugurated a similar regimen for NCOs. But the exigencies of the war with Spain, along with increasing commitments for deployments to East Asia, made the luxury of the School of Application unlikely. In 1901, a new Commandant of the Marine Corps, Brig. Gen. Charles Heywood, ordered the course suspended, and it was not reestablished until 1903. While Ellis's formal military education certainly suffered from the temporary suspension of the School of Application, other young officers of the era—many of whom would become the luminaries and icons of the Corps for the next generation, such as George Barnett and John A. Lejeune—did not attend either. The rudimentary and informal instruction that

Ellis, Hughes, McAllister, and Noa (and other young officers) received in Boston would have to suffice.[2]

Having satisfied Colonel Pope, the quartet of new second lieutenants reported to Marine Barracks, Washington, on 7 March 1902, pending an assignment overseas. On 1 April a troop train transported a replacement battalion consisting of 6 officers, 150 enlisted men, and a surgeon to San Francisco. There the Marines embarked on the *Sheridan* for the journey across the Pacific. On 1 April the Army transport steamed out of the bay. The vessel stopped in Honolulu to take on coal, and again in Guam to drop off an officer and twenty-five enlisted Marines. The ship rolled considerably in the swells of the heavy seas, especially while transiting the Pacific beyond Hawaii. Of the 800 soldiers and 150 Marines who had embarked in San Francisco, most suffered at times from seasickness. Ellis and the other junior officers inspected the Marines each morning and then exercised them in the afternoon. He noted with disgust that the embarked Army officers treated the sojourn as a pleasure cruise, generally ignoring the soldiers under their command. On schedule, the battalion marched ashore on 13 April 1902 at Cavite, the American naval base in Manila Bay in the Philippines. Since the first of the year, 17 officers and 620 enlisted Marines had returned home from the Philippines, while 23 officers—including Ellis—and 500 men had been sent out to replace them.[3]

In 1898 the old Spanish naval arsenal at Cavite had been seized by the Americans, and Adm. George Dewey left a small force of Marines to guard it. But Cavite Province proved to be a rebel stronghold when an insurrection against American rule broke out less than a year later. In response to the security threat, Secretary of the Navy John D. Long ordered the deployment of a Marine battalion to Cavite. This small force arrived on 23 May 1899, and a second battalion joined it on 21 September of the same year. A third battalion of Marines arrived on 15 December as the force continued to expand. By 1900 the leatherneck contingent in the Philippines had grown into a two-regiment brigade. Much of the force deployed to China during the Boxer Rebellion in that year, but Secretary Long ordered all leathernecks returned to Cavite on 28 September.

Although the Marines had deployed to provide security for the new naval facility, they took to the field in skirmishes against native insurgents in the region. Guerrillas protesting the American occupation cut off the naval base from U.S. Army headquarters in Manila. On 13 June 1899 a battalion from Cavite, reinforced by a landing party of bluejackets from the *Petrel* and an additional leatherneck contingent from the *Helena,* assaulted rebel positions at Novaleta. These and other actions by the U.S. Army in the islands led to the collapse of Filipino resistance in the Cavite area by January 1900. Within a year, 64 officers and 1,934 enlisted Marines served in the Philippines—roughly a third of the Marine Corps's total strength of 171 officers and 5,694 men. By the time of Ellis's arrival on the scene, the Navy had taken over the governing of Cavite Peninsula and the Marines had assumed control of many local governments. In addition, a prison to house rebellious Filipinos had been constructed at Olongapo, and it fell to the leatherneck brigade to provide the guards.[4]

A Chinese-Filipino room boy who took Ellis in tow saw him installed into his room in the officers' quarters. This primitive facility differed from the enlisted barracks only in that the structure had been divided into approximately thirty rooms. Ellis proclaimed his quarters "very comfortable" in his first letter home. The room boy explained the nuances of the social scene and emphasized the requirement to maintain an ample supply of alcoholic beverages so as to entertain visiting officers properly. The cost of entertainment did not appear onerous, even for a second lieutenant, because Scotch sold for fifty cents a quart and London gin for only a quarter. On weekends Ellis and the off-duty officers took the eight-mile tugboat ride across the bay to Manila. Drinks and dinner at the Hotel Orienti, followed by strolls down Luenta Boulevard, usually preceded more serious pursuits: chance introductions to the many beautiful young women drawn to the mainstay of the American social arena at the mouth of Manila Bay. In one of his first letters home, Ellis recalled for his mother a recent encounter with a pretty Filipino girl: "I told her that she had the most beautiful eyes that I had ever seen and that I was madly in love with her—then found out she didn't understand English."[5]

In the early years of the American occupation, local officials attempted to elevate the social scene of Manila. Doubtless Ellis witnessed what one journalist recorded as the transformation of Manila from "a drowsy, uncleanly, and undesirable place" into a modern city with "much gaiety and as much social charm as any European or American city." Manila, the journalist noted, boasted an active women's social club that sponsored musicals and cultural activities; its cotillion, held on New Year's Eve, was the social highlight of the season. By the time of Ellis's arrival at Cavite, the Army-Navy Club in Manila had become the cornerstone of military and naval society.[6]

On the day Ellis arrived at Cavite, the Army transport *Warren* departed Subic Bay for home with Maj. Littleton Waller Tazewell Waller and the survivors of the infamous Samar expedition. The previous fall, a band of Moro insurgents had massacred a luckless Army detachment in the southern reaches of the archipelago. In response to the atrocity, Maj. Gen. Adna R. Chaffee, military commander in the Philippines, ordered the formation of a brigade to seek retaliation. Although the admiral commanding the Asiatic Fleet had been reluctant to authorize participation by naval forces in the pacification effort, he relented in this instance given the brutality of the guerrilla action. To support Brig. Gen. Jacob H. "Howling Jake" Smith's 6th Separate Brigade, the admiral sent a battalion of leathernecks—15 officers and 300 men—under Waller along with a patrol boat. In the next eleven days, Waller's battalion burned Filipino homes, destroyed rice caches, shot water buffalo, and seized native boats. Later, Waller claimed that Smith had ordered him to "make of Samar a howling wilderness" and otherwise to wreak havoc in the countryside. Waller's small force followed Smith's dictum to the letter. At a battle at Sajoton near Bassey on 17 November, the Marines destroyed three Moro camps, killed thirty rebels, and captured a sizable store of bamboo guns and rice. Although it lost only two Marines in enemy action during the campaign, Waller's battalion accounted for a total of thirty-nine Moros killed and eighteen prisoners.

Then, part of the force—led by Waller himself—took off on an exhausting march through the jungle to the southern reaches of the island, ostensibly to map the interior and to determine a route for a telegraph line. As the strength of the tiny force ebbed in the inhospitable climate and terrain, Waller concluded that his Filipino bearers had become mutinous. Thereupon, he executed eleven of them; later, his adjutant shot another. Upon the return of the battalion to Cavite, Chaffee ordered a court-martial. In his defense, Waller claimed that Smith had ordered the punitive actions taken. Specifically, Smith had told Waller (and, fortunately, another officer who could bear witness) that he "wanted no prisoners," adding, "I wish you to kill and burn. The more you kill and burn, the more you will please me." Waller was ultimately exonerated. By the time Ellis arrived at Cavite, gossip about the infamous Samar episode prevailed. In one his first letters home, Ellis demonstrated a vicious streak of old-fashioned imperialism. To his mother, he opined that "tales of torturing natives do make the finest of campaign material, especially when they are true . . . subduing savages is a new thing to the American people and they *will* howl at the necessary adjuncts." Ellis emphasized that if America had been at the business of colonizing as long as Great Britain, its citizens would understand the problems and difficulties. As for the atrocities alleged in Samar, Ellis exclaimed that "Waller only did what others have done—except that he failed to kill them all—if he had done the latter, who would have told the tale? Whatever you do; do thoroughly!"[7]

Ellis's brigade commander, Col. James Forney, assigned him to the important post of adjutant for the 1st Regiment under Lt. Col. Mancil C. Goodrell. Lt. Col. Otway C. Berryman commanded the 2nd Regiment at Olongapo. By the time of Ellis's posting to the Philippines, the strength of the Marine Corps in the islands had increased to 59 officers and 1,547 enlisted men. Besides the large contingents at Cavite and Olongapo, posts had been established at Port Isabella on Basilan and at Polla on Mindanao. In addition to the burgeoning commitment of the Corps's meager assets, 6 officers and 396 enlisted Marines served in the ships of the Asiatic Fleet, and another 8 officers and 175 men occupied the barracks in Guam. The strength of the entire Marine Corps in June 1902 was only 191 officers and 6,031 men.[8]

Mornings at the barracks at Cavite began with officers' call at 6 A.M.—approximately twenty-five officers served with the brigade at Cavite at any one time during Ellis's tenure—followed by drill for the troops. Classes on general military subjects were held each day for the officers, but apparently they did not amount to much—at least as Ellis remembered. Ellis spent his afternoons seeking relief from the heat and humidity, usually relaxing in an easy chair or playing baseball with his troops. There appeared to be few demands on him professionally. Like the other lieutenants, Ellis stood duty one out of every four days. To his mother, Ellis exuded contentment: "I think that this is the laziest life that a man could find—there is not a blamed thing to do except lay around, sleep, and go 'bug house.' But just the same, I am helping to bear the 'White Man's burden.'"[9]

Whatever effort Ellis applied to his duties satisfied Goodrell, who rated him as "excellent" in his first fitness report—the highest category. Ellis's regimental commander took the opportunity to comment on the young officer's growth potential, something that not every reporting senior was inclined to do: "Lieutenant Ellis is an excellent young officer in all respects, and with experience, could be intrusted to perform any duty."[10]

The longer he served in the Philippines, the more Ellis became acclimated to the oppressive heat and the relaxed atmosphere that prevailed in the tropics; at one point he compared it to that of Washington in the summer and therefore tolerable. Enforcing good sanitation in an attempt to ward off tropical diseases occupied much of the attention of the officers. Malaria was rife, and strict discipline to avoid infection through mosquito bites was emphasized. At least once a year, cholera struck Cavite with a vengeance. Ellis noted ruefully that the waterborne pathogen could be fatal, but with prompt treatment at the onset of the disease, surgeons enjoyed a success rate of more than 75 percent.[11]

The Brigadier General Commandant had emphasized repeatedly that Marines deployed overseas or in the ships of the fleet would serve tours of two and a half years, and not more. After the initial euphoria following the Spanish-American War and the Relief Expedition to Tientsin, Marines began to loathe the alternating stints away from home. An anonymous doggerel of the era captured the dislike for assignment to America's far-flung possessions:

> *When I came to the Philippines in 1899*
> *I didn't think they'd keep me here till the sun had ceased to shine*
> *But it seems that they've forgotten that they sent us here at all*
> *So I guess we'll have to stay until General Recall.*
>
> *But when my time expires, and I am once more free*
> *I'll turn my back upon the mob, my face no more 'twill see.*
> *For I'm tired of bootleg coffee and the commissary bean.*
> *Oh! may the devil take me if again I become a Marine.[12]*

Even when the blessed relief arrived and the sunburned leathernecks returned home, many found the reception less than complimentary or appreciative. In 1903 the influential *Army-Navy Journal* heaped criticism on HQMC, the Department of the Navy, and a seemingly ungrateful government for its cavalier treatment of the veterans returning from the Western Pacific. In this account, a battalion commanded by Maj. Franklin J. Moses had arrived by ship at Oakland on 4 March 1903. Transferred to a slow-moving train, the draft crept across the continent to New York City at an agonizingly glacial pace of twenty miles per hour; worse, the Marines were fed only once every twelve hours. On the first day out of California, the initial fare consisted only of two slices of bread, a piece of pie, and a cup of coffee.[13]

As the months of his tour passed, Ellis became increasingly critical of the Filipinos. In one letter home he vented his disgust with the native youths, observing that most began smoking at an early age, then turned to gambling and petty thievery. In his admittedly parochial view, America's new colony needed an efficient government. He expressed the hopelessness of waging civilized warfare against "a pack of wild animals." Expanding on his venue, he called the Filipinos "primitive men when it came to fighting and [they] have about as much fairness as a cobra." A harsher colonial regime appeared to be more to his liking, just the prescription to solve the sociopolitical ills of the Philippines. By then organized insurgency resisting American rule in the vicinity of the naval base had ended, but roving bands of "ladrones" continued to infest many areas, vexing American military and naval commanders. For Ellis this meant deployment into the Cavite Peninsula to roust it of these petty thieves and social misfits.

At home, public euphoria over America's new possession began to wane with increasing criticism. One faultfinder scored the failure of the civil government, citing the "undue haste in establishing civilized institutions among races and tribes who are not yet able to comprehend or maintain them." To his father, Ellis opined: "I am not supposed to express an opinion but I will say this much, that the government of these islands is just about as rotten as any in the world today." Then Ellis flexed his neocolonial muscles: "What the islands need is military government á la Samar." At this juncture, Ellis had apparently become a confirmed imperialist. Racial slurs began to appear in his letters home with increasing frequency: "I wish that you could be with me so that you might meet your little brown brothers and sisters . . . they [Filipino children] remind me of a lot of little brown rats and they are just as plentiful too."[14]

The prospect of an extended tour in the Philippines caused Ellis to complain occasionally in his letters home. Although the Commandant promised tours of only two and a half years overseas or in the ships of the fleet, administrative and logistical shortfalls sometimes resulted in longer stints overseas. Learning of sizable leatherneck deployments to the Caribbean, Ellis wondered where HQMC might find replacements for those serving in the Philippines. From Ellis's perspective, the Commandant's dictum on the sanctity of the length of overseas tours appeared hollow. To his brother Ralph, he groused: "They send new men out here and then tend to forget them," adding, "some of the officers, due to go home, have had some hard service in China and the south [Samar] and are really in poor health." Barely a month after venting an apparent frustration to Ralph, he expressed satisfaction to another brother, Tad: "[I] am beginning to think that this is not such a bad place after all. . . . If I should say the foregoing to anyone in the [officers'] quarters, they would think that the climate was affecting me." To his father, Ellis continued to express contentment: "Everything is going nicely here—have no kick at all." But the nagging uncertainty over the length of the tours overseas continued to cause him to fret, a concern that Ellis shared often in letters home: "No Army or Marine officer is going to kick as long as there is fighting to do; but they do object to being posted in the bush and left to die of cholera."[15]

With easy access to the latest information pertaining to the Marine force in the islands, he learned of a possible posting to command the Marines in the battleship *Kentucky*. The detachment's commander, Capt. George A. Andersen, had received orders home without a relief available. Ellis enjoyed a good relationship with his

regimental commander and believed that Goodrell's friendship with
the admiral commanding the Asiatic Fleet, Robley D. "Fighting
Bob" Evans, had secured his assignment as the nominal relief for the
Marine detachment commander in the *Kentucky.*

At about the time of his relief and transfer to a new assignment,
Ellis reported to an examination board to determine his fitness for
promotion to first lieutenant. Although such boards rarely disquali-
fied candidates—promotion continued along a glacial path dictated
by strict seniority—examining officers put junior officers through
their paces with an exhaustive series of practical subjects. In Ellis's
case, he answered oral questions on administration, drill regulations,
small-arms firing, and signaling. Essay questions followed on the subjects of fire discipline, military field engineering, naval and military
law, tactics, naval gunnery, and military topography. Examiners
followed the completion of the written portion of the tests with
additional oral questions. Ellis earned an average of 81 percent on
the oral and written portions, and 84 percent on the practicum on
close-order drill. Examining officers took special note of an officer's
medical record, but at this juncture in Ellis's career his file disclosed
nothing unusual or disqualifying. By the end of this tour at Cavite
he had been treated for dengue fever—a common ailment—and several bouts with a variety of tropical fungi.[16]

On 21 January 1903, Ellis stood detached from the 1st Brigade
in the Philippines and reported to the captain of the battleship, then
at anchor in Manila Bay. He exuded pride in the assignment, especially since an officer with the rank of captain usually commanded
such a sizable unit; the Marine detachment in the *Kentucky* numbered seventy-three men, and it manned the 6-pounders at general
quarters. The mammoth battleship also carried four 13-inch, four
8-inch, and fourteen 5-inch guns. To his mother, Ellis boasted of his
new assignment but noted the burden of command: "It is up to me
to show that the responsibility was not misplaced." But the *Kentucky's* captain did not confuse youthful zeal and enthusiasm with

overall performance; he marked Ellis's first fitness report only "very good" in duties and abilities. But apparently the Fleet Marine Officer, Maj. George Barnett, spoke to the captain before the next semi-annual marking period. The captain noted this commentary and raised Ellis's marks to "excellent."[17]

The unusual assignment—unusual because of Ellis's rank—provided a bright spot for his future at this juncture in his career. Ellis received fitness reports during his tour as a battalion adjutant at Cavite marked "excellent," while his contemporaries commissioned from the enlisted ranks fared poorly. Both Hughes and McAllister had received orders as platoon commanders in a battalion commanded by Maj. Con Marrast Perkins, a graduate of the Naval Academy Class of 1881 and an officer with a reputation for unpredictable behavior. Perkins marked Hughes "not good" in general bearing and conduct and as "somewhat reckless and careless in matters other than of a military character, and with a disposition toward boisterousness not to my entire approval." Perkins claimed McAllister was "lazy, unreliable, lacked zeal, and performed his duties in a perfunctory manner." Both Hughes and McAllister rebutted the unflattering reports, arguing that the mercurial Perkins was unbalanced. Less than two years later, a medical board declared Perkins unfit for duty because of neurasthenia—a common euphemism for alcoholism.[18]

Ellis's medical record revealed no difficulties with alcohol abuse at this period in his career. Nonetheless, the officers' social scene included a heavy intake of liquor. Sometimes Ellis and the other officers gathered for formal dinners usually heavily laced with alcoholic beverages, not unlike the British mess nights adopted by Marines decades later. In an early letter home, Ellis recounted a farewell dinner for a group of officers departing Cavite: an estimated fifty officers from both of the sea services attended; captured Chinese banners from the Boxer Rebellion decorated the dining room, and a Filipino band played a mixture of Spanish love songs and American ragtime melodies. The gathering extended far into the night as Ellis

and the other officers toasted the Marine Corps, the departing officers, and the gallant dead of Samar and the Boxer Rebellion. Commentary on the heavy consumption of alcohol among the officers
prevailed in Ellis's letters, not necessarily in a disapproving tone, and
Ellis noted that apparently the senior officers established and encouraged the habit. In another letter, Ellis wrote that "Major [Randolf]
Dickens is here now, as well as ever, and with the same old capacity
for Scotch whiskey."[19]

During Ellis's first overseas tour, the helm of the Marine Corps
changed. With the approach of Heywood's sixty-fourth birthday in
1903, Col. George Reid, the Adjutant and Inspector, appeared as the
likely successor. The influential Reid enjoyed wide, bipartisan support, especially from a former Secretary of the Navy in a Democratic
administration, Hilary A. Herbert. A powerful Republican, Sen.
Marc Hanna, lent his influence in Reid's case as well. But the relationship between the Commandant and the Adjutant and Inspector
may have soured by then, for Heywood failed to argue Reid's case as
his successor. In addition, resistance to the selection of a staff officer
for the commandancy gained momentum from among line officers
of both branches of the naval services. Heywood retired on 3 October 1903, and Col. George F. Elliott succeeded him without dis-
cernible dissent or controversy. A veteran campaigner who had
accepted a commission in the Marine Corps in 1870 following his
expulsion from the U.S. Military Academy West Point for academic
deficiencies, Elliott had performed to the satisfaction of his superiors through long years of sea and expeditionary duty and with
increasing distinction during his field-grade years.[20]

Ellis welcomed the relief from the humdrum daily routine at
Cavite and the Spartan existence in the old Spanish naval arsenal.
During the first few weeks of his new assignment, the *Kentucky* con-
ducted exercises in Manila Bay and then entertained the visiting
British Far East Fleet. Near the end of February 1903, the battleship,
with the fleet commander and his staff embarked, stood to for

Borneo. A change in plans, however, saw the *Kentucky* steam directly for Singapore. The sparkling British colony just off the tip of the Kra Isthmus impressed Ellis. A sense of order and efficiency prevailed, in contrast to what he had witnessed in the Philippines. In a letter to his mother recounting the port visit for her, Ellis once again revealed that the spirit of neocolonialism and social Darwinism had captured his worldview: "Singapore is a much finer place than Manila but I suppose the latter will be just as good when we have occupied it as long as the English have this place."[21]

After a port visit there, the battleship stopped in Malacca and then set a course for Hong Kong, arriving in late March. From the British Crown Colony, the fleet flagship steamed north for the Chinese cities of Amoy and Chefoo. While in China, the admiral took a party to Peiping for an official visit, and Ellis had the opportunity to accompany it. The *Kentucky* then continued on to the Japanese port city of Yokohama. Ellis demonstrated a wry sense of humor in his worldview, noting that a "Rev. Mr. Austin is having church on board the ship this morning—he has a very slim audience, though—the men prefer to smoke and play cards rather than listen to an exhortation upon their sinful lives." At this point in his life, Ellis appears to have shed much of his evangelical upbringing. The previous August his brigade commander had embarked upon a program to improve the moral climate of the Marine garrison at Cavite. Colonel Forney considered the morals of his Marines to be of a low order, especially that of the officers. The brigade commander ordered the remodeling of a hall, fitted out for church services. Ellis apparently expressed his dislike for the scheme, because Goodrell excused him from participation. Disgusted, Goodrell instructed him to "have nothing to do with it."[22]

The uncommon assignment to command the Marines in the *Kentucky* proved fortuitous for Ellis in many respects. The Secretary of the Navy ordered the fleet flagship home to New York from Yokohama, and thus Ellis had circumvented the perfunctory length of an overseas assignment. Additionally, he had the opportunity to associate with the Fleet Marine Officer, Maj. George Barnett from the Naval Academy Class of 1881—one of the more promising officers of the Marine Corps. More than a decade later, Barnett would select Ellis as one his aides-de-camp when the former assumed the commandancy.[23] On 25 May 1904, Ellis stood detached when Capt. William H. Parker reported aboard to relieve him soon after the *Kentucky* steamed into New York Harbor. By this time Ellis had logged a total of one year, four months, and five days in overseas time instead of the customary two to two and a half years. Ellis's promotion to first lieutenant caught up with him on 15 March 1904 and established his date of rank as 3 March 1903.[24]

Reporting directly to the Commandant on 12 June 1904, as was the custom at the time, Ellis served then throughout the summer at Marine Barracks, Washington. After a lengthy leave visiting relatives in Pratt, Kansas, from 17 July to 13 August, he joined the barracks at Mare Island, California, reporting on 25 September 1904. Given an assignment as quartermaster for the command, Ellis chafed and attempted to avoid the assignment. Despite his discomfiture in the new assignment, from 31 September 1904 to 31 December 1905, Ellis managed to perform to the satisfaction of the barracks commanders. He continued to receive only the highest marks on his fitness reports. In his first evaluation, Lt. Col. Lincoln Karmany rated Ellis "excellent" in all categories and noted that he was "a reliable, capable, and efficient officer." The same laudatory remarks continued in his next evaluation. Earlier, at the Washington barracks, Ellis had earned similar marks under the supervision of Lt. Col. James E. Mahoney.[25]

By then the new Commandant had grown increasingly disconcerted over his inability to meet the demands placed on the small force. In testimony before the House Naval Affairs Committee, Major General Commandant Elliott noted that he was authorized only 255 officers and 7,329 enlisted men. From these meager assets, the Marine Corps counted 1,874 men in the ships of the fleet, 476 ashore in Panama, and the brigade in the Philippines. Despite Elliott's best efforts to reduce the length of the onerous tours in the Western Pacific, many Marines served up to three years in the islands while the Army kept its promise to keep the hardship tours limited to two years.[26]

Somehow, Ellis managed temporary duty as a recruiting officer in nearby Oakland during the summer of 1906. He was then detached for similar duties at the Marine Corps Recruiting Station in Des Moines, Iowa, from 31 July 1906 to 19 April 1907. In that era most junior officers spent repeated tours as recruiting officers, as the smaller of the sea services expanded significantly following the Spanish-American War. On the eve of the conflict with Spain, the strength of the Corps had stood at 4,700 enlisted men. A decade later that total had almost doubled, to 9,267. But despite the importance placed on recruiting duties, Ellis apparently failed to apply himself diligently. For the first time since his duties under instruction at the barracks in Boston, his marks on a fitness report fell from "excellent" to "good." In the spring of 1907 Ellis returned to Mare Island, but he received orders on 18 November 1907 returning him to the Philippines early in the winter of that year.[27]

Ellis arrived in Manila on 21 December 1907. The brigade commander, Col. William P. Biddle, ordered him to Olongapo. For the remainder of 1907 until 14 February 1908, Ellis served as adjutant of the 2nd Regiment under Lt. Col. Hiram I. Bearss. Olongapo stood at the end of Subic Bay and housed the huge floating dry dock that serviced the Asiatic Fleet. The Marine regiment served as the expeditionary force in support of the fleet in the Western Pacific. On 21 July 1903 the Department of the Navy ordered the consolidation of Marine Corps forces in the archipelago: Cavite, Olongapo, Basila, and Pollic. With a total strength of fifteen hundred men assigned, the Secretary of the Navy directed the positioning of at least a thousand leathernecks at Olongapo in readiness for immediate deployment to China. But by the time of Ellis's return to Subic Bay in

1907, the size of the force at Olongapo had slipped to 23 officers and 849 enlisted Marines.[28]

Ellis apparently performed to the expectations of the demanding Bearss, known throughout the Marine Corps by the sobriquet "Hiking Hiram" because of his penchant for speedy route marches in the field. Bearss marked Ellis's first semiannual fitness report with both "excellent" and "good" marks, and the regimental commander noted that Ellis demonstrated "ability in road-sketching and mapping." Significantly, item five, with regard to intemperance or the use of drugs and alcohol to excess, was marked "none."[29]

An increasing estrangement with the Empire of Japan—especially following Japan's angry response to the 1906 decision of the San Francisco School Board to segregate children of Asian descent—prompted U.S. military and naval planners to scrutinize the defenses of the Philippines anew. The admiral commanding the Asiatic Fleet developed plans to fortify Grande Island, a strategic landmass at the mouth of Subic Bay. On 14 February 1908, Bearss ordered Ellis detached from his headquarters to assume the duties as the executive officer of Company "E" on the island. Both Company "E" and Company "F" had the mission of emplacing naval guns sited seaward, as well as laying protective minefields, mounting searchlights, and positioning other equipment to protect the strategic harbor. By the following fall, senior Army officers had concluded that the forces under their command were inadequate to defend Subic Bay in the event of an enemy invasion. To the dismay of senior Navy officers, President Roosevelt agreed and ordered work at Subic Bay suspended pending a more thorough study and final decision.[30]

Meanwhile, Bearss rotated home and was relieved by Lt. Col. James E. Mahoney. Then the latter became ill and returned to the United States, resulting in the assignment of Maj. John A. Lejeune to command the expeditionary regiment at Olongapo. Shortly thereafter Biddle departed the Philippines without a nominal relief arriving on schedule, and Lejeune assumed the duties of Marine Corps brigade commander in the Philippines. Hindsight suggests that it was Lejeune who selected Ellis to command a company in the advanced-base force emplaced on the island. During this tour in the Philippines, Ellis's superiors marked him generally "excellent" in all categories on fitness reports.

For his command of Company "E" from 1 July to 30 September 1908, Ellis was noted to be "a zealous and efficient officer." While he was observed as the commanding officer of Company "F" from 12 November to 4 December 1908, his reporting senior apparently referred to the earlier report and marked Ellis the same; this time, however, he also described him as "an efficient and zealous officer." During the short interval between the two reporting periods, Ellis performed special duties involving the litigation of land cases with local Filipinos.[31]

That fall Ellis underwent his second formal examination for promotion. Just as before, the board began with a scrutiny of his medical record but found nothing unusual or untoward. Ellis answered questions to demonstrate his knowledge on the regulations governing small-arms firing and field engineering. On the second day of his appearance he wrote responses to questions on military law and naval ordnance and gunnery. The examining officers were satisfied and, declaring Ellis fit in all respects for promotion to the rank of captain, sent his name forward to the Commandant. When the warrant finally arrived, HQMC directed a date of rank of 18 May 1908; Ellis stood eighty-seventh out of the Marine Corps's ninety captains on that date.[32]

By the beginning of 1909, Ellis's professional zeal had apparently convinced Lejeune that he could be trusted with increased responsibilities. From 1 January through 31 May, Ellis commanded Company "F." Then he took over Company "E" for the entire month of June. The latter assignment included commanding the body of Marines as before, but also required his direction of the fortification effort and management of the local post exchange as well. It is at this juncture that Ellis supposedly shot the glasses off a table during a boring and strained dinner with a visiting Navy chaplain. But this story is unattributed, except in a journalist's account.[33]

Early in the spring of 1910, Ellis relinquished his duties on Grande Island and returned to Olongapo. By then a normal rotation of senior officers had occurred: Col. Lincoln Karmany, a heavy-drinking officer who had just scandalized genteel naval circles with a stormy divorce, arrived to assume command of the brigade. Lejeune had rotated home the previous summer. Lt. Col. Joseph H. Pendleton commanded the 2nd Regiment at Olongapo, and Ellis returned to familiar duties as adjutant. Even then Ellis retained a hand in the activities of the advanced base by supervising the storage and maintenance of equipment. Pendleton approved of Ellis's performance and took the opportunity to extol his subordinate's professional virtues in glowing terms: for the period from 1 October 1910 to 12 January 1911, Pendleton noted that "this officer's active, intelligent, and careful work in the Advance Base cannot be too highly commended. . . . I only regret that there is no higher term than 'excellent' to apply to this officer."[34]

Ellis stood detached from the brigade and sailed from the Philippines on 12 January 1911. Initially he had orders in hand to return to the barracks at Mare Island—a post that he apparently loathed—but by the time the ship docked in San Francisco a change in orders directed him to the barracks in the Washington Navy Yard. On the day he reported to the barracks, 22 March 1911, Ellis exhibited the career frustrations that would punctuate the remainder of his career. After almost a decade in uniform, only his work with the advanced-base concept in the Philippines had apparently stimulated his interest and intellect. In the entirety of his commissioned service, he had commanded companies of infantry for less than a year, and a seagoing detachment for a shortened tour. His remaining assignments had been on the staff. Perhaps disheartened at this juncture, Ellis penned a letter to the Major General Commandant requesting assignment to aviation duties.[35]

Headquarters Marine Corps apparently ignored the unusual request, and any response emanating from Washington has not survived. Clearly, Ellis thought himself at the crossroads of his career. But from the time of his assignment in the preparation of an advanced base in Subic Bay in support of the Asiatic Fleet and his arrival in Washington, several seemingly mutually exclusive events had transpired that would have a marked impact on his future as a Marine Corps officer. Ultimately, corollaries of these developments, and the bureaucratic machinations that accompanied them, would propel Ellis into professional prominence; at the same time, a growing dependence on alcohol would undermine his career expectations.

3 ~ Increasing Responsibilities 1911–1916

EARL H. ELLIS REPORTED, in compliance with his modified orders, to the Commandant of the Marine Corps on 22 March 1911. His date of rank as a captain, 13 May 1908, placed him number eighty out of ninety-one officers of that rank. Given the melancholy fact that promotions followed strict seniority on the lineal list, Ellis most likely resigned himself to remaining a company-grade officer for perhaps another decade before even becoming eligible for promotion to the rank of major. By then he would have been in a Marine Corps uniform for almost twenty years. When Ellis joined in 1900, the muster rolls listed 174 officers and 5,240 enlisted men. In 1911 that figure had increased to only 328 and 9,282, respectively. Perhaps reflection on his career and the potential for promotion prompted Ellis's request for a change in duties. Just two months after returning from the Philippines, he submitted a request for assignment to aviation duties.[1]

Even as Ellis pondered his career prospects in the smaller of the naval services, anxieties over the future of the Marine Corps and its role with the Navy dominated professional thinking during the closing years of the decade. He returned from this second tour in the Philippines hard on the heels of two events that would have far-ranging effects on both his career and the future of the Marine Corps. The first fractious issue focused on the leathernecks' traditional assignment of providing detachments in the warships of the fleet, something that many reformers within the Navy considered an anachronism remaining from the age of sail.

The most articulate and vociferous spokesman for the reformist element in Navy circles, William F. Fullam, had argued since the 1890s that the Marine guards in the ships of the fleet actually contributed to disciplinary problems by promoting the infantilism of the sailors. While interservice journals and major newspapers focused on the hyperbole of the protagonists, the underlying basis for the brouhaha appeared to be a desire for the Marine Corps to embrace a new mission in support of the fleet. The "Fullamites," as they came to be known pejoratively by a generation of senior Marine Corps officers, envisioned a Marine Corps organized into battalions for embarkation onto Navy transports as advanced-base units in support of the fleet. After almost a decade of interservice wrangling and political posturing, the issue came to the forefront of Washington politics in 1908 when a sympathetic Pres. Theodore Roosevelt ordered the creation of an independent commission to examine the organization of the Department of the Navy.

The Fullamites now had the momentum they thought they needed. In a series of bureaucratic maneuvers beginning that fall, Roosevelt approved an order removing the Marines from all warships. The Major General Commandant, George F. Elliott, responded with gruff determination to what he and his coterie interpreted as nothing less than a veiled attempt to disband the Marine Corps altogether. Then, Maj. Gen. Leonard Wood—an Army officer and a close friend and confidant of President Roosevelt—entered the fray with an innovative solution to the dilemma. Wood, an indefatigable

political schemer and meddler, proposed the amalgamation of the
Army's coastal artillery with the Marine Corps. Congressional watch-
dogs on naval affairs questioned the legality of transferring the
Marine Corps to the Army by executive fiat. Undeterred, General
Wood argued that the leathernecks were basically infantry and could
thus provide ten new regiments for the Army.[2]

What Ellis thought of the political infighting raging within the
Marine Corps hierarchy he never recorded or commented on in his
personal correspondence. But John A. Lejeune, then only a major,
confided to his sister that removal of the Marines from the warships
of the fleet, and subsequent transfer to the coastal artillery, meant the
end of his beloved Corps as a distinct entity. Ultimately, the Marine
Corps turned to its powerful friends in Congress, especially those on
the naval affairs committees. Measures passed both houses of Congress calling for the return of the Marines to the fleet. Even then,
Roosevelt's Secretary of the Navy attempted, albeit in a lame-duck
gesture, to find some sort of loophole to defeat the edict. Obdurate
to the end, Roosevelt signed an executive order directing commanding officers of ships to determine the duties of their Marines rather
than adhering strictly to tradition. The new President, William H.
Taft, brought the contentious affair to an end with the cancellation
of Roosevelt's final executive dictum. Quickly following the controversy over Marines serving with the fleet, events toward the end of
the decade drew unwanted attention and congressional scrutiny into
inner circles of the Marine Corps hierarchy. The events that unfolded
threatened to tarnish the leatherneck image, at least as viewed from
Capitol Hill, and set in motion bureaucratic processes that would
serve to propel Ellis's career ahead at a dizzying pace.[3]

In the same year that the controversy over Marine guards serving
in the warships of the fleet ended, the perennial conflict between staff
officers and officers of the line erupted anew. Staff officers—adjutant
and inspectors, quartermasters, and paymasters—served by appointment, usually for the entirety of a career, and at headquarters in

Washington. Often the designation meant an accelerated promotion. Obviously, such details precluded arduous duty in the field, at sea, or on expeditionary duties overseas. A century of this "staff system" had produced a group of officers who usually became entrenched in building up their own fiefdoms at the expense of the Corps. Some line officers used the term "staff" as a derisive epithet. Heretofore, the eruptions between line and staff at Headquarters Marine Corps (HQMC) were settled through the quiet intervention of the Secretary of the Navy.

Late in 1909, a simmering controversy between Major General Commandant Elliott and a senior member of his staff erupted with such ferocity that HQMC became an object of public ridicule and congressional scrutiny. Elliott, well known for his volcanic temper and impulsive character, upbraided the Adjutant and Inspector, Col. Charles H. Lauchheimer, over an alleged breach of deference and propriety. Lauchheimer sought redress, using the influence of powerful political friends, especially in the Jewish community. His supporters charged that the affair was nothing less than an example of religious bigotry on the part of the Commandant. Initially, Secretary of the Navy George von Lengerke Meyer censured both Lauchheimer and Elliott for their "disgraceful conduct." Lejeune considered the entire episode unsavory and unprofessional, and noted with disgust in a letter to his sister that "fortunately, the real Marine Corps is elsewhere and consists of the 10,000 officers and men who are scattered around the world doing their duties."[4]

The sordid affair mushroomed in the Washington press and garnered attention on Capitol Hill, especially among members of the naval affairs committees. Von Meyer ordered a formal board of investigation, which wound up faulting everyone involved. While acknowledging Elliott's contributions to the Marine Corps, the board criticized his failure to maintain order at HQMC—especially the maintenance of proper respect for the Commandant and his office. Insiders were aware of Elliott's predilection to seek solace in alcohol, a habit that contributed to his sometimes erratic behavior. Since both the Commandant and the Adjutant and Inspector had already been upbraided by the Secretary of the Navy, the investigative board advised no further disciplinary action or courts-martial. It did, however, recommend the detachment of Lauchheimer and other officers who appeared to have been contributors to the controversy from their duties in Washington.[5]

When Elliott reached age sixty-four and applied for retirement in the fall of 1910, the Taft administration pondered a replacement. The Secretary of the Navy's difficult experiences with the departing Commandant caused him to ignore strict compliance with seniority and consider all of the colonels and even lieutenant colonels of the line. But despite the supposed nonpartisan deliberation, politics came to quickly dominate executive decision making in the search for a new Commandant. Rep. John Weeks, a Republican from Massachusetts, championed the cause of Col. George Barnett, his roommate from the Naval Academy Class of 1881. The Virginia congressional delegation lined up in support of Col. Littleton Waller Tazewell Waller, the Marine Corps's most colorful campaigner. The powerful Sen. Boies Penrose urged the appointment of Col. William P. Biddle, the scion of the powerful Philadelphia family of the same name. In an audience with the President, supporters were allowed to argue the case for their respective candidates, after which President Taft excused everyone except Senator Penrose. According to a social aide who witnessed the exchange, Penrose promised to support Taft's legislative program in exchange for Biddle's appointment, and the President acquiesced. Thus Biddle came to the commandancy on 10 February 1911, and it fell to him to determine Ellis's new assignment.[6]

By the time Ellis reported in person to the Major General Commandant to discuss his next assignment, both controversies appeared to have subsided. At least neither episode prompted him sufficiently to comment on them in letters home. Ellis's request for aviation duties may well have inspired Biddle to cast about for a posting more to the liking of the brainy Ellis; clearly, the continuing round of barracks duties, punctuated with overseas assignments in the Philippines, had run their course for the near term. Given the sacrosanct adherence to an officer's date of last return from duties outside the continental United States, orders to Marine Corps outposts in the Caribbean seemed unlikely. As Biddle reviewed his personnel requirements, a unique possibility appeared seemingly tailored for someone with an intellectual bent. In his audience with the Commandant, Ellis held a distinct advantage because Biddle had commanded the brigade in the Philippines during the latter's recent tour and thus knew of the superlative fitness reports Ellis received while involved with advanced-base work. During the short period that Ellis served at the Washington barracks upon his return from overseas, his reporting senior continued to mark him 4.0 and "excellent" on all fitness reports. Significantly, there was no indication that Ellis returned from the Philippines with an alcohol problem.[7]

Biddle suggested that Ellis take the summer course at the Naval War College, and his ambitious subordinate leapt at the opportunity. He was detached from the Marine Barracks, Washington, on 27 May with orders to report to Newport by the end of the month. At the time, the institution offered only the four-month short course, but beginning in the fall of 1911 it expanded the curriculum into a full year's study. The president of the college, Adm. William L. Rodgers, asked the Commandant to retain Ellis and another officer, Randolf C. Berkeley, for participation in the longer course (11 September 1911–28 October 1912). At the time, the Naval War College constituted the only war-planning body in the Navy, because the general staff had been discarded and the college's faculty and students comprised the Navy's only strategic study group. The long course consisted of a main battle problem, representing hostilities between Blue and Orange. The curriculum included chart maneuvers, tactical games on the maneuver board, lectures by the staff of the college, topics of general interest, and international law.[8]

Ellis prepared several papers, all of which focused on advanced-base scenarios: "Naval Bases—Their Location, Resources, and Security"; "The Denial of Bases"; "The Security of Advanced Bases and Advanced Base Operations"; and "The Advanced Base Force." At the conclusion of the long course, Admiral Rodgers requested that Ellis remain as a member of the faculty. The president of the college held a very high opinion of Ellis's professionalism, apparently, and consistently marked his fitness reports 4.0 and "excellent." Comments such as "bold," "calm," "meticulous," "even-tempered," "forceful," "painstaking," and "industrious" reflected the hallmarks of Ellis's career to date and showed no indication of the intemperance that would cloud his professional future. With Biddle's concurrence, Ellis remained in Newport as a lecturer and seminar leader from 29 October 1912 until 16 October 1913.[9]

His next assignment reflected both his experiences at the Naval War College and his keen interest in the concept of advanced bases in support of the fleet. Although it appears that Admiral Rodgers selected Ellis simply because he had no other officer available to send to the maneuvers of the Advanced Base Force in 1913, in hindsight the choice appears prophetic. During Ellis's previous tour in the Philippines, the Marine Corps Adjutant and Inspector had visited the command at Olongapo and noted, with approval, the progress of the advanced-base work. The report Ellis filed upon his return to Washington prompted Colonel Lauchheimer to write an official letter of commendation over the Commandant's signature for Ellis's promotion file: "The Advanced Base Outfit appears to be in efficient condition and it is believed that if called upon for use it would be found thoroughly satisfactory. This condition is mainly due to the excellent work of Captain Earl H. Ellis."[10]

Four days after departing the Naval War College, Ellis reported to the newly formed Advanced Base Force at the Philadelphia Navy Yard. Shortly after the turn of the century, the Navy's new General Board addressed the obvious requirement for support of the fleet in worldwide operations. To operate any distance from the shores of the United States, the fleet needed either an extensive supply train or advanced bases established to provide supplies, munitions, and repair facilities for the ships and amphibious forces. Proponents pointed to the successful seizure of Guantánamo in support of operations in Santiago during the Spanish-American War. At the first meeting of the General Board of the Navy, in April 1900, Col. George C. Reid argued for the "organization of a force of Marines sufficient to hold each of three positions: Culebra [Puerto Rico], Samana [Dominican Republic], and Guantanamo [Cuba]; composition of this force as to infantry and artillery to maintain a position against cruisers or naval brigades landing to attack it." A year later, the board ordered the organization of a fixed defense regiment of a thousand men to be trained at Annapolis and Newport. Throughout the decade, ships of the fleet experimented in the landing of naval guns ashore, and naval planners formulated lists of equipment for advanced-base outfits.

Ellis's work at Subic Bay, along with efforts begun in 1907 prior to his assignment to Olongapo, demonstrated that advanced bases were necessary. Personnel increases for the Marine Corps reflected these requirements. In 1910 the Secretary of the Navy ordered the Commandant of the Marine Corps to organize and equip two advanced-base outfits, one on each coast of the United States. In response, however, a base on the West Coast was set aside in favor of the existing force at Olongapo. In 1911, Biddle ordered the establishment of an Advanced Base School at the Philadelphia Navy Yard. The Navy, in turn, fitted out the *Hancock* to join the *Prairie* as the only two readily available amphibious troop transports. On the eve of the maneuvers in Culebra, Barnett, who commanded the Marine Barracks, Philadelphia, and the Advanced Base Force during the maneuvers in Culebra, acknowledged serious problems in a letter to the Secretary of the Navy. He noted the difficulty in moving naval guns and troops ashore and recommended the acquisition of motorized tractors.[11]

That frequent critic of the Marine Corps's preparedness to support the fleet, Captain Fullam, penned a scathing report on the condition of the Advanced Base Force at Philadelphia. In a subsequent report he blamed the unprofessional and untoward situation on the frequent transfer of officers, personnel turbulence, inadequate preparation of the instructors, and total unpreparedness. For Fullam and his coterie, the seeming lackluster response by the Marine Corps to the mission of advanced bases supported contentions that the smaller of the naval services remained wedded to anachronistic missions associated with the age of sail.[12]

Fullam, now the Aide for Inspections for the Department of the Navy, heaped criticism on the Marine Corps for the lack of progress in developing the advanced-base force. Following an inspection of the Philadelphia Navy Yard in May 1913, he growled that "practically nothing [with regard to the advanced-base force] has been accomplished during the past thirteen years." That fall, Fullam intoned that "the present lack of adequate material [for the advanced-base force] clearly indicates the condition of unpreparedness for meeting the demands of war."[13]

By midsummer of 1913, the General Board of the Navy had taken a firm position with regard to the employment of the smaller of the naval services in support of the fleet. It recommended the establishment of a Marine expeditionary force, to include the regiment currently at the Philadelphia Navy Yard. Moreover, the board recommended that the force be exercised during the 1914 winter maneuvers in the Caribbean. Specifically, and for the first time, the board asked the Secretary of the Navy for authorization to study organization, transportation requirements, and equipment assigned to the advanced-base outfit. Most importantly for the Marine Corps and for visionaries like Ellis, the board hoped for an examination of "the duties of Marines and their connection with advanced base outfits."[14]

Fullam and his supporters continued to argue for a new Marine Corps mission in support of the fleet, one that was commensurate

with the precepts of the age of Alfred Thayer Mahan and in anticipation of engagements between entire fleets. Immediately after the
brouhaha of 1908, no less an icon and luminary than Adm. George
Dewey wrote to Fullam to lend his support. Dewey posited that
Marines be employed both as an expeditionary force and an
advanced-base outfit. The venerable admiral argued that Marines
organized as battalions afloat presented a more advantageous force
than the customary organizations of shipboard detachments assembled into ad hoc battalions and regiments. In the months just prior
to the fleet maneuvers in Culebra, Fullam suggested the formation of
a specialized flotilla in conjunction with the advanced-base outfits.
Seizing on the imagination of Mahan, apparently, Fullam envisioned
the flotilla consisting of a battleship, minelayers, submarines, a division of torpedo boats, and the troop transports *Hancock* and *Prairie.*
By late fall 1913, Fullam was suggesting the permanent deployment
of the advanced-base outfit in the aging transports—the mobile regiment on the *Prairie* and the fixed regiment on the *Hancock.* Fullam
thought both ships, with Marines embarked, should be kept in New
Orleans except to join the Atlantic Fleet during summer maneuvers.[15]

Ellis's arrival at the Philadelphia Navy Yard coincided with the eve
of the force's first maneuver. By then the force had mushroomed into
a headquarters and two thirteen-hundred-man regiments: one, a
fixed defense regiment composed of coastal artillery, searchlights,
mining companies, machine guns, and harbor-defense mines; the
other, a mobile defense regiment consisting of six companies of
infantry reinforced by field artillery and machine guns to repulse an
enemy landing force. As in the past, HQMC obtained the personnel for the force by scouring the barracks. To man the formations in
late 1913, Lieutenant Colonel Lejeune brought three hundred men
from his barracks in New York to join six companies from Colonel
Barnett's barracks at the Philadelphia Navy Yard. In addition, the
barracks at Annapolis, Washington, Portsmouth, and Boston contributed personnel to raise the total to twelve companies of Marines.[16]

The previous July, Barnett and Assistant Secretary of the Navy Franklin D. Roosevelt had chosen the tiny island of Culebra, sixteen miles east of Puerto Rico, as the site for the Advanced Base Force maneuver. Although the staff of the Atlantic Fleet prepared the overall scheme for the fleet maneuver, the Advanced Base School in Philadelphia drew up the plans for the exercise. Ellis was assigned to the headquarters as the intelligence officer and is presumed to have had significant input into the planning. On 1 November 1913 he journeyed to Culebra for a reconnaissance of the artillery positions and campsites. Upon his return to Philadelphia, he confirmed the feasibility of the exercise on the island. The scenario involved a declaration of war by the "red" nation (clearly, Germany) on 15 December 1913; the Atlantic Fleet (of the "blue" nation) would concentrate on Culebra to meet the enemy fleet and then steam north to defend the eastern coast of the United States. The semiofficial *Army-Navy Journal* trumpeted that "the exercise at Culebra will probably be the most important from a tactical standpoint that has ever been undertaken by the Marine Corps."[17]

On 27 November 1913 the Mobile Defense Regiment (27 officers, 798 enlisted men), commanded by Lejeune, steamed out of Philadelphia for New Orleans on the transport *Prairie,* prepared to deploy either to Culebra for maneuvers or to Mexico in the event of hostilities. In mid-December the Fixed Defense Regiment (33 officers, 861 enlisted men), under Lt. Col. Charles G. Long, began its embarkation. On 3 January 1914 Long's regiment left Philadelphia on the *Hancock.* Also embarked on the same convoy were the force headquarters, commanded by Colonel Barnett, a small aviation detachment, and a field hospital. The amphibious shipping left much to be desired, even by the standards of the era.

Launched in 1890 as the SS *El Sol,* the *Prairie* was purchased by the Department of the Navy in 1898 for conversion into an auxiliary cruiser. Decommissioned the following year and sent into mothballs, it underwent refit as a transport for the Atlantic Fleet.

The even more aged *Hancock* had slid down the ways in 1879 as the *Arizona,* then became a receiving ship in 1903. A decade later the ancient vessel went to the Philadelphia Navy Yard as a troop transport. Lt. Col. Wendell C. Neville, commanding a battalion in the Mobile Defense Regiment, complained that "the troop officers quarters in the *Prairie* could be compared to that in a cheap Bowery lodging house."[18]

On 7 January 1914 the amphibious task force dropped anchor off Culebra and began to fortify the small island in earnest. Two weeks later to the day, the opposing fleet arrived on schedule, and the Advanced Base Force defended the island vigorously. The chief umpire, Capt. William S. Sims, declared a victory for the defending forces and proclaimed success for the concept of defending advanced bases. After the ships turned away, the force spent the next two weeks camped on the small island engaged in target practice and other training. Fullam argued prophetically in the months just prior to the Culebra maneuver that the advanced-base concepts ought to become the raison d'être for the Marine Corps: "The Advance[d] base duty and expeditionary work of [the Marine] Corps should be considered as its true field, the one most useful and [the] most important purpose for which it can possibl[y] be assigned."[19]

Finally, on 9 February 1914, the Advanced Base Force returned to New Orleans in anticipation of possible deployment to Mexico in the face of heightened tensions in the region. Barnett prepared Ellis's fitness report following the exercise at Culebra, and Ellis had apparently impressed the commander of the Advanced Base Force, an officer who would play a significant role in his future: "[Ellis] performed in an excellent manner, and will no doubt add very greatly to the success of the expedition to Culebra. Considering the short time he had to make the reconnaissance [of Culebra], his work is quite remarkable."[20] When the ships tied up, both Ellis and Barnett received orders detaching them from the force: Ellis's orders were for an assignment in Guam, and Barnett's were to succeed Biddle as Commandant of the Marine Corps. The latter assignment underscored significant changes for the Department of the Navy.

President-elect Woodrow Wilson's Secretary of the Navy, Josephus Daniels, arrived in 1913 determined to bring order and efficiency to the department. A year with Daniels convinced Biddle of the advantages of retirement, and in late 1913 the quest for a successor began. A glance at the lineal list of that year revealed that the roster of contenders had not changed appreciably. Waller's record book arrived on the Secretary's desk along with a letter from Sen. Claude A. Swanson of Virginia to President Wilson containing the endorsement of all thirty-one Democrats in the Senate; John Weeks, now a senator, championed his old friend Barnett again. Two newcomers appeared. Lieutenant Colonel Lejeune, the commanding officer of the Marine Barracks, New York, and a recent graduate of the Army War College, threw his hat into the ring. Biddle supported Col. Lincoln Karmany, the commanding officer of the Marine Barracks, Mare Island. A veteran campaigner like Waller, Karmany had a reputation for hard drinking and womanizing. And, like Barnett, he had a diploma from the Naval Academy.

As Secretary Daniels considered his choices and prepared to make a recommendation to the President, he found little alternative but to select Barnett. Although Lejeune was an attractive choice and likely the best-qualified candidate of the lot, his rank eliminated him at the outset. Karmany's recent, messy divorce in order to marry another woman made him unacceptable to the moralistic Daniels. Waller lost out simply because the Wilson administration had just announced a new and progressive program with regard to the U.S. administration of the Philippines, and it made poor political logic to appoint an officer who had been accused of inhumane treatment of the Filipinos. Thus, Daniels's choice narrowed to Barnett, although the Secretary felt far from comfortable with the selection. Daniels later recalled his reservations about choosing Barnett, even though at the time it made good political sense to nominate an officer with strong Republican support to serve in a Democratic administration. Moreover, Barnett had an excellent record, albeit with few powder burns or tropical sweat stains on his uniforms, and he had a diploma from the Naval Academy. On 25 February 1914, Barnett took the oath of office as the twelfth Commandant of the Marine Corps. Then, while Barnett basked in the warm glow of congratulations and tributes, Ellis returned to the Pacific for a new assignment.[21]

Ellis's orders transferring him from the Naval War College came about in response to a request from Rear Adm. Bradley A. Fiske, Aide for Operations. On 23 January 1914, Fiske asked Biddle for Ellis's services as a member of a special committee established by the Joint Army-Navy Board to study the defenses of Guam. At the time, Ellis ranked sixty-eighth out of ninety-four captains on the lineal list; he had credit for three years and ten months of overseas duty and one year and four months of sea duty. These totals were not considered excessive or onerous at the time, and thus Ellis appeared a logical candidate for another tour overseas. On 3 March, Ellis joined the other members of the board, headed by Capt. William J. Maxwell, the governor-designate of Guam, and steamed west with them on an Army transport two days later. Shortly after the ship docked on 26 March, Ellis met with his committee to begin their investigative deliberations. Even though more than a decade had passed since the United States acquired Guam from Spain, the island was still governed as a naval station. Some of the naval governors had performed in less than a superlative manner, at times insulting the populace with their autocratic mannerisms. But Maxwell appears to have exhibited the most bizarre behavior and, in the process, sullied Ellis's professional image.

Observers believed that Maxwell suffered from mental deterioration of unknown causes. Claiming himself a devout Catholic, he attended mass irregularly and once even ordered the parish priest to stop ringing the chapel bells on Sunday. Subordinates noted a series of unusual, unpleasant, and incomprehensible orders emanating from the mercurial governor. Ellis earned Maxwell's wrath early in 1914, apparently after losing his temper in the presence of the governor. Maxwell must have remembered the sharp exchange, for he rebuked his subordinate on his next semiannual fitness report: "Ellis was called sharply to account for the manner of speaking to the Governor on one occasion. I considered Captain Ellis's manner and tone disrespectful, and I called him to account for it. He explained in a satisfactory (acceptable) way and the same condition has not been repeated."[22]

Despite the apparent lapse in military decorum, Ellis remained assigned to Guam following the completion of the mission of the Army-Navy Board's ad hoc committee. As a basis for its study, the group used an earlier defensive plan for the island, which called for 60-inch searchlights, mines, a mobile defense force of eighty-five hundred troops, and the installation of large-caliber naval guns on Orote Peninsula. Further development of naval facilities on the island failed to survive senatorial scrutiny, however, and extensive construction work on the base did not begin until 1940. Inexplicably, Maxwell assigned Ellis as his secretary and aide-de-camp, with additional duties as chief of police, registrar of the civil government, and intelligence officer. Undeterred by the cavalier and perfunctory work of the investigative committee that had brought him to Guam in the first place, Ellis continued an independent study of Guam as a site for an advanced base in support of the fleet. In March 1915, Ellis and a group of Marines tested the feasibility of moving 4.7-inch naval guns from ships to a shore emplacement. War had broken out in Europe the previous August, both Japanese and German warships were operating in the waters off the Marianas, and U.S. officials demonstrated concern for the security of Guam.

Ellis's report of a military reconnaissance of Guam reinforced earlier conclusions from both his tour at the Naval War College and as the intelligence officer for the Advanced Base Force in the Culebra maneuvers. At the outset he dismissed any notion of a piecemeal

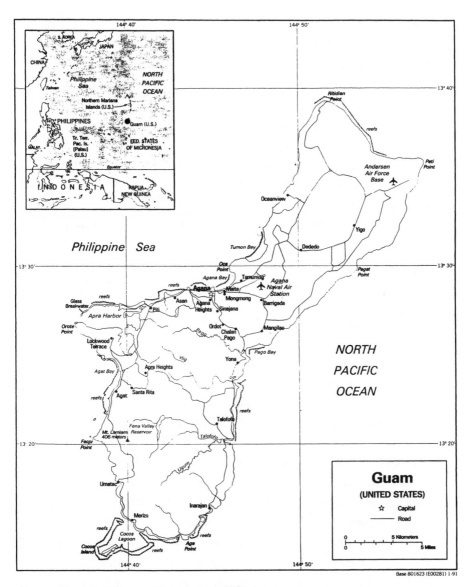

Guam (Suzzalo Library, University of Washington).

defense of the island, insisting that Guam in its entirety must be defended rather than merely Apra Harbor. Ellis envisioned a major line of defense at the water's edge to protect the harbor against enemy assault. He recommended a mobile defense to prevent amphibious landings on the island, and a mobile sea defense to supplement both the fixed and mobile defenses ashore.

Ellis considered the establishment of a stronghold on Orote Peninsula essential both to deny the harbor to the enemy and to retain a foothold for recapturing Guam should an enemy force succeed in establishing a beachhead ashore. In his detailed analysis, Ellis suggested sites for batteries of naval guns on both Orote Peninsula and nearby Cabras Island. His careful analysis included studies of approaches and egress to and from the positions. Ellis took issue with previous studies which concluded that outlying reefs prevented amphibious landings on Guam. He noted that between November and June, surf conditions were such as to allow the passage of small craft from transports to the reef; from there, troop formations could wade ashore without difficulty.[23]

At about this time in 1915, Ellis's health began to deteriorate. Shortly after the exercise to emplace the naval guns, Ellis reported to the naval hospital. His doctors diagnosed exhaustion, overexposure, and overexertion likely resulting from the strenuous nature of the maneuver. To make matters worse, he exhibited severe mental problems, characterized by fits of melancholia and crying, loss of self-control, and a tendency to hysteria. Confined to bed under a regimen of barbiturates, Ellis recovered sufficiently to return to duty after six days in the hospital. However, the diagnosing physician recommended a reduction in work-related activities. Significantly, the entries in Ellis's medical record and untoward comments on fitness reports during the tour in Guam suggest that his problems with alcohol abuse had become uncontrollable.[24]

In Ellis's first fitness report, for the period 1 October 1914 to 31 March 1915, Governor Maxwell marked him with a grade of 3.6, noting Ellis to be "calm, active, forceful" and commending him for his work on emplacing the naval guns ashore. The governor added that Ellis was "unusually well-qualified for intelligence duties in the field." But then Maxwell flayed Ellis on his next report, for the period 1 April to 29 September, writing that Ellis "has what is known as 'temperament' . . . high strung, verging on hysteria after great stress or after such stress . . . [became] sick [after] exhausting [himself] on duty which interests him." Under the rubric of "health," the governor marked Ellis "poor," with a grade of 2.0: "Captain Ellis's [medical] record shows no good reason for his temperamental qualities. They are therefore believed to be congenital." Significantly, Ellis refused to admit he had an alcohol problem and began a program of self-denial, a ruse common to alcoholics. Hospitalized again on 28 June 1915 for "nostalgia," he claimed his condition to be the result of morosity over the death of his mother; actually, Catherine Axline Ellis survived her son, dying in 1941.[25]

On 27 August 1915 the naval station received a cablegram detaching Ellis for duty in Washington. He obtained a berth on the Army transport *Logan* for Manila on 26 September, and from Manila he arranged for further transport on the steamer *Persia* for San Francisco. En route the *Persia* stopped at Yokohama, and Ellis disembarked for a side trip with a group of Japanese officers to the German naval station at Tsingtao on the coast of China. His bent for intelligence activities satisfied, at least for the moment, naval headquarters booked passage for him on the *Chiyo Maru* for San Francisco, which docked on 6 December 1915. After his perfunctory audience with the Commandant, Ellis received orders as one of the three aides-de-camp to Barnett. Significantly, Lejeune, promoted to colonel on 25 February 1914, now served as assistant to the Major General Commandant.

From the outset of his assignment to HQMC, Lejeune had harbored criticism with regard to the functioning of the staff. The appointed staff officers maintained the routine functioning of the smaller of the naval services, but they did not involve themselves in planning for war. Lejeune's tenure as a student at the Army War College during 1909 and 1910 had served to focus his attentions to prudent preparation for armed conflict rather than the scattershot approach used in the Spanish-American War. Besides the Commandant's aides-de-camp, no members of an executive staff existed at the time. When situations demanded additional officers for studies and special boards, personnel demands went out to nearby barracks for the loan of officers. Deeming the situation unworkable and inefficient, Lejeune began to use Barnett's three aides-de-camp as an ad hoc staff. Besides Ellis, Lejeune chose Thomas Holcomb and Ralph S. Keyser.

A fervor of thoughtful analysis and reflection gripped some Marine Corps circles by that date. In 1915, Lejeune and a group of senior officers founded the Marine Corps Association and began publication of a professional journal, the *Marine Corps Gazette*. In the first issue, Lejeune's essay on the mobile defense of advanced bases offered the opinion of the author that "the infantry of any military organization is not only the backbone of that organization, but possesses in a superlative degree, the very highest military qualities." In the next issue of the *Gazette*, Maj. John H. Russell criticized the absence of doctrine and military principles in the seemingly antiquarian Marine Corps. He called for the preparation and promulgation of new doctrine. The editor published commentaries on Russell's polemic, including one by Ellis.[26]

Whatever war planning occurred at HQMC by Ellis, under Lejeune's tutelage, stimulated little enthusiasm in naval circles. Just prior to relinquishing his office in 1914, Biddle argued for the addition of the Commandant of the Marine Corps to the General Board of the Navy. He noted that the board often made decisions of concern to the Marine Corps. In response to Biddle's memorandum, Capt. Victor Blue, Aide for Personnel, agreed, but only to allow the Commandant as an ex officio member. Rear Admiral Fiske enlisted the support of Admiral Dewey to oppose the move, and Secretary

Daniels acquiesced. As a counterproposal, the Secretary of the Navy added Barnett to his Council of Aides, a special advisory group: "In consideration of the important place of the Marine Corps in the organization of the Navy, which has been particularly exemplified by the present situation, Secretary Daniels today decided to add Major General Barnett, the Commandant of the Marine Corps, to his Council of Aides," the press release intoned.[27]

Although President Wilson argued consistently against involving America in the conflagration sweeping Europe—his first Secretary of State, William Jennings Bryan, was a pacifist—military and naval headquarters at home began to scrutinize assets and plan for an eventual entry into World War I. Ellis found HQMC buzzing with rumors and contingency plans in anticipation of a declaration of war. Even before the war clouds loomed, however, Congress approved the expansion of the Marine Corps in response to burgeoning naval requirements resulting from colonial infantry duties. In his final annual report to the Secretary of the Navy, Biddle underscored the fact that an increasing number of commitments for Marines had arisen without a concurrent rise in manpower. Ever since the Spanish-American War and America's increasing willingness to become involved in overseas affairs, both Congress and successive presidents appeared willing to commit naval forces as the spearhead of neocolonialism.

During Ellis's tenure as one of Barnett's aides-de-camp, no issue came to dominate the commandancy more than personnel increases. From an overly committed small force numbering approximately 10,000 officers and men in 1914, the Marine Corps grew to more than 70,000 by the end of World War I. For casual observers of the Corps's administrative scene, the quantum increases appeared tied to the commitment on the western front. However, long before "over there" became a household phrase in the United States, the Commandant and his staff had argued successfully for significant increases in numbers. Presumably, Ellis accompanied Barnett and Lejeune on their frequent trips to Capitol Hill to give testimony before either of the naval affairs committees, and most likely contributed to the staff preparations along with the other aides-de-camp.[28]

In October 1915, Barnett told Secretary Daniels of his concerns regarding personnel shortages. On the heels of a demand by the Navy for an increase of 7,500 men, Barnett argued for an increase in his ranks of 1,500, using the figure of 20 percent of Navy strength for the Corps, which he had cited in his annual report. On 3 February 1916 a special personnel board chaired by Assistant Secretary of the Navy Roosevelt made several far-reaching conclusions: the overall strength of the Marine Corps should be 20 percent of the Navy's, just as Barnett argued; officer strength should be 4 percent of enlisted strength; staff and line officers should be on the same list when considered for promotion; and finally, there should be one brigadier general for every four colonels. Roosevelt and the ad hoc group recommended the end of the special staff ranks. Significantly, the committee had taken note of the stagnation of the officers' lineal list with grave concern. In the committee's view, unless changes were made, by 1930 the average first lieutenant would be age forty-five and the average captain age fifty-one. The Assistant Secretary of the Navy noted ruefully that junior officers of that age would not be sufficiently fit to hike and march with their men.[29]

Even before the board met or reported out, Barnett appeared optimistic. The previous fall, he had indicated to his close friend and fellow Naval Academy graduate, Col. Joseph H. Pendleton, that he anticipated an increase of approximately two thousand officers and men along with authorization of two brigadier generals. The Commandant waxed optimistic: "No one can tell what Congress will do in the personnel way, but I fully expect to get something; in fact, I rather hope to get more than was allowed to go the estimates. If we get anything, I think we will undoubtedly get one or more brigadier generals, but, of course, about this no one can tell. I am sure that everyone in Congress is quite as much inclined to do something for the Marine Corps as for any branch of the military or naval service."[30]

In January 1916, Barnett testified before the House Naval Affairs Committee, which warmed to his plea for increases. Barnett informed the committee that unless company-grade officers received promotions at a more accelerated rate, the average captain would spend thirty-five years in uniform before becoming eligible for advancement to major. In just five more years he would be forced to retire for age! Barnett argued for Marine Corps regiments composed of 1,050 men, with 41 officers to lead them; in addition, a brigade headquarters required 11 officers.[31]

While the representatives appeared to agree with Barnett's argument, a member of the committee appeared ambivalent over at least one aspect of the Commandant's proposal. Rep. Thomas S. Butler argued against merging line and staff officers and spoke out strongly against allowing staff officers to become eligible for promotion to brigadier general. Doubtless the elder Butler reflected the histrionics of his restless son, the colorful Maj. Smedley D. Butler. When news of the Commandant's proposed legislation traveled to Haiti, the younger Butler lost no time venting his spleen in a letter home: "Tell him, the line officers . . . look upon this proposed Marine Corps personnel bill with suspicion . . . it promotes practically no one but staff officers who went into a staff department because they preferred an easy life."[32]

Barnett received even less support from Daniels and Roosevelt. Testifying on 28 February 1916, both officials agreed with the proposed increases in the size of the Marine Corps but expressed reservations over the figure of officer strength of 4 percent of enlisted numbers. Both the Secretary and his assistant appeared doubtful of the need to promote so many colonels to brigadier general. Nonetheless, congressional enthusiasm for such appointments in the Marine Corps had gained momentum since Barnett assumed the commandancy two years before.[33]

As Congress reviewed naval estimates in the final months of the session in 1916, HQMC reported a strength of 348 officers and

10,253 enlisted men, a total of 10,601 Marines. Of that sum, 1,966 served in the ships of the fleet and 2,776 in overseas stations in East Asia or the Caribbean. Barracks commanders on both coasts mustered only 4,823 Marines. Clearly, a disproportionate number of Marines served overseas or with the fleet, creating personal and family hardships and subsequent staffing difficulties for the Commandant. Given these onerous demands for personnel, Ellis could anticipate an assignment overseas following his tour as an aide-de-camp to the Commandant.[34]

On 12 May 1916 the House Naval Affairs Committee reported out its bill for naval appropriations for the following fiscal year to the floor of the House. Much to the surprise of Barnett and his staff, it called for an increase of 3,079 enlisted men for the Marine Corps, approximately 700 more than requested. In June the House passed the measure and sent it on to the Senate. Before the upper house could take up action on the measure, however, a fit of wartime hysteria appeared after Mexican revolutionary Pancho Villa's raid into New Mexico. Following Gen. John J. Pershing's punitive expedition across the border into Mexico, the Senate passed the naval appropriations bill on 22 July 1916, specifying an enlisted strength for the Marine Corps of 14,940, approximately 5,000 more leathernecks than called for in Barnett's original estimates. The bill also allowed the President to increase the size of the Marine Corps up to 17,400 men without further legislation in the event of hostilities.

Much to the delight of Barnett and the Corps's colonels, the Senate measure authorized the creation of eight brigadier generals—including three from among the staff colonels. When the bill became law on 29 August 1916, Barnett received immediate approval to recruit an additional five thousand men, to promote eight colonels to flag rank, to combine the line and staff officers on one list for the purposes of promotion, and to establish the Marine Corps Reserve. In his first term in office, Barnett had presided over a greater increase in the size of the Marine Corps than in any similar period in its history. However, as America drifted closer to war with Germany, the legislation of 1916 would only be the beginning of the expansion of the Corps. Passage of the bill meant that Ellis would be eligible for promotion to major. In a letter to his mother written earlier that summer, he indicated a preference for remaining a captain because of the duties the rank entailed. But Ellis apparently welcomed the opportunity to relinquish his assignment as one of the aides-de-camp to the Commandant: "I won't have to be an aide—I detest it. The general is fine, very fine, but the duty is not in my line. Too many women and too much politics."[35]

Ellis's cryptic comment with regard to women and politics doubtless referred to the Commandant's wife, a frenetic doyenne of Washington society. Keen observers of Marine Corps circles had noted that Lelia Montague Barnett pushed her husband and his career relentlessly into the commandancy with all of the charm and influence she could muster. Once Barnett had taken office in 1914, his ambitious wife turned "Eighth and Eye," the historic home of the titular head of the Marine Corps since 1806, into a site of social prominence. Few of Washington's influential citizens declined invitations to the Barnetts' lavish social functions at their stately quarters or at the palatial estate in nearby Wakefield Manor that Mrs. Barnett had inherited from her first husband. Guests enjoyed witnessing her sparkling repartee at the expense of pretentious politicians. Lelia Montague Barnett involved herself increasingly in service politics and in the internal affairs of the Marine Corps, at one point declaring herself "the Mother of Marines" and the champion of the enlisted ranks. Perhaps troubling to Ellis was the melancholy fact that whenever one of Mrs. Barnett's daughters required an escort and lacked a suitable companion, one of the aides-de-camp would be assigned the task.[36]

Ellis apparently found himself swept away by the frantic preparations at HQMC. He served on endless boards and special committees, responsible for examining contingencies for possible armed conflicts. Besides the commitment to the Western Pacific, which Ellis knew well, sizable contingents of Marines had deployed to the Caribbean. These and other personnel issues dominated Barnett's commandancy and most of the activities of his three aides-de-camp. The stress of his high-profile position apparently exacerbated Ellis's nervous condition and chronic alcoholism. In the early fall of 1916, while on temporary duty in Philadelphia, Ellis turned himself in to the naval hospital, complaining to examining physicians of depression and tension. His doctors noted that their patient behaved emotionally, exhibited muscular spasms, and spoke incoherently at times. Ellis exhibited frequent coughing, apparently without cause, and at one point exclaimed that "life was not worth living." He complained of insomnia, headaches, and anorexia. Failing to discern any plausible psychiatric symptoms, including alcoholism, Ellis's physicians treated him with a regimen of barbiturates. On 16 September they released him to full duty. Barnett continued to rate Ellis on his fitness reports as "excellent" and with grades of 4.0.[37]

Barely a month later, Ellis's case came before a board of examination for promotion to major. The spectacular increases in personnel had affected his status on the lineal list, but this time it required Barnett's personal intervention to explain away the untoward comment by Governor Maxwell on Ellis's first fitness report from Guam: "As the reporting officer [Maxwell] states in the report that the matter was explained in a satisfactory, acceptable way, I do not consider this entry as unfavorable . . . the candidate [Ellis] served under my personal command during the winter of 1913–1914, and is at present one of my aides-de camp. I know him to be an exceptionally-capable and efficient officer, thoroughly qualified in every way for promotion, and it is therefore recommended that the findings of the board in the case of Captain Earl H. Ellis be approved." Apparently satisfied, the board recommended Ellis for promotion to major. Barnett did note, however, that Ellis's health was only "fair" and that "he suffers at present from the bad effects of duty in Guam. He is improving." It would be extremely unlikely that any board of examination for a promotion of an officer would ignore an almost personal request from the Commandant, and Ellis's file went forward with a recommendation for advancement. His new rank became effective on 29 August 1916—backdated, as was the custom—and Ellis pinned on his new insignia of rank on 9 April 1917; America declared war on the Central Powers a week later.[38]

4 ～ World War I
1917–1918

THE AIDES-DE-CAMP TO THE COMMANDANT of the Marine Corps beseeched Maj. Gen. George Barnett for orders to join the force forming at Quantico. Earl H. Ellis, Thomas Holcomb, and Ralph S. Keyser knew that Barnett planned to offer a brigade of combat-ready Marines for service in France. The trio of young officers was aware that Barnett hoped desperately to involve his Marines in the initial contingent of troops sent to France. By then Ellis and the others had benefited from the unprecedented expansion of the Marine Corps with promotions to field-grade rank, and all of them hoped to command a battalion of infantry in the war. The fervor and excitement permeated all ranks. Career Marines clamored for an assignment to a unit earmarked for deployment to the American Expeditionary Forces (AEF); college students dropped out of school to enlist in an outfit for "over there."

The U.S. declaration of war against Germany in April 1917 offered Major General Barnett the opportunity to continue his spectacular expansion of the Marine Corps. Even the disclosure that the American involvement would be composed mostly of U.S. Army personnel—essentially an "all-Army show"—failed to deter the enthusiasm of the Commandant. In testimony before the House Naval Affairs Committee, Barnett posited that every military and naval asset should be made available in times of national emergency. He even took the unusual step of arguing with the Chief of Naval Operations, Adm. William S. Benson, over the issue of deployment of Marines as ground troops in the war. Fearful of burgeoning naval requirements, Benson wondered if ships' guards and barracks' detachments would be manned fully. Barnett assured a skeptical Benson that leatherneck commitments in support of the fleet would be kept. The Commandant noted for the benefit of the House Naval Affairs Committee that three brigades of Royal Marines served in the British lines in France. On 20 May 1917 the naval appropriations bill for fiscal year 1918 became law; significantly, it included provisions for an increase in the number of men wearing forest green to more than thirty thousand. Barely a month later, the General Board of the Navy expressed concern that, despite Barnett's assurances, Marine Corps's commitments to the fleet might not be kept. In this instance, the board urged that the naval strength of the Marine Corps be brought up to full force.[1]

Barnett convinced an unenthusiastic Secretary of the Navy Josephus Daniels to offer a brigade of Marines to accompany Gen. John J. Pershing and the initial contingent of the AEF to France. Daniels viewed any attempt at aggrandizement of personnel on the part of the Commandant with a chary eye, believing that Barnett would use any increase to support his pleas for more senior officers. But in this instance, Daniels agreed to the deployment and accompanied Barnett to an audience with President Wilson's Secretary of War, Newton D. Baker. Barnett prevailed on a reluctant Daniels to offer a brigade of Marines to accompany the initial draft of American troops to France.

Anxious to participate, Barnett agreed to several administrative changes to outfit and equip the token leatherneck force along Army lines. Because the typical Marine Corps brigade contained the same number of men as an Army infantry regiment, Barnett ordered the 6th Marines combined with the 5th Marines for the deployment. To give the outfit polish and grit, he ordered eight companies of seasoned veterans home from the Caribbean to form the backbone of the 5th Marines and infuse it with characteristic Marine Corps eccentricity and toughness. From the outset, however, the Army made the Marines feel unwanted, as Daniels noted ruefully in his memoirs: "When war was declared, I tendered, ready and equipped, two regiments of Marines to be incorporated into the Army. Senior Army officers were not keen to accept them."[2]

The obvious reluctance on the part of the Army and the Department of War to include Marines in the deployment failed to dampen spirits at Headquarters Marine Corps (HQMC). With his rank, diploma from the Army War College, and vantage as assistant to the Commandant of the Marine Corps, Brig. Gen. John A. Lejeune believed that he possessed the best qualifications to command the brigade. He communicated the news of the deployment excitedly to his friend in Haiti, Maj. Smedley D. Butler, along with an offer to obtain command of a battalion for the frenetic and ambitious son of Cong. Thomas S. Butler. When the brigade became only a regiment, Barnett selected a Naval Academy classmate, Col. Charles A. Doyen, to command it. Lejeune took the news stoically, simply because regiments are commanded by colonels, not brigadier generals. Butler fumed disgustingly from his lonely post, snarling petulantly to his powerful father: "News has just come that . . . Doyen is taking a regiment of Marines abroad right away, that is what you get by staying on duty around Washington. . . . [I have] far more hard work to my credit and get left out."[3]

Even though his hopes to command a brigade of Marines in France appeared dashed, Lejeune—as the assistant to the Commandant—prepared the roster of officers for the 5th Marines. Despite the hyperbole appearing since, Lejeune did not include either Butler or Ellis in his list of potential battalion commanders. Ellis's career, meanwhile, took another curious twist. His own request for orders to a unit earmarked for France resulted only in an assignment to Quantico. On 14 May 1917 the Department of the Navy leased six thousand acres in the woods of northern Virginia along the banks of the Potomac River. Promoted to the rank of major, Ellis received orders to the site to assist in the establishment of the new Marine Corps facility and then to serve as an instructor in the school for newly commissioned officers. Apparently Ellis's assignment came about following another bout of neurasthenia in June 1917. Convincing his physician that the nervous condition was precipitated by duties in close confinement, Ellis asked the hospital to send a letter to Barnett recommending orders to Quantico. In July, 250 new second lieutenants reported for training, and Ellis served as an instructor at the base until that fall. In a letter to his sister, Ellis scored a recent editorial in the *New York Herald* that criticized the harsh discipline and training of the various wartime military camps and argued that the purpose of such installations was to "inculcate the germs of devastation and assassination." Somberly, Ellis proclaimed that "if we don't win this war, we won't have any world at all."[4]

Barnett then selected Ellis for a liaison trip to France, apparently relying on his judgment on such matters as organization, training, and equipment. Ellis embarked on the *Von Steuben* on 25 October 1917, arrived in France to observe the formation of the AEF, and returned to New York shortly after the first of the year. By then the 4th Brigade (Marine), AEF, had taken up duties ashore far removed from what the Commandant or any of the senior Marine Corps officers had envisioned. Much to Barnett's disgust, Pershing and his staff deployed the leathernecks in a variety of rear-echelon assignments along the lines of communication as the initial contingent of the 1st Division, AEF, began intensive training for America's entrance into the western front. Pershing gave scant regard to the token force of Marines, but when attention was paid it contributed to a lack of interservice harmony. From the outset Pershing insisted on commonality among the units of the AEF. Doyen's Marines turned in their trusty Lewis machine guns for the less reliable Hotchkiss model. Much to their disgust, they learned to march according to the Army's style of close-order drill. When their distinctive green uniforms wore out, they donned Army khaki—but sewed their Marine Corps buttons onto the unpopular cloth.

The 1st Division, regulars in name only, failed to perform to Pershing's standards at that stage in the war. In his initial inspection visit to the units at Gondrecourt, the sharp-eyed Commander in Chief (CinC) noted with dismay that the interloping leathernecks appeared more soldierly than his own troops. But the unwanted regiment, foisted on him by the Department of the Navy, lent him a welcome surplus of trained manpower when such assets could not be obtained readily. Nonetheless, Pershing moved to end the deployment of the token force of Marines with a terse cablegram to the Adjutant General of the Army. In it the CinC repeated his desire for commonality. He cited an odd replacement system and the lack of supporting elements common to an Army division. Finally, he wondered, if such assets could be spared from naval duties, then they should become part of the national army forming for America's participation in the war. Pershing concluded his message by asking that "no more Marines be sent to France." To his dismay, however, the War Department informed him that the deployment had been directed by the President himself and could not be deterred. Moreover, Pershing surely must have bridled when the War Department directed that not only would the 5th Marines remain, but when the 6th Marines arrived, the two regiments and a machine-gun battalion would become an infantry brigade in the 2nd Division, AEF.[5]

From then until the spring of 1918, the token force of Marines gained Pershing's attention or earned his displeasure occasionally. At home Barnett vented his frustrations over the apparent lack of suitable duties for his leathernecks onto any congressman who lent an

ear. Such carping usually resulted in some sort of official correspondence from Washington, irritating Pershing and his staff. Many
senior Army officers considered the meddling merely patent exam-
ples of the Department of the Navy's attempt to intrude into an all-
Army show. But then command of the Marine brigade changed in a
dramatic way and set in motion events that would have far-reaching
consequences for the Corps.

The sharp-eyed Pershing grew increasingly chary over the physical condition of his senior officers. Many general officers appeared
obese, redundant, and doddering. The CinC directed a special medical team to examine his senior commanders; those appearing unfit
would be either transferred to the staff or sent home. Pershing's medical staff determined that Doyen, a stout and graying age fifty-nine,
had worn himself out and was not well. The CinC's laconic cablegram to Washington informed Barnett that Doyen had been relieved.
Although Pershing paid generous tribute to Doyen on his departure,
in truth the exacting CinC probably concluded that Barnett's Naval
Academy classmate "lacked the grasp," a pungent observation—
appearing often in Pershing's diary or in a memorandum to his chief
of staff—that meant the end of a senior officer's career.[6]

Pershing saw this as an opportunity to replace the veteran leatherneck with an Army crony. Brig. Gen. James G. Harbord, the first chief
of staff of the AEF, assumed command of the 4th Brigade (Marine),
AEF, on 6 May 1918. Despite Pershing's reluctance to have Marines
in the AEF, he considered the brigade an elite unit and a worthy
assignment for his old friend. Marines claim that Pershing admonished Harbord: "You are to have command of the finest body of
troops in France, and if they fail to live up to that reputation, I shall
know whom to blame." Harbord recalled simply that the CinC said
"he could give me no better command in France than to let me succeed General Doyen with the Marines."[7]

Languishing in frustration at Quantico, Ellis must have wondered
why Doyen returned to command the base. News of Harbord's

accession to command the Marines in France sent shock waves through naval circles in Washington. Pershing's compendious cablegram indicated that no replacement was required for Doyen; if HQMC sent out another brigadier general, he would receive an assignment on a staff or in the Services of Supply and not a command. Undaunted by the disappointing rejoinder, Lejeune renewed his quest for orders overseas. Although Barnett had rebuffed the entreaties of the uncommonly capable Lejeune and loathed losing his yeoman services, he retreated given the turn of events in France. Lejeune had commanded at Quantico since 27 September 1917, and apparently Ellis's friendship with one of the Marine Corps's luminaries grew stronger. Lejeune obtained orders to France and detached from Quantico on 23 May 1918; he took Ellis with him. Lejeune carried the verbal orders of the Commandant to encourage Pershing to markedly increase the number of Marines in the AEF, increases far more than anyone within government or naval circles could have imagined the year before. But as the disarming but calculating Lejeune prepared to depart, events in France put the capstone on leatherneck aggrandizement. Ironically, one of the Marine Corps's most heroic and costly victories spurred Pershing and his staff to dig in their heels and resist further deployment of Marines to France.

In response to the German offensive in the spring of 1918, Pershing released three of his divisions for duty in the lines to help the Allies stem the onslaught. While the 1st Division deployed to Cantigny north of Paris, the 2nd and 3rd Divisions took up positions at Château Thierry. On 2 June, Harbord's Marines dug in along the Paris-Metz highway just south of Belleau Wood. Over the next three weeks the leathernecks fought a series of pitched battles with the *feldgrau*-clad infantry, sustaining more casualties than in any other engagement in its colorful history; more than half the brigade were killed or wounded in order to secure the hellish ground. A grateful France renamed the contested terrain *Bois de la Brigade Marine,* but in a petulant gesture AEF Headquarters altered the name to *Bois de la Brigade Americains.* Just as forthrightly, the French changed it back.

The controversy over leatherneck élan and prowess on the battle-field continued to fester. When a beaming French president visited the 2nd Division, AEF, to congratulate it on helping to stem the threat to Paris, Harbord and his senior officers were not invited to participate in the audience. During the height of the assault to eject the Germans from the wood, an intrepid reporter for the *Chicago Tribune,* Floyd Gibbons, fell gravely wounded. Friends in the AEF censorship unit allowed Gibbons's particularly colorful account of the battle to be released intact. Because Belleau Wood constituted unfamiliar terrain to his readership, Gibbons chose to use the geo-graphical name for the entire area—Château Thierry—as the site of the battle. Thus, to the consternation of the remainder of the AEF, the unwanted Marines became the beneficiaries of a public-relations bonanza. Newspaper readers at home believed that the leatherneck brigade constituted the elite assault force of the AEF and had almost singlehandedly stemmed the tide of the German offensive. Barnett and other senior officers within the Department of the Navy rein-forced the notion. Marine Corps recruiting posters bleated "Don't wait to be drafted," meaning simply "Don't wait to be drafted into the Army." The interservice rivalry festered like a boil on the back-sides of many soldiers, but among the senior officers surrounding Pershing it became especially intense and irritating.[8]

Ellis and Lejeune arrived in France at the height of the brouhaha. The two Marines received a gracious invitation for dinner at Chaumont on 17 June 1918 with the CinC, and the following day Lejeune had an audience with Pershing. As instructed by Barnett, Lejeune broached the matter of employing additional Marines in the AEF; specifically, the Commandant wanted an entire division of leathernecks in the AEF. Pershing repeated his concerns for common-ality and support, especially the requirement for adequate replace-ments. The CinC believed, and Lejeune ruefully agreed, that it appeared unlikely that HQMC could provide the necessary man-power to replace losses in combat for an entire division. Concern over adequate replacements for anticipated combat losses remained a constant worry for Pershing and his staff. After receiving the dis-quieting notification that the 6th Marines and a machine-gun bat-talion would soon join the 5th Marines in France, Pershing requested three replacement battalions of Marines to support the brigade of leathernecks. After the horrendous losses in June 1918, the request increased to five battalions. By then an overseas depot had been estab-lished at Quantico to provide brief, intensive training for Marines slated for duty in France, and by midsummer 1918 two replacement battalions of Marines embarked for France during every remaining month of the war. While Pershing might have broached concerns over the potential attrition of personnel in his final meeting with Lejeune, the bitter bile of interservice rivalry remained in the mouths of many doughboys.

The interservice animosity following the epic battle for Belleau Wood contributed to Pershing's reluctance to accept additional Marines, and the hyperbolic journalism trumpeting leatherneck prowess and heroism exacerbated the problem. Lejeune left the meet-ing convinced that an obdurate CinC had no intention of accepting a Marine Corps division in the AEF, and he notified Barnett accord-ingly. Leaving nothing to chance, Pershing cabled Washington: "[Lejeune] brings up the subject of the formation of a Marine divi-sion for service here. . . . I am of the opinion that the formation of such a unit is not desirable from a military standpoint. Our land forces must be homogeneous in every respect. . . . While the Marines are splendid troops, their use as a separate division is inadvisable." The Chief of Staff of the Army, Gen. Peyton C. March, concurred, indicating that Pershing's opinion was "in harmony with the policies of the War Department in that matter."[9]

Other observers within the Department of the Navy interpreted Pershing's intransigence with regard to the formation of a Marine

Corps division as simply interservice rivalry at its lowest ebb. From his headquarters in London, Adm. William S. Sims waxed critical. While acknowledging Pershing's strong desire to avoid the intense rivalry among British, Australian, Canadian, and Indian Army units common to the Commonwealth forces, and repeating the theme of "commonality," Sims opined that "it does seem a pity that the spirit and esprit de corps that has grown up after a great many years in our Marine Corps should not be utilized by putting them in battle under their own organization."[10]

His errand completed, Lejeune—with Ellis in tow—sought an assignment within the AEF. Through friendships from his tour as a student at the Army War College, Lejeune received orders to command the 64th Brigade, 32nd Division. Ellis accompanied him as the prospective adjutant of the Wisconsin National Guard unit, then assigned to a French division in the lines between the Swiss border on the right and the Rhone River on the left. Meanwhile, Pershing had grown increasingly disconcerted with the Commanding General of the 2nd Division, AEF. In a stinging diary entry, he noted that "General [Omar] Bundy disappoints me. I shall replace him at the earliest opportunity." Pershing ordered Harbord promoted to two-star rank, shunted Bundy off to an insignificant position, and then gave command of the 2nd Division to Harbord. A requirement for a new commander of the leatherneck brigade resulted in a change of assignment for Lejeune, and he assumed command on 25 July 1918 just as the Marines marched into reserve; Ellis relieved Harry R. Lay as adjutant on 9 August; during the interval, he served as the division inspector.[11]

On 20 July the 2nd Division took up a rest position in the vicinity of Nantuil-le-Handouin, midway between Soissons and Paris. The strength of the 4th Brigade (Marine), AEF, had dropped to less than 50 percent since Belleau Wood and Soissons; replacements streamed into depleted units while veterans cleaned equipment and mended uniforms. Three days later, Harbord reported to Pershing at his headquarters. After perfunctory greetings and a few platitudes about the division's performance, the CinC shared his dissatisfaction with the Services of Supply (SOS) and its commander, Maj. Gen. Francis J. Kernon. By midsummer 1918 the SOS area behind the American units of the AEF had become so muddled and inefficient that Pershing's superiors in Washington considered sending over Col. George W. Goethals—the legendary builder of the Panama Canal— to take charge of the SOS in a command separate and distinct from Pershing's AEF. Considering such a proposal anathema, Pershing asked his old friend Harbord to relinquish command of the 2nd Division and straighten out the SOS for him. But the move might well have been the CinC's way to gently let down an old friend, because the performance of the 2nd Division at Soissons had been less than superlative. In any event, Harbord's loyalty to and friend-ship with Pershing outweighed any personal or professional goals that he had at the moment. As the senior brigadier general in the division, Lejeune assumed command pending appointment of a permanent replacement for Harbord.[12]

Even before departing for France, Barnett had told Lejeune in strict-est confidence that he could expect a second star because of strong support from Secretary Daniels, Congressman Butler, and the Com-mandant himself. Lejeune's elevation to two-star rank did not go uncontested, however. Littleton W. T. Waller, languishing in frustra-tion in command of the skeletonized Advanced Base Force in Phila-delphia, attempted to call in his political favors to gain the promo-tion for himself. Although Waller satisfied Secretary Daniels's dictum to "reward those who have been at the cannon's mouth," Lejeune's close friendship with the Secretary of the Navy made the promotion of the Marine Corps's senior officer in France a foregone conclusion.[13]

Apparently, when Pershing learned that the Department of the Navy intended to promote Lejeune, he elected to leave him in com-mand. Lejeune became the Commanding General, 2nd Division, AEF, on 29 July 1918; a week later he received his promotion to major general, with a date of rank of 1 July. Colonel Neville received his star at the same time and assumed command of the 4th Brigade (Marine), AEF. Whatever transpired between the two senior officers with regard to Ellis's posting is lost to the dustbin of history; however, Ellis remained as the adjutant of the brigade as it rested and re-outfitted. His own temporary promotion to lieutenant colonel had become effective on 1 July.

On the night of 30–31 July the brigade moved to Pont-à-Moselle in an area encompassing the French training cantonment of Bois la Haie l'Evêque. As the adjutant for one of the infantry brigades, Ellis drew up training schedules for his Marines. The division conducted extensive patrolling, apparently in support of AEF Headquarters's hope that the Germans would believe the next offensive would strike in that area. German units tested the mettle of the brigade with numerous forays at night, but casualties remained light up to the time the 82nd Division, AEF, took over the lines. Lejeune worked tirelessly to mold a cohesive team and otherwise put to rest the rancor resulting from the publicity earned by the leatherneck brigade at Belleau Wood. Ever since, doughboys had taunted Marines with a musical doggerel—usually a prelude to a fistfight—sung to the tune of "Mademoiselle from Armentiéres":

> *The Marines have won the Croix de Guerre, parlez-vous?*
> *The Marines have won the Croix de Guerre, parlez-vous?*
> *The Marines have won the Croix de Guerre,*
> *But the sons-a-bitches were never there.*
> *Hinky dinky parlez-vous?*

But Lejeune's division surgeon, Lt. Col. Richard Derby—Pres. Theodore Roosevelt's son-in-law—recalled that Lejeune "maintained among officers and men the same high standard of morale and cemented the ties of comradeship and respect between the two infantry brigades." Marine Corps swagger and a flaunting of leatherneck eccentricities, however, would aggravate the situation for the remainder of the war.[14]

In the first week of August 1918, the division moved to the Marbache area near Pont-à-Moussan in preparation for the first offensive
of the American Army in France. A standard U.S. infantry division
numbered 979 officers and 27,080 men—twice that of a British or
French division. Because of losses suffered at Soissons, the strength
of the 2nd Division had fallen to less than 22,000 men. Replacements arrived, many from drafts newly arrived from basic training
centers in the United States or gleaned from a scouring of the lines
of communications. The opposing Germans found the Americans a
tougher lot than anticipated, as a captured document indicated:
"The 2nd Division may be classified as a very good division, perhaps
as assault troops. The previous attacks of both regiments at Belleau
Wood [were] carried out with dash and recklessness." The intelligence report added that the "effect of our firepower did not materi-
ally check the advance of the infantry. The nerves of the Americans
are still unshaken."[15]

The Marines assembled at Toul. Then, beginning on 2 September,
they marched to Manonville. The contested salient, French territory
held by the Germans since the first day of the war, interrupted the
north-south railway line and allowed the enemy to interdict road
traffic on the Paris-Nancy highway. From a strategic perspective, the
German occupation of the salient prevented Allied offensive action
in Lorraine and the Meuse-Argonne. On the night of 11–12 September, the 2nd Division, AEF, marched into the lines to join twelve
other divisions for the assault. Ellis's primary duty as adjutant was to
prepare the operations order for the 4th Brigade (Marine), AEF, and
supervise its implementation. Because Lejeune and his Assistant
Chief of Staff, G3 (Operations), Col. James C. Rhea, selected the 3rd
Brigade to lead the initial assault, Ellis's contribution appears to have
been minimal. In any event, both Lejeune and Rhea had studied the
terrain as students at the Army War College as part of instruction on
the Franco-Prussian War.[16]

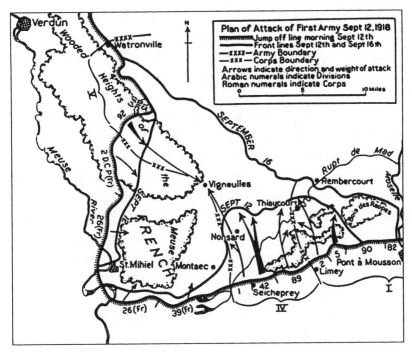

American operations in the St. Mihiel Region, 13–16 September 1918 (*Second Division: Summary of Operations in the World War* [Washington, D.C.: GPO, 1944]), p. 69.

The attacking forces stormed into the German lines, already weakened by an enemy decision to evacuate the salient. Late in the afternoon, Lejeune ordered the Marines to replace the 3rd Brigade in the assault, and by the following day they had fought their way up against the Hindenburg Line. The capture of the salient, along with numerous prisoners and an impressive pile of German material, resulted in a withdrawal of the 2nd Division, AEF, from the lines on 16 September. Despite the relative ease of the offensive, the 4th Brigade (Marine), AEF, appeared in poor condition as it marched to a rest area south of Toul. The nine days it had spent shivering in the freezing rain prior to the offensive had taken a toll; many of the Marines and doughboys had already been evacuated to the rear because of exposure and hypothermia. Ellis reported casualties of 3 officers and 129 enlisted men killed and 19 officers and 600 enlisted men wounded.[17]

The success of the first American offensive reassured the Allies. The French, weakened by four years of war and fielding an ineffective army racked by mutinous conduct, asked Pershing for assistance in their failed offensive to seize the heights of Blanc Mont in the Champagne area. Reluctantly the CinC relented, releasing both the 2nd and 5th Divisions to the French. From 24 to 30 September the 2nd Division moved by rail from Toul to an area just south of Châlons-sur-Marne. Until 2 October the troops mended equipment, absorbed replacements, and prepared to join the French offensive. By then the campaign—led by the 4th French Army—had stalled near Somme-Py; the 2nd Division, AEF, formed with XXI Corps for the attack. Three French divisions had already been shattered in futile attempts to seize the Essen Hook on the left of Blanc Mont, a hardened position bristling with strongly fortified German machine-gun emplacements. Gen. Henri Gouraud proposed using the Americans simply as replacements—merely the two infantry brigades—to reinforce his weakened 21st and 67th Divisions, a notion that Lejeune considered anathema. John W. Thomason, destined to become the Rudyard Kipling of that Marine Corps era, captured what Ellis and the other leathernecks must have felt as they surveyed the desolate terrain of Blanc Mont: "The rich topsoil that formerly made the Champagne one of the fat provinces of France was gone, blown away and buried under by four years of incessant shell-fire." He added that "areas that had been forested showed only blackened, branchless stumps, upthrust through the churned earth."[18]

The Commanding General, French XXIV Corps, André Naulin, proposed that the 4th Brigade attack frontally half of the distance to

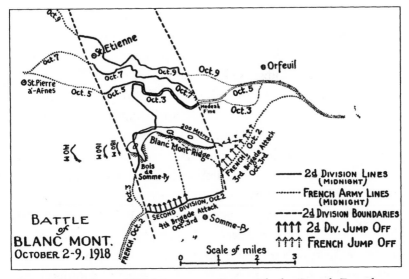

Blanc Mont, Second Division operations with the Fourth French Army, 2–10 October 1918 (John A. Lejeune, *The Reminiscences of a Marine* [Philadelphia: Dorrance, 1930]), p. 337.

Blanc Mont; then the 3rd Brigade would take up the assault with an oblique thrust. Lejeune opposed the plan, arguing that the excessively complicated maneuver presented the real danger of the 4th Brigade's fires impacting on the 3rd Brigade. Instead, Lejeune propounded that the 2nd Division's objective be split in half, with both infantry brigades attacking simultaneously. Perhaps baited by the canny Gouraud, Lejeune countered by promising to seize the heights of Blanc Mont if the 2nd Division, AEF, remained intact. At that critical conference, Lejeune's key commanders and staff accompanied him to meet with the French generals: Brig. Gen. Hanson E. Ely, commanding the 3rd Brigade, AEF; Brig. Gen. Wendell C. Neville, commanding the 4th Brigade (Marine), AEF; and Colonel Rhea, Chief of Staff, 2nd Division, AEF. Ellis apparently remained in the lines with the command post of the leatherneck brigade.[19]

In an unsubstantiated account, Lejeune returned to his head-quarters, pondering just how he could keep his promise to Gouraud. Summoning Ellis, Lejeune's aide-de-camp supposedly informed him that "the colonel is indisposed"—meaning, of course, that his erst-while subordinate was intoxicated. Apparently nonplussed by the dis-closure, Lejeune ordered Ellis to report forthwith: "Ellis drunk is bet-ter than anyone else around here sober."[20]

While this journalistic account is colorful, it is unlikely that Lejeune would ignore his own staff and commanders and turn to a staff officer in a subordinate unit for advice at this critical juncture in the offensive. Moreover, since the night of 1–2 October, the 4th Brigade (Marine), AEF, had occupied a three-kilometer front between Boyau de Austrine and Boyau de Bromberg; it is improbable that Ellis would be summoned away from his demanding duties in the line to confer with Lejeune at some considerable distance away. More-over, this vignette suggests that Lejeune had lost confidence in his Chief of Staff and former Assistant Chief of Staff, G3, Colonel Rhea, an officer he praised highly throughout and after the war. Whoever conceived the operation for the 2nd Division, AEF, inferred that the French divisions on both flanks could keep pace with the assault; this erroneous assumption resulted in the 4th Brigade (Marine), AEF, suffering more casualties in a single day than at any other time in World War I.

On 3 October a short artillery barrage precluded an assault on a three-mile front. Bypassing a German strongpoint between them, a heavily fortified position—named, appropriately, Bois de la Vipère—the infantry brigades maneuvered to seize the wooded heights south and southwest of Saint Étienne. Both brigades advanced in columns of regiments beginning at 0550, with battalions in column. Each brigade had a company of French tanks in support. As the 6th Marines stormed up the slopes of Blanc Mont, murderous machine-gun fire tore into their ranks. Col. Logan Feland's 5th Marines took the German threat under fire, and Feland ordered his 1st Battalion to swing to the left to clean out the Essen Hook. The failure of the French 21st Division to keep pace with the assault prompted Ellis to send a worried message to division headquarters: "Have you seen any of the French on our left?"[21]

As the 5th Marines fought to contain the devastating fires from their exposed flank, the 6th Marines took their first objective. By 0830 the leathernecks had captured the main battle line except for the western slope of Blanc Mont ridge. On 4 October the 5th Marines passed through the 6th and swung northwest down the slopes of the ridge. By then a fresh German division had been added to the order of battle, and the gallant regiment had suffered more than eleven hundred casualties. Just as the passage of lines began, the Germans counterattacked in an attempt to roll up the flanks of the 4th Brigade (Marine), AEF. The infiltrating 5th Marines stunned the bewildered enemy and drove them back. After a second counterattack late in the day, a concerned Ellis sent another message to division headquarters: "Have repelled two counterattacks, possibly three. We need all the artillery protection we can get . . . our losses are about 50 per cent, more among officers and sergeants."[22]

The bitter engagement allowed the 6th Marines to move forward and link up with the 3rd Brigade on the right of the division's front. On the night of 5 October, the 6th Marines assaulted the ridge. The 3rd Battalion led the attack on the ridge, while the 2nd Battalion swung left toward Saint Étienne. While the 3rd Battalion swept over the ridge, withering enemy machine-gun fire stopped the 2nd Battalion southeast of its objective. A day later, as the 2nd Division, AEF, began its withdrawal from the front, a fresh division—the 36th, AEF—continued the advance. A battalion of the 6th Marines remained with it to take Saint Étienne on 8 October.

The imaginative and bold offensive action came perilously close to complete disaster. The 2nd Division, AEF, and particularly the 4th Brigade (Marine), AEF, suffered casualties more akin to those of British and French divisions before the Americans entered the lines.

The leathernecks counted 494 killed and another 1,864 wounded. The entire 2nd Division, AEF, reported alarming losses: 41 officers and 685 men killed, 162 officers and 3,500 men wounded, and 6 officers and 579 men missing in action. Ellis reported a substantial share of the positive results for the 4th Brigade (Marine), AEF, in the total: the division claimed the capture of 48 officers and 1,915 men, 95 artillery pieces, and 332 machine guns.[23]

Lejeune chose not to report his heavy losses on 4–5 October, instead amalgamating them into the totals for the entire offensive. In his operation report for the period 15 September–9 October— prepared by Rhea but signed by Lejeune—he simply notes that "this operation was continuous from October 2 to October 10, both days inclusive. The troops were continually under fire and most of the time hotly engaged. Therefore, the report of casualties is not given by days but of the operation as a whole." More than two decades later, Lejeune only noted that "despite a considerable number of machine guns and a heavy artillery fire [the action of the division] brought about the most favorable results." But in a personal letter to a fellow officer at home, he noted sadly that "the Marine Corps has just cause to feel proud of its brigade . . . there isn't much left of the original crowd. [The hospitals] are full of wounded."[24]

A German participant's account offers little to support Lejeune's hyperbole: "Even when deploying, the enemy suffered bloody losses. The separate and isolated groups came in carelessly at first, were at once subjected to a withering concentration of light and heavy machinegun fire . . . gaping holes were torn in the line of riflemen, entire columns being mowed down." A secret staff study, prepared by an obscure officer in Pershing's headquarters, took issue with much of the inflated rhetoric espoused by both the 2nd Division, AEF, and the 4th French Army. The author argued that the French advance had not stalled but was advancing in small, steady gains all along the front in conjunction with assault elements of the 1st U.S. Army. The 2nd Division, AEF, was supposed to take the lead in order

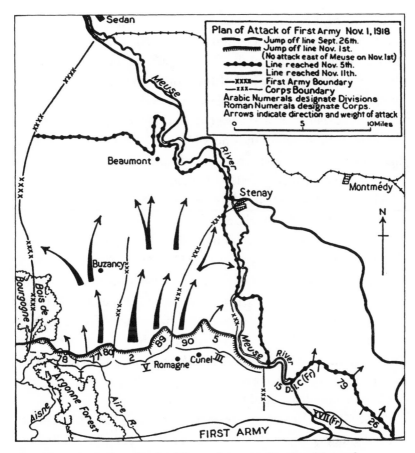

American operations in the Meuse-Argonne Region (*Second Division: Summary of Operations in the World War* [Washington, D.C.: GPO, 1944]), p. 127.

to allow adjacent French units to advance, but not necessarily abreast with the Americans. The anonymous officer preparing the study scored the notion that the Blanc Mont sector was more difficult than any other facing an American division. Finally, no evidence exists to support the contention that German forces were preparing to withdraw from the area.[25]

For the next two weeks, the weary leathernecks and doughboys recovered in the farms and meadows of the Suippes area. On 25 October operational control of the division passed to the 1st U.S. Army, then to V Corps. By the end of the month, the Allies intended for the 1st U.S. Army and the 4th French Army to launch an offensive to break the stalemate on the western front. I Corps, with three U.S. divisions, held the left of the line, while V Corps stood poised on its right with four U.S. divisions—including the 2nd. Ellis continued as the adjutant, 4th Brigade (Marine), AEF.

The 4th Brigade (Marine), AEF, recuperated from the bloody offensive and absorbed replacements into its badly depleted formations. By then the 2nd Division, AEF, had completed its transfer from the 4th French Army to the 1st U.S. Army, then in turn to V Corps. On 1 November the Marines reentered the lines for what many hoped would be the final offensive of the war. For their gallantry at Blanc Mont, a grateful France had bestowed a third Croix de Guerre on the Marines, thus entitling the brigade to wear the red and green shoulder cord of the *fourragère*. The 2nd Division, AEF, occupied a two-kilometer sector facing the Hindenburg Line, and on 1 November it attacked behind a rolling barrage.

Just as at Blanc Mont, the leathernecks charged on the left while the doughboys charged on the right. In the sector of the 4th Brigade (Marine), AEF, the 5th Marines assaulted on the right with the first battalion in the lead; the 6th Marines attacked on the left, with their first battalion taking point. Neville ordered his Marines to advance to the heights of Barricourt. By midafternoon they had seized their objective and advanced nine kilometers into enemy-held territory to take Landres et St. Georges, St. Georges, and Bayonville et Chénnery. The next day, the weary Marines rested while the 3rd Brigade led the assault, vaulting further into enemy-held territory as the Germans retreated rapidly. For four days, the leathernecks secured the left flank of the division because the adjacent 80th Division, AEF, failed to maintain pace. But the weakened German forces no longer had the capability to exploit the exposed flank as they had at Blanc Mont.

Shortly before noon on 4 November, the Marines had seized Ferme de Belle Tour, while the 23rd Infantry raced north that night. By daybreak on 5 November, the division's positions had been consolidated and infantry patrols looked for likely crossing sites over the Meuse. By the night of 6–7 November, the assault elements of the 2nd Division, AEF, stood hard on the river. Although Lejeune and his senior officers knew that an armistice was near and loathed incurring needless casualties in the waning days of the war, 1st Army and V Corps pressed their subordinate units to continue the attack. In the last eleven days of the war, the 4th Brigade (Marine), AEF, suffered losses of 277 killed and 1,263 wounded. Four infantry battalions made preparations to cross the river on pontoon bridges, but they wisely called off the attack upon learning that the opposite banks bristled with German machine-gun positions. Two other battalions of Marines did attempt a crossing at another location, suffering heavy—and many said needless—casualties.[26]

To earn the right to continue to exclaim "First to Fight," the Marines had paid heavily: 41 officers and 1,114 enlisted men lost their lives on the western front. Heroic Marines earned 5 Medals of Honor, 363 Distinguished Service Crosses, and 1,237 Croix de Guerre. Along with the 2nd Division, AEF, the leathernecks had advanced a total of sixty-one kilometers against the enemy—more than any other unit in the AEF. In a letter to Assistant Secretary of the Navy Franklin D. Roosevelt, Harbord cited the impressive list of decorations: "You will not be able to read them over without tears coming to your eyes in your pride in the gallantry of your countrymen."[27]

Ellis had performed to the exacting standards of his mentor, Lejeune, and his brigade commander, Neville. Both of these prominent Marines added Ellis's name to a small list of officers recommended for accelerated promotion, but Ellis never saw a colonel's

eagles on his uniform. Neville also recommended him for both the
Distinguished Service Medal and the Navy Cross, and a grateful
France presented him with the Croix de Guerre and the Légion
d'Honour (Grade of Chevalier).[28]

But in what must have been bittersweet success, Ellis had survived
the war without commanding anything; in fact, he had not held a
command position since serving as a junior officer in the Philippines
almost a decade before. His contemporary from the ranks, John A.
"Johnny the Hard" Hughes, had led a battalion of infantry. Both
Thomas Holcomb and Ralph S. Keyser, aides-de-camp to the Commandant of the Marine Corps with Ellis in 1915–17, commanded
battalions in the 4th Brigade (Marine), AEF. Nonetheless, Ellis's reputation as a planner and strategist had grown. What he learned on
the western front meant something to other Marine Corps officers.
Less than two years after the guns fell silent, Ellis's thoughtful observations on his experience in France appeared in the semiofficial
Marine Corps Gazette. In his monograph, Ellis argued persuasively
and convincingly that the new stress on maneuver warfare and skir-
mishing did not alleviate the exigency for fire superiority—artillery
was essential. The fighting in France underscored the requirement
for careful and ruminative operational planning. Finally, the thoughtful Ellis emphasized that there was no substitute for meticulous staff
planning.[29]

~ Earl H. "Pete" Ellis shown during the World War I era.

∿ Earl Hancock Ellis at the time of his graduation from high school, Pratt, Kansas, 1900. DOROTHY ELLIS GATZ

∿ The first photograph of 2nd Lt. Earl H. Ellis, probably taken in 1902 just as he reported to Marine Barracks, Boston. DOROTHY ELLIS GATZ

∼ Ellis and another officer, identified only as "Lieutenant Fay," seated on an old Spanish cannon at Cavite in 1902. DOROTHY ELLIS GATZ

∼ 1st Lt. Earl H. Ellis in 1904. On the back of the photograph he wrote, "a Marine boy raised on hay and whiskey." DOROTHY ELLIS GATZ

~ Ellis appears on the right in this photograph, taken in the Philippines in 1908, and assumes the demeanor of a no-nonsense tropical campaigner. To his right is Capt. John R. Right, probably the Commanding Officer, Company E, 2nd Regiment at Olongapo. Sgt. Peter H. Kerrigan stands behind them.

JAMES R. BOWEN AND JAMES F. CANAZZA, *THE MARINES IN THE PHILIPPINES: A SOUVENIR* (N.P., N.D).

～ Ellis and a group of officers on Grande Island, Subic Bay, Philippines, 1909. Ellis is in the center of the photograph, and the officer to his left is probably his regimental commander, Lt. Col. Joseph H. Pendleton. DOROTHY ELLIS GATZ

～ Ellis in Guam, 1915, seated on the extreme right at a table at the officers club.
PATSY PERRENOT

~ Lt. Col. Earl H. Ellis, Fourth Brigade (Marine), AEF, 1918–1919.
DOROTHY ELLIS GATZ

~ *Facing Page:* In a World War I photograph Barnett (front row, second from left), then Commandant of the Marine Corps (1914–1920), appears with Assistant Secretary of the Navy Franklin D. Roosevelt, Secretary of the Navy Josephus Daniels, and William S. Benson, Chief of Naval Operations (front row, far right). Later, Daniels would turn on Barnett and implement steps for his ouster as titular head of the Marine Corps. U.S. NAVAL INSTITUTE PHOTOGRAPHIC COLLECTION

～ Sometime during Ellis's tenure as one of the aides-de-camp to the Major General Commandant, the senior leadership of the Marine Corps appeared in this photograph at the barracks in Philadelphia. The Major General Commandant, George Barnett, is in the center; his assistant, Col. John A. Lejeune, is to his immediate right. NATIONAL ARCHIVES AND RECORDS ADMINISTRATION

~ A pensive Ellis, taken in France in 1918, perhaps on the eve of one of the three offensives in which he planned the activities of the Fourth Brigade (Marine), AEF. DOROTHY ELLIS GATZ

∼ Is this the "Rose Lady?" The subject of this photograph,
which was found in 1970 among Ellis's papers, could not be
identified by any member of his family. Quite possibly this
is Elizabeth Allen Rogers. When Ellis met and courted her,
1921–1922, she was the estranged wife of another Marine
Corps officer, Henry Sheldon Green. After Ellis's death,
she married William W. Buckley, a Washington attorney.

DOROTHY ELLIS GATZ

~ A group of officers in Germany, 1919. Ellis is at the extreme left. Others identified
include: Franklin D. Roosevelt (Assistant Secretary of the Navy), second from
right; John A. Lejeune (Commanding General, 2nd Division, AEF), third from
right; and Wendell C. Neville (Commanding General, Fourth Brigade [Marine],
AEF), third from left. DOROTHY ELLIS GATZ

~ The last known photograph of Ellis,
taken for his passport in 1921.
DOROTHY ELLIS GATZ

〜 The irrepressible and sometimes controversial Smedley D. Butler, left, poses
with John A. Lejeune at a sporting event at Quantico during the 1920s. Butler's
father, Cong. Thomas S. Butler, supported the ouster of George Barnett as
Commandant of the Marine Corps and his replacement by John A. Lejeune.
MARINE CORPS HISTORICAL CENTER

∿ Captain Lyman A. Cotten, USN, was the naval attaché in Tokyo when Ellis passed through Japan. He became alarmed upon learning that Ellis had disclosed aspects of his classified mission to companions in shabby drinking establishments in Yokohama. NATIONAL ARCHIVES AND RECORDS ADMINISTRATION

∿ Chief Pharmacist Lawrence Zembsch, who perished in the earthquake that struck central Japan in 1923 before he could reveal what he had learned in his mission to recover Ellis's remains in Palau. HARRY DAY

〜 Edwin H. Denby (1870–1929),
Secretary of the Navy, 6 March
1921–10 March 1924 U.S. NAVAL
INSTITUTE PHOTOGRAPHIC COLLECTION

〜 Adm. Robert E. Coontz
(1863–1935), Chief of Naval
Operations, 1 November 1919–21
July 1923 U.S. NAVAL INSTITUTE
PHOTOGRAPHIC COLLECTION

〜 Jesse Hoppin, a missionary in Jaluit who befriended Ellis. Known as "Mother Hoppin" to the Marshallese, she began her service in Micronesia in 1899 and remained until Japanese authorities forced all foreign residents to leave just prior to the war in the Pacific. HOUGHTON LIBRARY, HARVARD UNIVERSITY

〜 Felix Rechuuld, in 1968. He was Ellis's houseboy in Palau and obtained whiskey for him at the NBK store in Koror. DIRK ANTHONY BALLENDORF

~ Hans G. Hornbostel poses with the captain of a Japanese schooner, en route from Guam to Saipan in 1923. An old friend of Ellis and a former Marine, Hornbostel gathered information on the islands in the Central Pacific for the Office of Naval Intelligence during the 1920s while employed by the Bishop Museum in Honolulu. ELLIS COLLECTION, MICRONESIAN AREA RESEARCH CENTER

~ Oikong Joseph Tellei poses with Dirk Anthony Ballendorf at Koror in the area where Ellis's body was buried by the Palauans. Tellei served as chief of the native Palauan police during Ellis's visit in 1923, and recalled that the Japanese authorities ordered him to have Ellis watched "around the clock." ELLIS COLLECTION, MICRONESIAN AREA RESEARCH CENTER

~ Benjamin Lajipun, Ellis's houseboy in Jaluit, was tailed by the Japanese police. DIRK ANTHONY BALLENDORF

~ Metauie, Ellis's Palauan wife, in 1968.
DIRK ANTHONY BALLENDORF

5 ~ Transition to Peacetime
1919–1920

NOT ALONE AMONG THE LEATHERNECKS of the 4th Brigade (Marine), AEF, Ellis hoped for a speedy withdrawal from the lines, a train trip to the port of embarkation at Brest, and a troopship home. But Gen. John J. Pershing and his senior officers feared that, with the armistice, the discipline of the largely volunteer American Army might unravel. In selecting units to man the 3rd Army for occupation duties in Germany, the Commander in Chief (CinC) sought dependable, professional units infused with the character of old-time regulars. Not surprisingly, AEF Headquarters selected the 2nd Division, AEF—in which the Marines served—to remain in Europe until a defeated Germany had demonstrated acceptance of the terms of the surrender. Pershing's chief of staff cautioned each division commander on the heels of the cease-fire, emphasizing the high standard of performance the CinC expected: "There remains now a harder task which will test your soldierly qualities to the utmost. Succeed in these and little note will be taken and few praises will be sung; fail, and the light of your glorious advancements of the past will sadly be dimmed."[1]

From 11 to 16 November, Ellis and the 4th Brigade (Marine), AEF, rested and re-outfitted in the soggy marshes of the Beaumont area. Then on 17 November 1918, the 2nd Division, AEF, began the long, weary march from France through Belgium and Luxembourg to the Rhine. Soldiers and Marines displayed the effects of the final offensive to end the war. As the columns wound down the country roads, most of the doughboys and leathernecks marched as if in a stupor. Pauses for a rest break, or for a fitful night's sleep, usually witnessed most collapsing into a slumber as soon as the order to fall out was given. Although the brigade received the supplies necessary for the long march, much of it appeared inappropriate for a unit embarking on a trek of herculean proportions. Poorly fitting and uncomfortable English shoes had arrived, adding to the misery of the marchers. Between the armistice and the beginning of the trek into Germany, influenza had hit the AEF full force and hundreds of men were being evacuated to hospitals each day from among American units along the western front. Late in November, Pershing passed by the ragged lines in his staff car and expressed a general's displeasure at what he saw. Storming into the headquarters of the 3rd Army, he dictated a litany of discrepancies: men walking and slouching instead of marching, unshaven troops, and horses and mules requiring grooming. Perhaps unsaid was the unnerving fact that it was not the appearance of Ellis's 4th Brigade (Marine), AEF, but that of the soldiers of the 3rd Brigade, AEF, that had aroused Pershing's ire. Once again the exacting CinC was reminded that the interloping leathernecks appeared more soldierly than the doughboys.[2]

For almost the remainder of the month, the long columns marched through northern France, Belgium, and Luxembourg and finally reached the German frontier on 25 November 1918. On 10 December the first units of the division approached the Rhine River; the officers of one Marine battalion marched in formation to the banks of the historic waterway and urinated in it. Three days later the 4th Brigade (Marine), AEF, crossed the waterway into Germany and established its headquarters at Nieder Bieber. Three Allied armies formed the occupation force: the French 10th Army on the right facing Metz, the French 5th Army on the left opposite Bastogne, and the American 3rd Army beyond Luxembourg on the Rhine. Pershing selected the veteran 1st and 3rd Divisions to join the 2nd Division, AEF, for occupation duties; the 42nd Division, AEF, formed the final component of the 3rd Army as its reserve. For the remainder of the period of occupation, the 4th Brigade (Marine), AEF, remained along the Rhine, except for a brief period when all Allied units moved forward just prior to Germany's signing of the peace treaty.[3]

Ellis's Marines manned a river patrol along the Rhine, fought boredom, and complained about the inadequate delousing facilities. Officers kept contact with the docile populace to a minimum and attempted to keep the troops occupied with a training schedule reflective of a peacetime tempo. Some of the more senior officers received orders rotating them home ahead of the brigade in the spring of 1919, and the vacancies prompted several key shifts in personnel. On 17 March, Logan Feland received his promotion to brigadier general, and Col. Harold C. Snyder assumed command of the 5th Marines; Ellis became the regiment's executive officer. In the final months of its deployment in Europe, the 4th Brigade (Marine), AEF, hosted a variety of dignitaries: Josephus Daniels, Secretary of the Navy; Adm. William S. Benson, Chief of Naval Operations; Franklin D. Roosevelt, Assistant Secretary of the Navy; and General Pershing. Each visit required much preparation on the part of troops anxious to return home. Finally in August 1919, the doughboys and leathernecks began the rail trip to embarkation ports. After the division paraded through the streets of New York City, the 4th Brigade (Marine), AEF—never to be called that again—marched in review for President Wilson along Washington's Pennsylvania Avenue. The regulars of the brigade returned to peacetime duties at Quantico, and Ellis remained as the executive officer of the 5th Marines.

Ellis's mentor, Maj. Gen. John A. Lejeune, commanded at Quantico. The remnants of the brigade became an expeditionary force again, poised to renew its full-time commitment to the fleet. The 5th Brigade, organized and sent to France in September 1918, failed to deploy with the AEF; instead, it was broken up and its manpower frittered away as replacements for the heavy losses incurred by the 4th Brigade (Marine), AEF. The commanding officer of the 13th Marines, the frenetic Smedley D. Butler, gained his brigadier general's star but became the disgruntled commander of the AEF processing depot at Brest instead of leading an infantry brigade in combat. He considered failure to see action in the war an insult to his soldierly virtues and a smear upon his honor—he wore two Medals of Honor. To his powerful father, Butler snarled: "I feel at the present time . . . that my days of soldiering are over. For over twenty years, I worked hard to fit myself to take part in this war which has just closed, and now when the supreme test came my country did not want me." Many officers shared Butler's despondency over failing to serve in France during the war; however, Major General Commandant Barnett had promised to keep all of the Corps's commitments to the fleet, despite the draw on manpower to the AEF. Obviously, many ambitious officers had to remain either in skeletonized bases at home or with brigades and regiments deployed to the Caribbean.[4]

Ellis found little solace or satisfaction in his peacetime duties at Quantico. Lejeune responded to the frantic quest for the utilization of military skills in civilian pursuits, and the command embarked upon an ambitious regimen of vocational training that occupied half of every working day. The irrepressible Butler served as Lejeune's deputy, as the site in northern Virginia rapidly became the Marine Corps's most important and visible post. Apparently Ellis found little of interest at Quantico to arouse his enthusiasm; the letdown from

combat duties in France dulled his professional zeal. Just as Ellis and
the regulars returned to Quantico, the Secretary of the Navy informed
him that his four-year appointment as an adjutant and inspector,
dated 16 September 1918, had been revoked by order of the President. But no record of Ellis's appointment to such a position exists;
the "adjutant" position that he filled throughout most of the war was
not that of an "adjutant and inspector," the latter being an appointed,
semipermanent position to the staff. Ellis may well have received the
appointment without applying for it, perhaps resulting from a Headquarters Marine Corps (HQMC) examination of his career prospects
after almost a decade in uniform. By the end of 1921, Ellis had over
seven years of foreign duty and almost a year and a half of sea duty
to his credit; the total of more than eight years of service outside the
continental United States might explain why he never married. At
the time, he ranked number 2 out of 113 majors following the postwar reductions in rank.[5]

Then a chance opportunity for an assignment involving intelligence duties appeared. The war in Europe had shifted Washington's
concern from America's southernmost neighbor, but events in
Mexico, where a sizable amount of U.S. capital had been invested,
continued to be worrisome. The sorry nation had experienced no
fewer than ten presidents since U.S. warships blockaded Veracruz
and leathernecks and bluejackets marched ashore in 1914. During
the upheaval since, a revision of the constitution prohibited foreign
ownership of mineral rights. President Wilson protested, loudly but
feebly, to Mexico's current president, but to no avail. Ellis's minus-
cule role in the imbroglio remains obscure, but it appears that the
Major General Commandant summoned him to his office on 3 August 1919.

Barnett apparently instructed Ellis to travel to his home in Pratt
in a leave status, and there to prepare for an intelligence-gathering
mission at the behest of the Office of Naval Intelligence in conjunction with increased U.S. scrutiny and concern with regard to Mexico.

A Marine Corps regiment—later expanded to an entire brigade—had been stationed near Galveston, Texas, as a result of wartime concerns for the Mexican oil fields and fears of a German seizure of the vital facilities. In Pratt, Ellis apparently bided his time studying oil geology at the local library while waiting for orders. On 18 August 1919 he left Pratt for Galveston. At the end of the month he returned to his home, but on 21 September he journeyed to Galveston again. This time Ellis continued on to New Orleans, where he took passage on the SS *San Ramon* for Tampico, arriving at midnight on 28–29 September. He departed Tampico on the *George W. Barnes* on 9 November 1919 for New Orleans and returned to Pratt to continue his leave. Neither Ellis nor Barnett left any reports behind, and thus whatever feeble intelligence-gathering took place has disappeared into the dustbin of history.[6]

Upon his return to Quantico, Ellis received orders detaching him from the 5th Marines, effective 28 November 1919, for duty at HQMC. He took up residence, as before, at the Army-Navy Club in Washington. Barely a month later, the manager of the facility summoned medical assistance from the Washington Naval Hospital. A physician admitted Ellis and noted a depressed and nervous patient. Ellis exhibited tremors of the hands and face. He complained of mental retardation, inability to concentrate, and insomnia. On New Year's Day 1920, Ellis's doctors diagnosed neurasthenia and recommended a sick leave of three months. While Ellis recovered, first at his brother's home in Arizona and then in Pratt, Barnett took steps to stimulate his mercurial subordinate's career. On 13 April 1920 the Commandant sent a message to Brigadier General Feland, commanding the brigade in Santo Domingo: "Do you desire services of Major Earl H. Ellis as intelligence officer?" Barnett received a swift response: "Services desired and earnestly requested." Ellis returned from convalescent leave, and the naval hospital discharged him to full duty on 17 April; his orders to the Caribbean took effect the same day.[7]

While Ellis participated in the intelligence-gathering venture, events were set in motion that had the potential to dislodge his two most faithful supporters, Barnett and Lejeune, from the hierarchy of the Marine Corps. On 20 September 1919, Daniels summoned Lejeune to his office. After an exchange of pleasantries, the Secretary informed Lejeune that he intended to remove Barnett from office; the new Commandant of the Marine Corps would be John Archer Lejeune. In the conversation—which Daniels charged be kept confidential—he told his candidate of the circumstances surrounding Barnett's reappointment in 1918 and expressed his understanding that a change in the commandancy would take place after the war had ended. At the time, Daniels had decided on Lejeune once he returned from France. The only matter left unsettled was the approval of the President. The Secretary planned to gain that as soon as the Chief Executive returned from his speaking tour in the Western states. Wilson's subsequent illness and debilitating stroke prevented any decision. In mid-October, Daniels summoned Lejeune again and informed him that the plan to remove Barnett had gone awry because of the President's condition. After the conference, Lejeune motored back to Quantico with Smedley D. Butler, who confided that Daniels had informed his father of the plan and gained the enthusiastic approval of Cong. Thomas S. Butler.[8]

In May 1920, Daniels summoned Lejeune to his office and informed him that he had approved Barnett's request for a tour of inspection to the West Coast only to get him out of town and set the machinery in motion for Barnett's ouster. On 17 June 1920, Daniels met with the ailing President and gained his approval for the plan. At the meeting, the Secretary apparently informed Wilson of Barnett's earlier promise to step down upon the cessation of hostilities. In his office two days later, Daniels dictated a letter of dismissal; then he packed for a business trip out of the capitol, leaving instructions for a messenger to deliver the correspondence to the Commandant of the Marine Corps.

Ill with influenza, Barnett received news of his removal from office at "Eighth and Eye" at approximately 1:30 P.M. on Friday, 20 June 1918. The messenger had instructions to remain for an answer: did Barnett wish to retire effective 30 June 1920 as a major general, or remain on active duty as a brigadier general? Stunned, Barnett summoned his wife, and together they penned a response: the Commandant of the Marine Corps elected to remain on active duty and requested promotion to major general (a vacancy existed because of Lejeune's elevation to the commandancy), assignment to Quantico, and extended leave, as he had not used any since the beginning of the war.[9]

Daniels may have expected Barnett to bow out, but he underestimated his opponent's and Mrs. Barnett's fury. That evening the Barnetts held a council of war in their home, and President Wilson's personal physician, Adm. Cary Grayson, attended. A close friend of the Barnetts, Grayson had apparently witnessed Daniels's meeting with the chief executive on the previous Tuesday. From the Barnetts' view, Daniels's request to seek the Commandant's removal racked with duplicity. Grayson pledged the Barnetts to secrecy for his part in the revelation of what he had witnessed at the White House, and Barnett took the name of his informant to the grave. However, Mrs. Barnett revealed Grayson's name, unwittingly, in the table of contents to her unpublished autobiography. By the end of the evening, both Barnett and his wife had decided to fight the order of dismissal.[10]

On Capitol Hill, Barnett turned to his considerable array of Republican friends to seek redress, and they turned out in force. Henry Cabot Lodge indicated his support, and even a Democrat on the Senate Naval Affairs Committee, Claude Swanson, tried to help. Barnett's old roommate from the Class of 1881, Sen. John Weeks, led the charge. The Chief of Naval Operations (CNO), Admiral Benson, while congratulating Lejeune on the one hand and offering advice to Barnett on the other, suggested that the ousted Commandant call on Daniels to confront him. When Barnett did have his painful audience with Daniels, the Secretary refused to discuss the matter or to answer Barnett's questions, and dismissed the Commandant curtly. Meanwhile, events moved closer to the change in office.

Barnett's letters of sympathy and concern came mostly from Republican friends, classmates from the Naval Academy Class of 1881, and relatives. Lejeune's mail burst with warm notes applauding his appointment, sent by every important senior officer in the Marine Corps and Navy except one: only Brig. Gen. Joseph H. Pendleton expressed sympathy for Barnett's plight and remained aloof from the controversy. Others, such as Charles H. Lyman and Ben H. Fuller, dashed off letters of condolence to Barnett, then wrote to Lejeune to congratulate him! Meanwhile the Butlers relished in the event, and Congressman Butler's letter of congratulations to Lejeune exuded warmth and promised a smooth relationship with the House Naval Affairs Committee: "We are going to have a Marine Corps . . . commanded by a real soldier. My I am pleased with your appointment & mean to assist you in any way to make your administration a great success. . . . [T]he right thing has been done. Tell me always when I can serve you."[11]

Mrs. Barnett ordered a party for their close friends on their last day in the historic home of the Commandants. All of the Barnetts' possessions had been moved, and the furniture and trappings of the old mansion had been put away; the walls remained bare except for a photograph of Daniels inscribed affectionately to Barnett. None of the guests missed the point. The next day, Lejeune arrived at HQMC at 11:30 A.M. for the change in command. Two versions of the strained event survive. One aide-de-camp, Clifton B. Cates, recalled that Barnett asked Lejeune why, as an old friend and fellow officer, he failed to inform him of the plot. Lejeune only replied lamely that his hands were tied. The other aide-de-camp, Charles I. Murray, recalled that Barnett ordered Lejeune to stand at attention in front of his desk, refusing to give up the office until twelve o'clock sharp and accusing his successor of disloyalty. As the clock struck noon,

Barnett ordered Murray to remove one star from each shoulder and walked outside a defeated man. Across the street, Smedley Butler sat in a parked car to relish in the scene, a bit of petulant behavior recorded by his own aide-de-camp.[12]

Meanwhile, Daniels refused Barnett's request for a promotion and assignment to Quantico and penned a negative endorsement to the ousted Commandant's letter of grievance to the President. Senator Weeks gathered support for Barnett as best he could. Lejeune sought to end the controversy fairly and with dispatch by suggesting to Daniels that, first, Barnett be assigned to a new post as Commander, Department of the Pacific, in San Francisco (and far from his seat of political power); and second, that Barnett receive the promotion to major general that he had requested. Righteous in his wrath, the Secretary agreed to the transfer but not the promotion. Meanwhile, the Republicans took the White House in the elections of 1920, and the Senate set aside the appointment of a new Commandant of the Marine Corps for the pleasure of the new administration. Angry Barnett supporters in Congress, now in the majority, presented the real possibility that Lejeune's nomination might become a casualty of partisan bickering. And it appeared unlikely that, having been removed, Barnett would return to the commandancy.

Barnett took up his post in San Francisco alone; Mrs. Barnett would have none of his exile, and the general spent the next two years living at the Bohemian Club. When a new administration took office in 1921, Secretary of the Navy Edwin H. Denby approved Barnett's promotion to major general. In 1923, Barnett reached the mandatory retirement age of sixty-four and retired to his new home in Washington. The former Commandant worked on his memoirs in his final years, but in 1929 he suffered a debilitating stroke. His last year was spent mostly in the Washington Naval Hospital, and his wife probably completed much of the autobiography for him. Kidney failure followed the stroke, and the twelfth Commandant of the Marine Corps died on 30 April 1930. Mrs. Barnett survived her

husband by twenty-nine years and continued to lash out at her ene-
mies while attempting to salvage his reputation.[13]

Ellis's personal correspondence fails to reflect undue concern at
this juncture, but he must have felt somewhat uneasy. In a rapid
series of political events, his two most important and prominent supporters appeared to have run afoul of Washington politics: Barnett,
ousted by a vindictive and scheming Secretary of the Navy; and
Lejeune, appearing as the unwitting candidate of a Democratic
administration about to be supplanted by a Republican in the Oval
Office. Should Lejeune follow Barnett into obscurity, only Neville—
himself hardly certain to ascend to the Commandancy—remained
as Ellis's admirer and supporter among the Corps's major generals.
The soothing transition, fashioned by Secretary Denby's wise decision to return Barnett's second star, cooled senatorial ardor to seek
redress at the expense of the ailing President Wilson. Lejeune served
as Commandant of the Marine Corps from the day of Barnett's dismissal in 1920 until the inauguration of Pres. Warren G. Harding
on 4 March 1921; on that day, Denby asked Lejeune to stay on as
Commandant.

As the machinations of intraservice politics ran their course in
Washington, Ellis's tour in Santo Domingo began and ended in short
order. He embarked on the troop transport *Kittery* in Charleston,
South Carolina, on 20 April 1920 and reported to Brigadier General
Feland on 10 May. By then the Marines were attempting to garner
a modicum of success out of America's heavy-handed intervention
that had begun in the previous decade. In 1916 continued unrest in
the eastern half of Hispaniola grew worrisome to Santo Domingo's
powerful neighbor to the north because of the sizable Yankee invest-
ment in the native economy. Two companies of leathernecks sent
over from nearby Haiti as a temporary measure increased quickly
into an entire brigade. While initial successes appeared promising,
the shift in focus to America's entry into the war in Europe had a
debilitating effect on the naval mission in Santo Domingo. The

replacement of seasoned Marine veterans with wartime recruits who enlisted to fight the Germans contributed to the problem, as did a new set of officers lacking the experience of the old-time regulars.

Brigadier General Feland welcomed Ellis's organizational skills and bent for intelligence, contributions sorely needed to bolster the flagging U.S. intervention by 1920. Since the Marines had marched ashore in 1916, senior officers hoped to emulate the successful strategies applied in nearby Haiti, especially the formation of a Guardia Nacional, similar to the successful Gendarmerie d'Haiti. But the Marine force had no long-range program to improve the social and economic fabric of the country, nor did the succession of brigade commanders have any such mandate. By 1920 senior officials within the Wilson administration had expressed concern for the lack of tangible results in the strife-torn land and indicated a likelihood of the withdrawal of American troops. Whatever Ellis and Feland contributed to the naval mission to Hispaniola, their early departure was preordained by Lejeune's ascendancy to the commandancy. Nonetheless, Feland lauded Ellis's performance in Santo Domingo in a letter of commendation to the Commandant: "The effect of his [Ellis's] thorough knowledge of intelligence duties and of his hard work in training his subordinates became apparent almost at once. The intelligence reports, which had been a mass of unrelated and generally unimportant scraps of information, became well-compiled and well-digested reports of the condition in Santo Domingo."[14]

Near the end of his tour in Santo Domingo, Ellis apparently concluded that his professional future lay in intelligence duties. In confidential correspondence with the Major General Commandant—now Lejeune, not Barnett—he requested orders to organize a reconnaissance of both South America and the Pacific. In his unusual application, Ellis offered "to adopt any personal measures (submit undated resignation, travel as a civilian, etc.) which the Major General Commandant may deem necessary to ensure that the United States shall not become embarrassed through my operation." Lejeune directed a member of his staff to send the correspondence on to the Office of Naval Intelligence: "Information is requested as to whether or not the service rendered by this officer can be utilized to advantage."[15]

By the time Ellis returned from the Caribbean in the fall of 1920, Lejeune had already directed a major reorganization of HQMC. Initially he moved to eclipse the power of the appointed staff officers by creating additional divisions whose directors reported directly to the commandant. While serving as the assistant to the Commandant from 1914 to 1917, Lejeune had urged Barnett to form a planning section at HQMC. On 1 December 1920, the new Commandant ordered the expansion of the planning section into the Division of Operations and Training (DOT). This new organization had responsibility for operations, training, military education, intelligence, and aviation. Brigadier General Feland became the director of the DOT, and Ellis headed the intelligence section. Maj. Gen. Wendell C. Neville served as assistant to the Commandant. Thus the most influential officers at the seat of power all knew and admired Ellis; all could be counted upon to promote his career, while at the same time overlooking his increasing dependence upon alcohol.[16]

Even before Ellis's return from the Caribbean, drastic retrenchment programs had passed Congress. On 11 December 1918 the wartime strength of the Marine Corps peaked at 74,832 officers and men. Following the armistice, that figure plummeted. On 30 June 1919, planners at HQMC counted 48,834 leathernecks; within weeks, Congress passed legislation establishing the peacetime strength of the Marine Corps at 1,093 officers and 27,400 enlisted men; by then the 269 women reservists ("Marinettes") had been released from active duty. By 30 June 1920 personnel rosters revealed further reductions: 1,104 officers and 16,061 enlisted men. Reducing the size of the enlisted ranks posed little difficulty, however, because most of the men had joined up either in a burst of wartime patriotism or to avoid being drafted into the Army. Thus, much of the excess in the ranks simply returned home without significant impact on the

Marine Corps. But the dilemma of a burgeoning officer corps continued to vex senior officers.

In April 1917 only 341 officers—including Ellis—wore forest green; by the end of the war the ranks had increased to more than 2,400. To fill the vacancies, HQMC had turned to meritorious non-commissioned officers and applicants attending colleges and universities. Many of these temporary and reserve officers sought to remain in uniform. First Barnett and then Lejeune faced the unpleasant task of deciding who should remain while mustering others out of uniform.

A board convened during the closing weeks of Barnett's commandancy and stunned the officer ranks by "plucking," or reducing in rank, many officers with distinguished combat records. Disappointed observers charged that the board had concentrated too heavily on education and pedigrees. An unattributed source reported that Col. John R. Russell, the board's chairman, had admonished the conferees to "select those officers whom you would invite into your homes, and that you'd want to marry your daughters." Sensing a sharp division among his officers, Lejeune ordered a new board. Chaired by Neville, the new group included Butler and the former commanding officer of the 6th Marines in France, Col. Harry Lee. When this board reported out in May 1921, its recommendations surprised few observers: officers who had demonstrated courage and decisiveness under fire received preference for retention and promotion. The deliberations had nothing whatsoever to do with Ellis's failed career aggrandizement, because he had already been reduced from lieutenant colonel to major through peacetime reductions. Four brigadier generals were reduced in rank to colonel as a result of postwar cutbacks.[17]

Ellis's return to Washington on 11 December 1920 and Lejeune's ascendancy to the Commandancy the previous summer coincided with significant and far-reaching changes in the American political scene. Disillusioned by the world war and its aftermath, the body politic rejected both the Democratic Party and the League of Nations. The new Republican administration responded in kind to the American people with promises of normalcy and isolation. A clamor for disarmament grew with increasing momentum following a joint congressional resolution in June 1921. The following August the U.S. Secretary of State invited nine major naval powers to send representatives to a disarmament conference in Washington. At the opening of the plenary session on 12 November 1921, Secretary Charles Evans Hughes startled the conferees by proposing a limitation on naval construction. He propounded that the United States, Great Britain, and Japan together scrap a total of sixty-six ships equaling 1.87 million tons. Hughes suggested a ratio of 5 (U.S.): 5 (Great Britain): 3 (Japan); later he added 1.7 (Italy) and 1.7 (France) to limit naval construction among the major powers.

Within a month, the major powers generally agreed to the stunning proposal. Even the most militant navalists understood that a continuation of the arms race would be ruinous to their nations' respective economies. But as the agreements evolved into treaties, American naval strategists especially expressed shock and dismay when the United States agreed not to fortify the Philippines, Guam, Wake, and the Aleutians. Great Britain followed suit by agreeing to suspend fortification of Hong Kong, Borneo, the Solomons, and the Gilberts. A reluctant Japan promised not to expand naval holdings in Formosa or the mandated islands in the Central Pacific. Assurances by the Empire of Japan did little to deflect the shock of senior American naval strategists. For them, America's rush to disarmament and isolation had left its naval bases in the Pacific marooned and indefensible. The treaties signed in Washington appeared to acquiesce to Japanese naval supremacy in the Western Pacific.

Capt. William Veazie Pratt, who represented the office of the CNO at the conferences, remained ambivalent. While in his unpublished autobiography he attempted to maintain a lofty, philosophical stance, clearly his manuscript reflected the frustrations of fellow navalists at the apparent sellout of American naval supremacy. Assistant Secretary of the Navy Theodore Roosevelt, Jr., embraced the goals and aspirations of the conferees wholeheartedly and dismissed any contention from senior U.S. Navy officers as unrealistic, impractical, and shortsighted. But the CNO, Adm. Robert E. Coontz, sputtered discontentedly: "Had there been a naval officer among our delegates . . . I do not think we would have agreed to article 19 [the nonfortification clause] of the treaty." Most navalists noted with dismay that the conferees focused on the tonnage of ships while demonstrating an abominable ignorance of the importance of naval bases in support of the fleet.[18]

Although the treaties appeared to abrogate claims to American naval supremacy in the Pacific, U.S. navalists continued to clamor for a continuation of the Wilsonian naval construction program of 1916. The General Board of the Navy argued that the naval limitations endangered America; only by increasing its naval strength could the United States maintain its national security. American representatives at the conference adopted a more parsimonious stance. Assistant Secretary of the Navy Roosevelt contended that the nonfortification treaty left the United States in a better position than it did Japan. In his view, America had traded fortifications not yet completed for base expansion that Japan would most certainly have finished. While the United States retained a major naval facility in Hawaii, Japan would be relegated to naval expansion only in the home islands. Roosevelt's colleague at the historic conference, Captain Pratt, supported the U.S. position rather than coming to the side of his fellow navalists: "Guam and the Philippines never were, and never would be, adequately fortified by us in peace, as they might be by a more military government."[19]

Despite the gloomy perspectives of 1921, strategists within the Department of the Navy responded stridently to the specter of a wholesale abrogation of American naval strength in the Pacific. Even before the conferees agreed to the contentious provisions of the treaties, planners had begun to scrutinize existing war plans in light of postwar initiatives and imperatives. In early January 1920 the CNO, Admiral Coontz, alerted Lejeune that a major revision to War Plan Orange had begun. Coontz noted specifically that "provisions are made for the capture of certain bases in the Carolines and Marshall Islands as the fleet advances over the Pacific." The CNO suggested two Marine Corps expeditionary forces, one on each coast, with a state of readiness of forty-eight hours to embark. Coontz added that he anticipated Army forces would take over Marine Corps duties in Haiti, Santo Domingo, and Cuba, thus releasing Marine manpower for expeditionary duties and for continuous service in the ships of the fleet. The following April, Col. Ben H. Fuller, the Marine Corps representative on the War Plans Division, General Board of the Navy, wrote Lejeune to report excitedly on the implications of the revisions to War Plan Orange as they pertained to existing plans for advanced bases: "There is now being prepared at [the Naval War College] a very comprehensive problem covering all of the operations connected with a campaign for the control of the Western Pacific, including as one of its important plans the occupation and defense of advanced bases in the Marshalls or Carolines."[20]

Barely a month after signatories agreed to the three treaties—one limiting naval tonnage, a second forbidding further construction and expansion of existing naval facilities in the Western Pacific, and a third guaranteeing the sovereignty of China—Lejeune responded to concerns within naval circles. The Commandant laid out the capabilities and limitations of the Marine Corps in support of fleet operations within the parameters of the treaties. Lejeune emphasized that the strength and organization of the Marine Corps should be determined by both peacetime duties and missions in time of war. While peacetime missions remained essentially the same, including the manning of garrisons overseas, the Commandant recognized the need for a mobile expeditionary force for carrying out U.S. foreign policy. The farsighted Lejeune concluded that "the primary war mission of the Marine Corps is to supply a mobile force to accompany the fleet for operations on shore in support of the fleet; this force should be of such size, organization, armament, and equipment as may be required by the plan of naval operations." Ellis had arrived at HQMC at a seemingly propitious moment.[21]

Sometime shortly after Ellis's return to Washington near the end of 1920, he met the woman who might have changed his life and deflected the spiral into debilitating alcoholism. Robert H. "Hal" Dunlap's wife, Katharine, apparently introduced her dressmaker to the morose bachelor. Elizabeth Allen Rogers, nine years younger than Ellis, was the estranged wife of Lt. Col. Henry S. Green. Commissioned in 1905 after a brief stint as a student at Princeton University and then as a bond salesman in Manhattan, Green earned an unsavory reputation because of indebtedness and for writing worthless checks. At about the time that Ellis returned from Santo Domingo, the Marine Corps had witnessed enough of Green's disquieting personal life and dismissed him on 12 December 1920. Betty Allen Rogers probably married the lackluster Green in 1911, but before the end of the decade the marriage had floundered.

Beginning in early 1921, the romance between Betty—sometimes she called herself Betty Allen Rogers, at other times Elizabeth Allen Rogers-Green—and Ellis blossomed. Both Betty's dress shop, "The Book and Gown" on 17th Street N.W., and her residence lay near the Army-Navy Club. Ellis courted her through a series of candlelight dinners and evenings at the Knickerbocker Theater. She doubtless told him that her father was William Allen Rogers (1854–1931), the celebrated political cartoonist for the *New York Herald*. Ellis's relatives recalled only one other woman who might have gained a permanent place in his life, and that romance had stalled years before. In a letter to his brother John written late that spring, Ellis referred to Betty Allen Rogers as "the future Mrs. Earl." She indicated in a letter to Ellis, written while he was abroad, that her divorce from Green had become final on 15 May 1922.[22]

As Ellis settled into HQMC on 23 December 1920, the initiatives and imperatives of the new world order influenced the smaller of the naval services. As the intelligence officer for the DOT, Ellis's role in Marine Corps planning for the postwar era became increasingly pronounced. Initially his intellectual focus scrutinized leatherneck roles as America's colonial infantry following the Spanish-American War. Although much of the altruism that clothed Yankee imperialism in the first two decades of the twentieth century had been discredited and abandoned by the end of the world war, Ellis's fellow Marines appeared especially suited as a neocolonial naval force. Ellis's views on this thorny subject appeared in the pages of the semiofficial *Marine Corps Gazette.* The date of official approval for the publication of the jingoistic essay indicates that Ellis prepared it prior to embarking for Santo Domingo, and thus much of the cynicism contained in what appeared in print reflects conclusions harbored from his two tours in the Philippines.[23]

The stimulus for Ellis's literary effort may well have been increasingly shrill criticism of U.S. policies in Haiti, Santo Domingo, and the Philippines. Denunciation of America's neocolonialism—and especially of the role of the Marine Corps personnel as the instruments of Western imperialism—had increased markedly by 1920. In his essay, entitled "Bush Brigades," Ellis reminded readers that his fellow Marines served as the agents of neocolonialism at the behest of the government of the United States. He underscored the benevolent motivation for the involvement; however cynical the politicians might be, individual Marines tended to believe the altruistic rhetoric emanating from Washington. As with much of his intellectual forbearance, Ellis's prophetic analyses placed his varied theses decades beyond situations at hand. Many of his sage observations of 1921 appear, in hindsight, more valuable to another generation of Marines landing in Nicaragua in 1927, or their great-grandchildren marching ashore in Vietnam in 1965.

Ellis described in painstaking detail just what military and civil operations might be required to accomplish such a mission. He noted what a future generation learned with chagrin in Vietnam—that in the process of eradicating subversion and insurgency, the friendship of the people the military or naval force had come to assist may be forfeited permanently. In a rather harsh tone, Ellis proclaimed the necessity to hunt down and kill the insurgents, and to destroy their homes and property. Such sentiments are generally consistent with views expressed in letters home from the Philippines two decades before, when Ellis expressed approval of Waller's punitive actions during the infamous march across Samar. He noted that "mothers in these countries particularly are prone to nurse hatred and pass it along to their children." For a generation after the first U.S. intervention in Nicaragua in 1910, native mothers quieted their unruly children with a timeless admonition: "Hush, Major [Smedley D.] Butler will get you." Politics aside, Ellis's compendium underscored the necessity for complete and thorough intelligence in a counterinsurgency environment. As for the violence accompanying these foreign interventions and imbroglios, Ellis ended his polemic with a professional tongue-lashing for knee-jerk liberal critics: "Yes, the Marines are down in jungleland, and they did kill a man in a war, and a great many people did not know anything about it. This is most unfortunate, but—the Marines are only doing their job as ordered by the people of the United States."[24]

Ellis's spirited defense of colonial infantry roles in imperialistic duties appeared at a propitious moment. The Marine Corps had been buffeted with allegations of brutality and wrongdoing in Haiti just as Lejeune took the reins of the Marine Corps. Near the end of his tenure as Commandant, a stunned Barnett had expressed outrage over an allegation of "indiscriminate killing of natives" by Marines assigned to the Gendarmerie d'Haiti. According to the material in a transcript of a court-martial sent to the commandant for approval of sentence, two Marines had summarily executed a pair of native insurgents. Shocked at what he read, Barnett ordered an official investigation. He then followed his correspondence with a "confidential and personal" letter to the Marine Corps commander in Haiti to express his concern. The second letter cautioned Col. John H. Russell to take whatever action was necessary to ensure that such atrocities did not recur. The matter might have ended then and there, except for mounting opposition to American involvement in Haiti—especially during a U.S. presidential election.

Criticism of U.S. intervention in Haiti increased in intensity in 1920, especially from political organizations representing African-Americans. Political advisors to presidential hopeful Harding hoped to embarrass the Wilson administration by revealing a series of provocative materials at the height of the election. In the summer of 1920 a journalist returned from a fact-finding trip to the troubled nation and reported in a weekly magazine that "I have heard officers wearing the United States uniform [presumably Marines] in the interior of Haiti talk of 'bumping off gooks' as if it were a variety of sport like duck hunting." The reporter added that reports of torture and murder by Marines were commonplace. He concluded his scathing report by suggesting that the Marines assigned to duties in Haiti were, for the most part, "ignorant and brutal."[25]

Sensing a major political controversy in the making, Secretary of the Navy Daniels ordered Barnett to prepare a detailed report on the history of Marine Corps activities in Haiti. In compiling the information, as directed, Barnett added a copy of his "personal and confidential" correspondence to Russell. Apparently Daniels overlooked the inflammatory letters, but an enterprising journalist spotted the material, or perhaps a vengeful Barnett pointed it out. In any event,

the revelation added to mounting criticism of the Wilson administration's foreign policy and involvement in the region. Harding
delighted in telling eager crowds that "thousands of Haitians have
been killed by American Marines." But a special investigation of
leatherneck misconduct in Haiti, conducted by Lejeune and Butler,
unearthed only a few instances of misconduct since 1916, and every
case had resulted in prison sentences. Most observers remained
unconvinced, however, and criticism of U.S. intervention in the
Caribbean continued to aid the Republicans through the presidential election of 1920.[26]

Following the successful printing of "Bush Brigades," Ellis penned
a stronger diatribe on the same subject. While this essay has been lost
to history, it apparently contained sufficient militaristic and imperialistic commentary to frighten politically sensitive reviewers who
hoped to distance President Harding from such controversial material. Strident imperialism, however practical it might appear to a seasoned veteran like Ellis, was deemed politically incorrect by the
Harding administration. The new Secretary of the Navy, Edwin H.
Denby, took his cue and responded according to the wishes of the
Oval Office. In this instance Ellis was officially informed that he
could not offer "Bush Brigades and Baby Nations" for publication.[27]

Toward the end of 1920, a variety of initiatives served to focus the
attentions of Lejeune and his senior officers on war planning in the
event of hostilities in the Pacific against the Empire of Japan. Revisions of War Plan Orange were well under way. Then, indications that
U.S. diplomats appeared willing to bargain away possible strength-
ening of fleet anchorages in the Western Pacific at the conference
table stimulated the mercurial Ellis's intellectual bent. Whether his
superiors directed the study of the Marine Corps's role in amphibious operations in the event of war, or if once again Ellis demonstrated that he marched to a different drummer, is unknown. It is,
however, unlikely and improbable that Ellis would immerse himself
in such monastic fashion in staff work of this magnitude without the

direct approval of Brigadier General Feland, his nominal superior in the DOT, and the tacit sanction and approbation of the Commandant of the Marine Corps himself.

The document produced by Ellis, "Advanced Base Operations in Micronesia," was actually the third part of a secret war plan of the same name. The first part, prepared by an anonymous staff officer, was entitled "War Portfolio." These few pages simply set the parameters for Ellis's much larger study, first with a purpose: "To guide and coordinate training and activities of the Marine Corps in peacetime so as to be ready to execute war plans." The portfolio assumes that a personnel strength of 27,400 Marines will be available, but notes that an additional 5,000 recruits would be required to bring the brigades up to full strength. At this time the Marine Corps counted brigades at Quantico and San Diego, and overseas in Haiti and Santo Domingo. Ellis's work constitutes the next eighty pages of the prophetic document.

Ellis posited that in order to impose the will of the United States upon Japan in the event of hostilities, advanced bases would be required to support the fleet. Geographical distances and the weaknesses of existing bases in the Philippines and Guam prompted Ellis to conclude that facilities in Hawaii constituted the only support for the U.S. Navy in the Western Pacific. At the same time, Japan's occupation of the former German holdings in the Marshalls, Carolines, and Palaus flanked U.S. lines of communications in the region by more than twenty-three hundred miles. Perhaps reflecting the Mahanian influence at the Naval War College during his tenure there, Ellis predicted that Japan would keep its fleet in home waters until a meeting engagement with the U.S. fleet was foreseen.

Ellis then offered a series of analyses: the sea, the air, the land, and the native population. In the latter section, the racial and ethnic biases from two tours in the Philippines are found to remain, and Ellis elects to denigrate the native populations, noting that they exchanged barbarous vices and virtues for Western vices: "[The] lazy and deceitful qualities of the usual native convert [are displayed] . . . lately, their mental indigestion has been further complicated by the occupation of the Japanese." In his analysis of the enemy, Ellis states boldly that he anticipates Japan to initiate the war. But he writes that the United States has "advantages over the enemy . . . generally common to the Nordic races over the oriental: higher individual intelligence, physique, and endurance." Ellis concludes that "these superior qualities will manifest themselves directly in our superiority in the use of hand weapons and in staying power." Continuing in this vein, he sullies the potential foe even further: "The Japanese sometimes reach a high peak of morale, but react quickly and, being excitable, they become rapidly disorganized—not only in defeat, but often in victory."

At this juncture Ellis's study makes a radical departure from accepted doctrine. Heretofore planners had emphasized the defense of advanced bases in support of the fleet. Marine Corps units would deploy to take up a purely defensive position, with the assumption that the sites were essentially available for the taking without forced entry. Now, because Japan had occupied the geographical locations under discussion, it appeared necessary to reduce and occupy the islands in the Central Pacific. Ellis predicted three phases in such a naval campaign: first, reduction of the Marshalls; second, seizing of the Carolines west as far as Yap; and third, the taking of the remainder of the Carolines, including the Palaus. Ellis emphasized that the tactics of feint and maneuver were important because of anticipated strong resistance at Kusaie, Ponape, Truk, and Babelthuap. The difficulties inherent in an opposed landing prompted Ellis to conclude at this point that "only men trained along Marine Corps lines can succeed." Overall, he emphasized the value of the element of surprise and rapidity of execution, as well as the importance of naval gunfire in the preassault phase. Ellis admonished fleet commanders to approach the amphibious objective area under cover of darkness and to land at daybreak: "Night landings in force are dangerous unless the coast conditions and the enemy defenses are well known." His disquisition on tactics concludes with the advice for quick offensive action inland: "[It] confuses the defense in general but the counter-attack forces in particular."

Ellis emphasized that the primary mission for the amphibious force was to secure and then protect a suitable advanced base for the fleet. An unfettered innovator, he argued convincingly for a landing force that was task-organized. Ellis predicted the requirement for landing regiments of Marines, each numbering approximately 2,000 men: headquarters company, 125; supply company, 125; 37mm gun company (12), 125 each; 75mm gun company (8), 125 each; machine-gun company (30), 125 each; and three infantry battalions, 500 each. The melancholy fact that the Marine Corps had nowhere such numbers of men in uniform failed to dissuade Ellis in his analysis; on 30 June 1921 the active-duty strength of the Marine Corps was only 22,990 officers and men!

Ellis anticipated the requirement for nine such landing regiments: three each for Wotje-Mille and Eniwetok-Likieb, two for Jaluit-Elmo, and one in reserve. Once the amphibious force had seized an advanced base, he emphasized, the primary objective became the defense of the site, not the destruction of the enemy. Although Ellis emphasized mobility and flexibility in the defense, he prescribed a substantial number of naval guns emplaced ashore: twelve 7-inch, tractor mounted; twelve 5-inch, pedestal mounted; twenty-four 5-inch antiaircraft guns, pedestal mounted; twelve 3-inch antiaircraft guns on ground mounts; and eighteen 30- and 36-inch searchlights. He anticipated a mobile defense at sea, as well as that ashore.

Ellis's conclusions to "Advanced Base Operations in Micronesia" place him at the forefront of naval strategists of the era: a major fleet action would decide the war in the Pacific; the U.S. fleet would be 25 percent superior to that of the enemy; the enemy would hold his main fleet within his defense line (meaning, Japan would keep the fleet in home waters); fleet units must be husbanded; preliminary activities of the U.S. fleet must be accomplished with a minimum of assets; Marine Corps forces must be self-sustaining; long, drawn-out operations must be avoided to afford the greatest protection to the fleet; sea objectives must be isolated; and sea objectives must include a fleet anchorage. Ellis concluded that the great losses to the amphibious forces would occur in what he termed the "ship-shore belt." And he advised planners to avoid blue-water transfers, to form task forces prior to leaving base ports, and not to divide units up among several transports.[28]

Ellis apparently completed the draft of his prophetic study before the end of spring 1921. Subsequent analyses by Feland, Neville, or even Lejeune are unrecorded. Ellis is known to have conferred with his old friend Col. Robert Dunlap at Quantico during the preparation of the study. Dunlap had studied at the Naval War College with Ellis a decade before; many considered him, along with Ellis, one of the Marine Corps's most promising luminaries. Sometime in late April the plan to send Ellis on a covert mission to examine the Marshalls and Carolines firsthand was formulated. On 9 April 1921, Ellis submitted a pro forma request for three months' leave to visit Europe in a tourist status. On 4 May, Assistant Secretary of the Navy Theodore Roosevelt, Jr., approved the request as the acting Secretary of the Navy.

By then Ellis had suffered another bout of neurasthenia but recovered sufficiently for the naval hospital to discharge him on 4 May 1921. The following day he reported to HQMC for a personal audience with the Commandant. What transpired between the two is unknown, but transmittal of an undated letter of resignation apparently took place then.[29]

6 ∽ Mission to the Central Pacific 1921–1923

BY EARLY 1921, Ellis's furtive mission to visit the Japanese mandates in the Central Pacific had received official permission from his superiors in the Marine Corps chain of command. At Headquarters Marine Corps (HQMC), Ellis's nominal supervisor, Brig. Gen. Logan Feland, must have been a party to the affair from the outset. Col. Robert H. "Hal" Dunlap, an old friend, appears to have played a role in the sub-rosa affair. It was Dunlap's wife, Katharine, who apparently introduced her dressmaker, Betty Allen Rogers, to Ellis. Dunlap reported to Feland in the latter's capacity as Director of the Division of Operations and Training, which held responsibility for operations, training, military education, intelligence, and aviation. Approval by Feland was a sine qua non even before the unusual request reached the desk of the Commandant of the Marine Corps, Maj. Gen. John A. Lejeune. From Feland, Ellis's request, stamped "Confidential," passed to the assistant to the Commandant, Maj. Gen. Wendell C. Neville, another senior officer who knew and admired Ellis. The correspondence asked simply that Ellis receive permission to travel in Europe in a leave status for a period of three months.[1]

Hindsight suggests that Lejeune alerted Adm. William Veazie Pratt, the Chief of Naval Operations, to the request and that Pratt turned the matter over to the Office of Naval Intelligence (ONI). That the mission gained tacit approval in the chain above HQMC seems axiomatic; no fool, Lejeune could not jeopardize his office and expose the Marine Corps to another scandal. Already in the first year of his commandancy, HQMC had been buffeted, first by the sacking of Lejeune's predecessor and then by a scandal alleging atrocities committed by Marines in Haiti. Whether the Secretary of the Navy, Edwin H. Denby, or his assistant, Theodore Roosevelt, Jr., knew of the plan remains a mystery. However, since assuming office, both senior civil servants had focused their attentions on the potential for a naval war against Japan in the Pacific, and especially the implications for the Navy emanating from the Washington Naval Arms Limitations Conferences. Thus, any information provided by Ellis that revealed construction of fortifications and fleet anchorages in the Central Pacific by the Japanese would support assertions by some officers in the Department of the Navy that the provisions of the various treaties served to strengthen Japan at the expense of the United States.[2]

The most important treaty to emerge from the Washington Naval Arms Limitations Conferences of 1921–22 was the Five-Power Naval Treaty of 6 February 1922. The United States, Great Britain, France, Japan, and Italy agreed to curtail the rush to construct naval tonnage in capital ships by setting a ratio among the major powers. An important caveat forbade the competing powers from fortifying their possessions in the Pacific further and required that they maintain their remaining defenses. Although limiting the capital ship tonnage of the Imperial Japanese Navy to only 60 percent of that of either the United States or Great Britain, the nonfortification clause precipitated alarm among American naval strategists. Naval war plans for further development of U.S. holdings in the Philippines and Marianas were put aside. Worse, it meant that neither Subic Bay nor Guam could be defended in the event of Japanese attack, as operations in East Asia from America's distant naval base at Pearl Harbor, Hawaii, appeared too distant and impractical.[3]

Ellis and his superiors prepared a suitable cover for the mission. John A. Hughes, commissioned from the ranks along with Ellis in 1902, had been medically retired in 1920 as a result of wounds and injuries sustained in combat. The colorful Hughes, known as "Johnny the Hard" because of his gruff demeanor, returned to Manhattan and joined his father in the import-export business. Conveniently, Ellis became a representative of the Hughes Trading Company. He obtained a copy of the Navy's F2 codebook, presumably from ONI. His plans made and his personal affairs in order, Ellis then asked for a three-month leave to visit Belgium, France, Germany, and England as a cover to explain his absence from HQMC. The speed with which the routine administrative request received the approval of Lejeune and Denby supports the contention that the latter knew of the intelligence-gathering mission.[4]

Even as Ellis prepared to depart, his frequent bouts with alcoholism resulted in another incidence of neurasthenia. Ellis was confined to the Washington Naval Hospital, and medical records reveal him "nervous and tense, and emotionally unstable." He complained of "insomnia, nausea, and an irritative cough." The admitting physician noted the onset of delirium tremens, manifested by the "shakes." But as before, after a regimen of hypnotics and an absence of alcohol, he recovered sufficiently to be discharged to duty on 4 May 1921. These episodes, occurring with alarming frequency since his initial assignment to HQMC in 1915, foreshadowed disaster—especially for someone charged with a dangerous and sensitive mission. Between September 1916 and August 1921, Ellis had been ill for a total of 282 days. Because of alcohol abuse, he suffered continually from nephritis, a painful inflammation of the kidneys.[5]

On 5 May, Ellis signed out of HQMC on leave. Before departing he stopped by Lejeune's office to pay his respects and say good-bye. The Commandant's secretary observed that Ellis handed Lejeune an envelope, which the Commandant placed into a desk drawer without apparent comment or unusual interest. The urgency that Ellis attached to his ill-fated quest was underscored by the fact that on the day he chose to depart Washington, he was scheduled to appear before a board of examination to determine his fitness for promotion to lieutenant colonel—he never appeared, but received the promotion anyway.[6]

Ellis boarded a train in Washington and returned to Kansas to visit his family. Since his last visit home his father had died, but his mother still lived in the old home. Ellis told most relatives and friends that he planned to travel for his health and that they would be unable to contact him because of his frequent moves. He anticipated returning in approximately eight months, but in no instance were they to ask Marine Corps or civilian superiors of his whereabouts. Ellis emphasized, above all else, that no inquiries were made to either of Kansas's senators or his congressman. The excuse that his poor health required the lengthy sojourn appeared plausible, especially to Ralph Ellis. Ellis's older brother expressed alarm at his unhealthy condition, especially the symptoms of alcoholism, and begged him not to attempt the mission. Inexplicably, Ellis waited until returning to Pratt before applying for a passport. Perhaps it conformed to the subterfuge he was involved in, for he swore before the District Court of Pratt County that he was a commercial agent residing permanently in Pratt, Kansas.[7]

Ellis departed home on 28 May 1921, traveled to San Francisco, and booked passage through the American President Line on a ship to Australia. In an attempt to obtain visas to almost anywhere in the Pacific, he inquired at a number of consulates in San Francisco. To his dismay, Ellis discovered that such applications had to be made at the proposed point of departure—in this instance, Sydney. While in the Bay area he telephoned Hans G. Hornbostel, a Marine he had known during his tour in Guam. Hornbostel had left the Marine Corps and taken a job as chief forester on Guam, and Ellis pumped his old comrade for information on the Marianas. Inexplicably, Ellis revealed details of his classified mission. Since Hornbostel planned to take up a new position as a collector for the B. P. Bishop Museum in Honolulu, the old friends agreed to meet again soon somewhere in the Pacific. The brief chat ended with Hornbostel confiding to his wife that Ellis thought he "might not return from the trip." Ellis also paid a perfunctory call at the district naval headquarters, where he made an appointment with Comdr. Wallace Bertholf, the resident agent of naval intelligence for the 12th Naval District, and again revealed his purpose in passing through the Bay area. Thus, since leaving Washington, Ellis had revealed his classified mission to two civilians and then to a fellow naval officer—all of whom had no "need to know." Apparently the contact with Commander Bertholf was to establish a commercial banking repository for the funds to finance the mission. Before leaving Pratt, Ellis asked his mother to inform all correspondents that he was in Europe.[8]

Ellis's odyssey took him first to New Zealand, and then on the SS *Maheno* to Australia, arriving 28 September 1921. During his stay at Usher's Metropolitan Hotel in Sydney, Ellis advised his brother John of his whereabouts and asked that no more mail be forwarded to him. He planned to sail on the SS *Suva* to Fiji, Tonga, and British Samoa on 25 October. Ellis still believed he could obtain passage from the British Pacific islands to the mandates. But several weeks of a sleepy voyage in the South Pacific failed to spark his interest, and he returned to Australia. To his mother, Ellis added to the mystery of the journey: "If you don't hear [from me] for quite a while, it will be because I am well into the islands where mail boats don't happen."[9]

In Sydney he inquired at the Japanese Consulate for permission to visit the Carolines and Marshalls. On 25 October 1921 the consul-general passed on the request to Tokyo. A day later the Japanese

Foreign Office asked the Imperial Naval Ministry if it had any objection. With none reported, the consul-general issued the necessary visa. But to Ellis's dismay, no steamship service existed from Australia to the mandates. Undaunted, Ellis cabled Hal Dunlap: "Impractical here, proceeding Japan, everything all right, cable club Manila if not agreeable." Privately, however, Ellis found the experience of the journey exasperating and frustrating. To John Ellis he proclaimed that "I think my get-a-long is good. I'm never going to try it again—too old to be so damned adventurous." In the same letter, he asked his brother to file everything that he mailed, explaining that "some of the correspondence may contain *information*."[10]

Ellis became ill in Sydney with a septic toe, and the attending physician confined him to a hospital. After recovery and release, he took passage on the SS *Tango Maru,* disembarking in Manila. By then the symptoms of neurasthenia had returned, and Ellis entered a hospital in Manila. While visiting the city, a friend, Maj. Howard W. Kipp, learned of Ellis's visit and arranged for his transfer to the naval hospital in Cavite. The symptoms had not changed: "Complains of nervousness, restlessness, twitching of the muscles of the face and arms . . . diagnosis changed to nephritis, acute." Following his release, Ellis prepared a message to HQMC: "It is essential to reach objective by northern route. I have gained complete authority and I do not think there will be any further difficulty. Delayed here while ill but all well now. I desire to continue, and if necessary to take six months extension time. I possess necessary funds. Your reply is desire[d] by radio to NavSta [Naval Station] Cavité."[11]

Despite his professed love for Betty Allen Rogers, Ellis apparently never corresponded after December 1921. Perhaps in his twisted perspective and amateurish approach to covert intelligence operations, he chose to shield her from anything untoward. Her letters, beginning in January 1922 and through the spring, were filled with affection and longing: "The rose lady loves you, as always . . . all the men who take me out seem so flat and stupid after knowing you. . . . I want just you and will be so glad when you get home." In March 1922 she announced that her divorce from Henry Sheldon Green had become final. Strangely, Ellis never corresponded, although he referred to her as the "future Mrs. Earl" in a letter to Ralph Ellis. In a final letter, written just before departing Australia, he asked her not to write to him except in care of John Ellis in Pratt.[12]

Undaunted, Betty wrote to John Ellis near the end of 1921 to inform him of her address for the Christmas holidays, should "Pete" happen to correspond. In her letter she mentioned receiving letters from Ellis but offered no details. Apparently he failed to correspond after departing Australia for the Philippines. A few months later Colonel Dunlap sent Ellis a newsy, chatty letter in care of John Ellis. In it he noted that "Katharine sees Betty often and they always talk of you—you had better come back and settle down on the farm."[13]

Into midsummer, Ellis remained in Manila in the guise of a commercial agent and recovered his strength. In late July 1922 he departed the Philippines on the SS *President Jackson* for Yokohama with through passage to San Francisco. Apparently, HQMC remained confident that the mercurial Ellis could remain sufficiently sober to continue the mission, for a cable reached him in Manila before embarkation: "Extension granted for period of six months or as much of that time as may be necessary." Significantly, the assistant to the Commandant, Major General Neville, signed off on the cablegram. Thus it may be assumed that everyone in Ellis's Marine Corps chain of command—Dunlap, Feland, Neville, and Lejeune—knew of his whereabouts and the status of the mission. Whether the Commandant informed Commander McNamee, Admiral Pratt, Assistant Secretary Roosevelt, or Secretary Denby of Ellis's status at that juncture in the mission is unknown, but may be presumed. The amateurishness of Ellis's spy mission continued unabated; from Manila, he cabled John Ellis to declare, "[I am] proceeding Japan."[14]

In Yokohama, Ellis made final preparations to enter the Central Pacific. With visas in hand, he booked passage with the Nanyo Boeki

Kaisha Line for a ship transiting the mandated islands. Then, reverting to pattern, Ellis began to drink heavily. Quickly, word of his bizarre activities, including patronage of shabby bars and geisha houses along the waterfront, reached the American embassy in Tokyo. To the alarm of the naval attaché, Capt. Lyman A. Cotten, Ellis was reported to have disclosed aspects of a classified mission to his drinking companions. Cotten ordered his assistant, Lt. Comdr. Garnet Huling, to monitor the case. Once again, Ellis checked himself into the U.S. Naval Hospital in Yokohama, suffering from neurasthenia. Capt. Ulysses S. Webb, the director of the tiny medical facility, examined the troublesome patient. On 12 August 1922 he noted that Ellis weighed 145 pounds and stood 71 inches in height, had graying hair and blue eyes. Inexplicably, Dr. Webb failed to note a diagnosis of neurasthenia or any of the debilitating symptoms of alcoholism on the examination report. After the usual regimen of rest, hypnotics, and an absence of alcohol, Ellis was released from the hospital.[15]

Ellis's deteriorating condition disturbed Dr. Webb. Summoned shortly thereafter by the manager of the Grand Hotel in Yokohama, Dr. Webb found Ellis gravely ill and exhibiting the symptoms of delirium tremens again. In his stupor, Ellis revealed the secret mission to the alarmed physician. On 1 September 1922 he was admitted to the naval hospital for treatment again. Upon his release he claimed to have obtained passage on a steamer departing 14 September, but he failed to appear for the passage to the mandated islands. On 20 September a Japanese taxi dropped Ellis off at the naval hospital, and he underwent treatment for alcoholism again. Between Dr. Webb and Captain Cotten, the decision to order Ellis out of East Asia and home on the next military transport seemed prudent. They offered Ellis the choice of voluntarily returning on the next available civilian shipping or returning under orders on a military transport.[16]

Ignoring the direct orders of his superiors, Ellis cabled his bank in San Francisco for a draft of a thousand dollars, packed his luggage, and took the train to Kobe. From there he departed for Saipan on the next leg of his confused odyssey. Meanwhile the naval attaché in Tokyo reported Ellis's disappearance from the hospital. Captain Cotten reported no trace of Ellis since the evening of 6 October 1922. The erratic spy had mentioned his intent to traverse the Caroline Islands to someone at the naval hospital, and this disclosure—along with the revelation that Ellis had a "good supply of ready money"— doubtless fueled concerns in Washington. A copy of the cablegram was signed off by Major General Neville. The Director, ONI, admonished the naval attaché in Tokyo to "handle with great caution and under no circumstances inform any Japanese of his presence or movements."[17]

On the third day out of Japan the *Kasuga Maru* stopped briefly in the Bonins, and Ellis had the opportunity to take a stroll around Chi Chi Jima. Two more days' steaming brought the ship to Saipan, where it anchored in Tanapag Harbor. Ellis moved ashore to a shabby hotel in Garapan, apparently planning to remain in the Marianas for a while. Hornbostel had advised him, once established, to contact an old friend, Kilili Sablan. Ellis sought him out for information on Saipan. Meanwhile, ONI attempted to locate Ellis through withdrawals from the special bank account he had established with the funds ONI provided for the covert mission.[18]

Magellan laid claim to the Marianas, comprising a land mass of approximately forty-six square miles, in 1521. After the Spanish-American War ended in 1899, Germany took control until supplanted by Japan in 1914. By the time Ellis stepped ashore at the Port of Tanapag, Saipan, the Japanese were using the island as the hub of their activities in Micronesia. Sugarcane, grown for export, covered most of the cultivated land. Garapan, where Ellis stayed briefly, served as the site of the island's main port and constituted the largest town in the mandated Marianas.

Ellis's presence on the island quickly came to the attention of the Japanese authorities, and police agents began to follow him. Sablan recommended that Ellis move out of the Koakien Hotel, and arranged for him to live with the family of Nanna and José Ada. Despite the change in living quarters, native policemen continued to dog Ellis's footsteps. For the next three weeks he traveled throughout Saipan, preparing detailed maps and charts. He learned that the Japanese planned construction of a railway line to support the growing and processing of sugarcane. Tracking down the proposed site of the rail line occupied much of his amateurish intelligence-gathering efforts. Confident and enthused in his work, Ellis apparently refrained from alcohol abuse during his three-week stay in Saipan. On 3 December 1922 he boarded the *Matsuyama Maru* for the Carolines and Marshalls.[19]

The ship steamed past Rota and Guam without pausing, then stopped at Yap. On 6 December, Ellis stepped ashore at the port of Colonia. A local copra trader, Henry G. Fleming, greeted him and assumed the role of Ellis's guide. A Marshallese-German, Fleming spoke some English and escorted Ellis on a brief tour of the tiny island—comprising only forty-five square miles. Ellis demonstrated sufficient knowledge of the copra trade to convince Fleming that he was a bona fide entrepreneur. Ellis apparently found little to hold his interest on the sleepy island, and he saw no evidence that the Japanese had undertaken any activities to disturb the extensive grasslands of the flat terrain. He did ask Fleming to escort him on a lengthy tour of Yap, but the knowledge that few ships stopped in Colonia prompted Ellis to reboard the *Matsuyama Maru* on the evening of the day he arrived. Yap lay 466 nautical miles from Guam.[20]

That night the cargo vessel stood to and steamed southwest for Koror in the Palaus with Ellis aboard. Ellis moved ashore into a local hotel in the bustling Japanese trading entrepôt. The Palaus constituted the westernmost group of islands in the Carolines. Koror lay seven degrees north of the equator and six hundred miles east of the Philippines. The Palau archipelago stretched more than four hundred miles in a north-south direction. After 1920, Palau became the

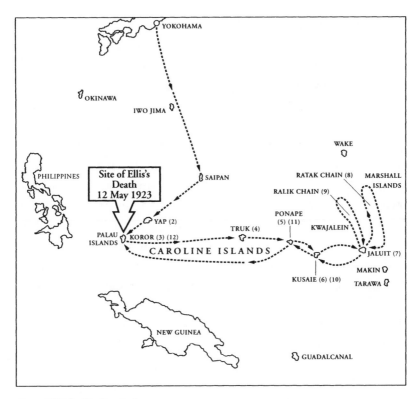

Pete Ellis's final mission

seat of the Japanese government in the mandates. Intensive economic development had begun under the Japanese by then, far surpassing anything undertaken by Spain or Germany. At this point in his tortuous quest, Ellis got the idea of taking passage from Yap to New Guinea or the Celebes, where he could find a ship to Jaluit, return to Koror, and then book passage south. At the hotel, Ellis met James Gibbons, the son of a Jamaican who had jumped ship in the Palaus. Again relying on someone local who could speak English, Ellis received the Gibbons's assurance that quarters ashore and assistance in surveying the area would be obtained upon his return. The immediate availability of shipping further east, and the absence of any vessels plying the commercial trade to the south, prompted Ellis to opt for a berth on the *Matsuyama Maru* to Truk on 13 December 1922.[21]

It took the Japanese cargo vessel more than four days to transit the distance through the west passage to Truk, and it tied up in the harbor of Dublon Island. By 1922 and Ellis's brief stop at Truk, the Japanese had begun development of the island as a major port. Truk lay 650 nautical miles southeast of Guam and 1,400 nautical miles north of Papua New Guinea. Dublon, or Tonoas as it was known locally, had become the center of Japanese administration in Palau by the time of Ellis's arrival. The Japanese had established a coaling station on the island, and the harbor constituted a busy entrepôt for trading activities in the region. Authorities prevented foreigners from leaving the dock area, and a frustrated Ellis could only pace the deck of the small trader or walk around the pier. On 18 December the ship steamed east to Ponape, paused briefly, and then steered a course for Kusaie.

Midafternoon on 20 December, Ellis came ashore. The easternmost of the Carolines, Kusaie—or Kosrae—was a high island covering an area of eight and a half by ten miles. Two rugged basaltic mountainous masses, punctuated by steep ridges and deeply eroded valleys, presented the dominant terrain. By the time of Ellis's brief sojourn, the coastal plains had been developed extensively into a network of mangroves and coconut palms. At the small settlement of Lelu he encountered two men engaged in the copra trade, Arthur Hermann and his nephew Victor. Since the *Matsuyama Maru* planned to remain overnight or perhaps longer, Ellis accepted the Hermanns' invitation for dinner and lodging. Over the conviviality of drinks and dinner, the Hermanns aired their dislike for the Japanese authorities and imperial interference in their commercial affairs. Warmed, perhaps by the friendly political overtones of the conversation as well as the consumption of copious quantities of alcoholic beverages, Ellis revealed his true identity and informed his startled companions that he was on a special mission at the behest of the American Secretary of the Navy. The Hermanns arranged a gala Christmas celebration after dinner for their guest, and everyone became uproariously drunk. The younger Hermann recalled that the Japanese had embarked on an extensive operation to dredge the harbor at Palau. He later remembered Ellis's remark that it appeared as if the Japanese were constructing a base at the site. At an interview taken at naval headquarters in San Francisco shortly after Ellis's death, though, Hermann claimed no knowledge of Ellis's clandestine intelligence-gathering activities. He did suggest that the Japanese authorities believed otherwise, however.[22]

On the morning of 29 December 1922, the *Matsuyama Maru,* with Ellis aboard, steamed out of Kusaie and continued east. As a gesture of friendship, Victor Hermann gave Ellis several bottles of whiskey. During the two-day transit from Kusaie to Jaluit, Ellis apparently confined himself to his cabin and consumed the cache of spirits. Alarmed at the condition of his occidental passenger, the captain of the *Matsuyama Maru* radioed authorities in Jaluit that he had an American businessman aboard who required medical attention. An ambulance waited on the dock and transported Ellis to the local hospital on New Year's Eve 1922. Several interested spectators witnessed the strange disembarkation of the Western passenger, including Tanaka Shoji, the district police chief, and Jesse Rebecca Hoppin, an American missionary who had resided in the islands since 1880.[23]

Because "Mother Hoppin," as she was affectionately called, spoke both Marshallese and Japanese as well as English, Tanaka apparently asked her to accompany him to greet the ship and act as interpreter. Jesse Hoppin recalled that at the hospital, the Japanese district health officer, Dr. Uichi Ishoda, examined Ellis and diagnosed alcoholism. As Ellis recovered slowly, Hoppin visited him often and admonished the inveterate alcoholic for his intemperance. Upon his release from the hospital, she offered to provide for his care at the mission with the understanding that Ellis was not to consume alcohol. Ellis acquiesced, perhaps because he desperately needed an ally at this point in his flawed mission; in addition, Ellis sensed a dislike by Hoppin for the Japanese and perhaps believed that he had found in Mother Hoppin a confidant at this juncture in his erratic mission. Fellow missionaries stood in awe of her lifetime of service in Micronesia and attributed to Mother Hoppin qualities of "patience, persistence, good sense, wisdom, and above all love which suffereth long and is kind." The editor of the American mission's *Newsbulletin* added that "her long years of service there has given her a knowledge of the island peoples which few white people have ever had."[24]

Sometime in January 1923, Ellis left the hospital and Mother Hoppin installed him in a native house in the mission compound. He appeared to thrive in the religious environment and, with the absence of alcohol, his health improved rapidly. Ellis disclosed the nature of his secret mission to Micronesia to Jesse Hoppin, another civilian with no "need to know." Mother Hoppin continued to entreat Ellis with regard to his "wicked habit," and she mentioned that Tanaka had asked her to observe his movements and report them to the chief of police. Tanaka revealed to her that he had also made inquiries about Ellis to his superiors in Tokyo. Mother Hoppin had a way of causing every conversation with Ellis to turn to his perennial bouts with alcohol abuse. Always contrite, Ellis told Mother Hoppin of his repeated hospitalizations for neurasthenia and his understanding of the fatal implications of alcoholism. Convinced that the end of his life was growing close, Ellis hoped desperately to complete his intelligence-gathering mission. From the perspective of the mercurial Ellis, a failed mission and a return home because of alcoholism meant disgrace and probably early retirement; he "would rather be dead," she recalled him exclaiming morosely.[25]

The next morning, Tanaka appeared and offered the help of his office. Ellis, still in the guise of a commercial agent, informed the Japanese chief of police that he intended to visit the coconut plantations on Jaluit with an eye to the Hughes Trading Company entering the copra business. Ellis refused Tanaka's offer of assistance, because by now he had concluded that the Japanese authorities harbored suspicions about his presence in the region. He inventoried his meager possessions and decided that the two weapons in his luggage—a .38-caliber revolver and a .45-caliber pistol—represented nothing more than a foreigner's desire to protect himself. Ellis's major concern was his codebook. He had pasted the copy of the F2 naval code obtained from ONI in the back of a worn copy of *Bentley's Business Code.* Since he feared it might fall into the wrong hands, he gave it to Mother Hoppin. Ominously, Ellis asked her to deliver the codes and all of his personal possessions to John Ellis should a misfortune strike.

Over the next few weeks, Ellis surveyed the Marshalls, using Jaluit and Mother Hoppin's compound as a base of operations. Spanish explorers discovered the Marshall Islands in 1529. German trading companies were active in the Marshalls from the 1850s. In 1885, Germany established a protectorate over the Marshalls and the Carolines, although Spain held ownership of the latter archipelago. In 1899, Spain sold all of her Micronesian holdings to Germany, which developed the region until the islands were lost to Japan in 1914. Under the Covenant of the League of Nations, Japan held a mandate over the Marshalls after 1920. Two chains of islands constituted the Marshalls: Ratak or Sunrise chain, running north to south; and Ralik or Sunset chain, running south to north and west. The Marshalls lay two thousand miles southwest of Hawaii and thirteen hundred miles southeast of Guam.

Ellis remained sober and attended church services with Mother Hoppin. The minister's daughter, Myra Heine Nelson, remembered Ellis's fine, strong voice and his joy in singing the hymns. Ellis told her that it reminded him of church services for the troops in France and Germany during the war. Rev. Claude Heine escorted Ellis around

Jaluit and accompanied him on short trips into the lagoon. Feeling
stronger, Ellis obtained passage on the *Caroline Maru,* a small sailing
vessel that plied the interisland trade in the Marshalls. Mother
Hoppin arranged for several young boys from the mission to accompany him when he left Jaluit. Soon his prolific note-taking and chart-
making became public knowledge, and Tanaka began to appear on
the interisland schooner when Ellis left Jaluit. As Ellis began preparations to travel through the rest of the Marshalls, the Japanese
attempted to hinder his journey with bureaucratic hurdles. When
Ellis attempted to arrange passage on the *Caroline Maru* for its swing
north through the Ralik and Ratak chains to pick up copra, the
Japanese booking agent attempted to dissuade him with a litany of
difficulties: no room aboard suitable for a Westerner, and no potable
water. Obdurate, he and a Marshallese, Benjamin Lajipun, obtained
berths and slept on tatami mats on the main deck. At each stop, Ellis
questioned Western traders and missionaries and continued sketch-
ing lagoons and harbors. At Kwajalein his presence and inquisitive-
ness aroused the suspicions of the Japanese authorities, but no one
attempted to prevent his further passage in the islands. On the final
leg back to Jaluit—two days' steaming—the main deck was covered
with copra, and Ellis and Lajipun spent the trip standing up![26]

By the time Ellis returned to Jaluit, the urge to imbibe in alcoholic
spirits began to overtake his resolve. During his absence, Dr. Ishoda
and Mother Hoppin had removed the bottles of liquor from his
room. Then they asked the native shopkeepers in the area not to sell
Ellis alcohol. But the furtive Ellis found a local entrepreneur who
could speak some English. Then, with the assistance of Benjamin
Lajipun, hired by Mother Hoppin as a houseboy for her guest, Ellis
arranged for the purchase of liquor delivered to the mission compound concealed in cartons of foodstuffs. Benjamin recalled that
Ellis drank whiskey from a teacup with his meals, washing it down
with beer. Then, perhaps mindful of the damage to his system, Ellis

filled the cup with lemon juice, water, and Epsom salts. Predictably and within minutes, he would vomit the contents of his stomach, then drift into a troubled sleep. Ellis's behavior became increasingly bizarre and erratic. Once when Ellis's room was unguarded, Tanaka gained entrance and saw the hand-drawn charts; in a fit of temper after learning of Tanaka's intrusion, Ellis threw his weapons at Benjamin for the houseboy's failure to watch over his quarters.

Ellis next sought passage on the *Caroline Maru* as the ship transited the Carolines. He told Mother Hoppin that from Koror in the Palaus he might travel through the Pacific and then return to America. Although Mother Hoppin offered to send some of the boys along to provide for his safety and comfort, as she did during his trips in the Marshalls, Ellis declined the generous offer and assured the faithful missionary that he could manage all right.[27]

On 26 March 1923, Ellis departed for Palau. The interisland steamer stopped at Kusaie for a few days, and Ellis visited the copra plantation of Capt. Johann V. Millander, whom he had met on his previous visit to the island. Millander's adopted son, a ten-year-old Micronesian named Hilton Philip Millander, accompanied Ellis on the voyage from Kusaie to Ponape. During the short stop in Kusaie, Ellis attempted to resume his surveying and charting, but the Japanese police restricted his visits. Victor Hermann also departed Kusaie with Ellis on the interisland steamer, probably in the first week of April 1923. During brief stops at Ponape and Truk, after four days steaming, no foreign passengers were allowed to disembark. Hermann claimed that the Japanese had installed gun emplacements on Truk, though he had never actually seen them. After drinking heavily, Ellis became ill and in one drunken stupor expressed a desire to stay in Palau for a while and then continue to the Celebes and New Guinea. As Hermann intended to continue to Japan and then the United States, Ellis gave him an envelope to mail to his brother Ralph. Upon arriving at Koror, Ellis sought out William Gibbons, who found a house for him. Gibbons also introduced Ellis to Metauie, a beautiful young Palauan woman who became his "Palauan wife" during his stay in Koror.

Ellis attempted to obtain permission to visit Babelthuap, the largest island in the Palaus, but the Japanese authorities denied his request. Still determined to accomplish his mission, he turned his attention to a survey of Koror, Ngrmid, and Arakabesang. The chief of the native police, Joseph Tellei, recalled that he and four members of the native constabulary received orders from the Japanese authorities to follow Ellis whenever he left the house. There appeared little subtlety in the surveillance, and once Ellis whirled on a policeman and asked him point blank if he were following him. When Tellei reported the incident to the Japanese authorities, he was told merely to continue following the foreigner. Meanwhile, Ellis's drinking became more prolonged and severe. A Japanese physician, Isake Shoji, tried to see him but Ellis refused treatment. Gibbons introduced Ellis to Felix Rechuuld, and the islander moved in with Ellis and Metauie as a sort of houseboy. Felix remembered Ellis as being sick with fever and eating very little. More often, the ailing leatherneck drank copious quantities of beer, vomited, and then drank more. Dr. Isake appeared often and pleaded with him to come to the hospital, but Ellis remained obstinate.[28]

By then Ellis had a coterie of native boys who would buy whiskey and beer for him at the local store. One of the youths, Antonio Ngirakelau, recalled that the Japanese authorities prohibited the sale of alcohol to Palauans. Undeterred, Ellis marched his native cohorts to the Nanyo Boeki Kaisha general store and informed the manager that the boys would be making purchases for him. For the remainder of Ellis's days, the native boys obtained the noxious beverages for him. Decades later, Antonio insisted that the bottles procured for Ellis came from the same cartons that were sold to the Japanese.

Metauie prepared Palauan food for Ellis, but he had no appetite. Years later, she estimated that Ellis drank an average of three hundred bottles of beer a week. His behavior became increasingly irrational. He talked to himself and marched around his bedroom barking military commands. Once he shoved his fist through the wall. Dr. Isake persisted in another attempt to treat him, but Ellis refused to accept advice or medication. According to witnesses, shortly after Ellis's fruitless ransacking of the Gibbons's home in search of alcohol the Japanese authorities disposed of the troublesome Marine by simply delivering two bottles of whiskey to him. Ellis drank them both and died on 12 May 1923. His Palauan wife and friends attended his final hours as best they could, recalling that Ellis called out the names of his parents and cried. At one point he blurted out that he was an "American spy sent by higher authorities from New York."[29]

A Palauan men's club constructed a coffin for Ellis and buried him in the Japanese cemetery. The Palauans who had befriended Ellis participated in the brief funeral service. Half a world away, Ellis's superiors continued in the belief that nothing untoward had befallen the erratic leatherneck. The day before Ellis died, Logan Feland responded to John Ellis's worrisome inquiry: "I don't think there is anything any of us can do except wait to hear from him. I am sure if he was in any trouble he would communicate with you or me." Less than two weeks later, Lejeune informed Mrs. Ellis of her son's death.

In 1924 a Japanese Navy officer appeared at ONI headquarters in Washington. Lt. Comdr. Laurence F. Safford recalled that the seemingly diffident visitor appeared somewhat uneasy. After perfunctory introductions, the nonplussed Japanese handed Safford a small package: "Here is something we know you wouldn't want to fall into the wrong hands." Examining the parcel, Safford found Ellis's codebooks; the Japanese officer departed without further comment or explanation. Inexplicably, this bizarre incident failed to find its way into any of the voluminous files on the Ellis saga—Marine Corps, Department of the Navy, Department of State, ONI, or Imperial Japanese Navy.[30]

7 ~ Epilogue

THE POTENTIAL FOR A POLITICAL BROUHAHA over the ill-fated and poorly conceived Ellis mission disappeared quickly into the dustbin of Washington politics. John A. Lejeune's forthright admission of the role of Headquarters Marine Corps in the genesis of the venture served to dampen journalistic ardor for subsequent inquiry. Although Ellis's friends and family urged further investigation and argued incessantly that the mercurial leatherneck had died at the hands of the Japanese, Lejeune allowed the matter to end with the return of Ellis's ashes for interment in Pratt. Other matters, ostensibly more weighty, demanded the attention of the Commandant of the Marine Corps. The possibility that the entire Department of the Navy might have played a part in the venture, and any link to the contentious Washington Naval Arms Limitations Treaties, failed to stimulate the fourth estate.

Edwin Denby resigned his post as Secretary of the Navy on 17 February 1924 in the backlash of the scandal surrounding the lease of the Navy's oil reserves. Although no taint of corruption was laid to the Secretary, the public humiliation took its toll. Denby died of a heart attack on 8 February 1929. Theodore Roosevelt, Jr., left office before the end of the Harding administration and turned to other pursuits. He returned to active Army service in World War II, served as an assistant commander of an infantry division in the invasion of France in 1944, and lost his life on the beaches of Normandy earning the Medal of Honor. Robert E. Coontz completed his tour as Chief of Naval Operations on 21 July 1923, returned to the fleet for subsequent duties, retired in June 1928, and died on 26 January 1935. None of these officials within the Department of the Navy left their handprints on the disturbing demise of Earl H. Ellis, except in the most circuitous fashion.

Even though senior officers within the Department of the Navy noted Japan's rush for naval dominance in the Pacific, the retrenchments mandated by the President and Congress during the 1920s continued unabated. Although commitments overseas and at sea with the fleet resumed or actually increased, Lejeune saw his Marine Corps reduced in size even further. Nonetheless, he was able to establish the primary mission of the smaller of the naval services as an amphibious assault force with approval by the Joint Army-Navy Board in 1927. Lejeune served three terms at the helm of the Marine Corps, but in 1929 he opted to step down in favor of naming his own successor. A coincidental opening of a position as superintendent at the Virginia Military Institute provided the popular Marine with employment in retirement, and he held that position until ill health forced his second retirement in 1937. In 1942, Lejeune died following surgery for the removal of a malignant prostate; shortly before his death, Congress approved his promotion to lieutenant general on the retired list. The last thing Lejeune wrote for publication was a hagiographic account of the offensive to seize Blanc Mont. He followed up the submission of his missive with a similarly laudatory piece for his official record, a compendium that included copies of letters of praise from senior French Army officers. The timing of the submissions suggests that the horrendous casualties suffered by the Marines troubled Lejeune almost to the end of his days; ironically, Ellis was purported to be the architect of the Second Division, AEF's, plan of attack.[1]

Like Commandants before him and since, Lejeune coped continually with the fragile egos and career aggrandizements of his officers. Postwar retrenchment reduced promotions to the glacial pace of the period preceding the Spanish-American War. Most successful officers found patrons, either in uniform or on Capitol Hill, to promote their respective careers. Lejeune sought, albeit unsuccessfully, to obtain legislation to mandate promotions through the recommendation by selection boards rather than by adhering to strict seniority. While the Naval Affairs Committee in the House of Representatives dutifully approved the scheme and passed it onto the floor for speedy passage, the Senate Naval Affairs Committee found faults with the notion and allowed it to die in the committee. While some officers languished in their postwar rank for a decade or more, others took steps of their own. Smedley D. Butler, perhaps confident of the influence of his father, Cong. Thomas S. Butler, even had the temerity to inform Lejeune that if his name did not appear on a proposed list of new major generals, he had no intention of asking his father to support the authorization for the increases.[2]

By the close of the decade, Lejeune felt serious misgivings about the state of the Marine Corps. Increasing commitments overseas and in support of the fleet continued, despite decreases in appropriations for manpower. The death of Congressman Butler, an unflagging admirer of Lejeune and supporter of the smaller of the naval services, on 26 May 1928 and the election of Herbert Hoover that fall prompted the venerable Lejeune to not request a fourth term as Commandant. Given Hoover's promise of military and naval retrenchment, the tepid support from the Senate Naval Affairs Committee, and the absence of Congressman Butler to steer the House Naval Affairs Committee, the likely frustrations of another stint in office appeared too onerous.

Although Wendell C. Neville appeared as Lejeune's logical successor, the nomination of the popular Marine was far from certain. A Democrat like Lejeune, the gregarious Marine had few if any powerful political favors to call at this important juncture in his career. Fears that the new Republican occupant of the White House might derail Neville's elevation to the commandancy ultimately prompted Lejeune to relinquish his post before Pres. Calvin Coolidge and Secretary of the Navy Curtis D. Wilbur left office; the latter official was Lejeune's Naval Academy classmate. At the same time, Lejeune feared for Neville's ill health and his comrade's inability to control his hypertension. James G. Harbord, now in retirement from Army service and enjoying important Republican friendships, quietly supported Lejeune's choice of a successor while deflecting Logan Feland's maladroit attempt to gain the commandancy for himself.[3]

In 1930, barely a year into his own tenure at the helm of the Marine Corps, Neville suffered a debilitating stroke and died. Although Feland's quest to become Commandant had been muted following Lejeune's retirement and Neville's nomination, he entered the intense competition with renewed vigor. From the perspective of most observers, the competition appeared to rest between Brig. Gen. John H. Russell and the increasingly controversial Smedley D. Butler. Ultimately, however, President Hoover and Secretary of the Navy Charles Francis Adams chose to nominate an obscure and seemingly compliant brigadier general, Ben H. Fuller, to succeed Neville. Senior officials chose Fuller over Feland because the latter lacked a diploma from Annapolis; Butler appeared as a distant third choice, as Secretary Adams and the coterie of admirals surrounding him considered the feisty and outspoken leatherneck anathema, and the least likely to comply with President Hoover's plan for cost-saving retrenchment.[4]

Bitter and chagrined, Feland completed his full career in uniform and retired in 1933. To the end of his days, he blamed Lejeune for failing to rally to his cause and probably never understood that the former Commandant harbored grave concerns over Feland's own dependence on alcohol. Feland died on 17 July 1936. Equally disappointed, Butler became increasingly outspoken and controversial. He marched noisily into retirement in 1931 following a threatened court-martial for inopportune and inappropriate remarks concerning Italian dictator Benito Mussolini. Butler involved himself in intraservice politics one last time by attempting to derail Russell's appointment as Fuller's successor to the commandancy. As his own ill health worsened, Butler slipped from public view, and he died of stomach cancer on 21 October 1940. To the end, he decried the ascendancy of the succession of Annapolitans to lead his beloved Marine Corps at the expense of veteran campaigners with tropical sweat stains and powder burns on their uniforms.[5]

Robert H. "Hal" Dunlap, Ellis's contemporary and close friend, appeared as the logical successor to Neville at the time of Lejeune's retirement. For critics of the seemingly endless cycle of graduates of the Naval Academy heading the Marine Corps, Dunlap—commissioned directly from civil life in 1898—appeared an ideal candidate to thwart the desire of the admirals to maintain the progression of Annapolitans at the helm of the smaller of the naval services. In 1930, Fuller posted Dunlap, newly promoted to brigadier general, as a student to the prestigious École Supérieur de Guerre. Some observers viewed the assignment as a ploy to remove Fuller's likely successor from the vicissitudes of Washington politics. Sadly, however, the promising officer died on 19 May 1931 in a heroic rescue attempt to save a French woman trapped in the collapse of a cave dwelling.

The Dunlaps were living in Peking, where he commanded the barracks, when the news of Ellis's death reached them. As Betty Allen Rogers's close friends, it must be presumed that they told her the sad news via the slow transit of a steamship letter. The *City Directory* for Washington reveals that she continued in her partnership in "The Book and Gown" on 17th Street, N.W., with Louise Stephensen through at least 1923 or 1924. In the latter year, Betty Allen Rogers listed her residence at the same location. In 1925 she probably married William W. Buckley, a patent attorney with the firm of Munn and Company. Betty Allen Rogers still resided in Washington when her father died on 20 October 1931.[6]

Virtually all of the Micronesian islanders who knew Ellis when he traveled on his mission through the Japanese mandates are now gone. Some were important people, such as William Gibbons, the *Ibedul* (highest chief) of Koror, and his wife, Ngerdoko, the *Bilung* (highest woman of the *Idid* clan) of Koror. Metauie, Ellis's Palauan wife while he lived during the final weeks and days of his life in Koror, was also a member of the *Idid* clan and held the title of *Sumech* (the second-highest woman). William Gibbons passed away before the war, but both Ngerdoko and Metauie lived long afterward.

Houseboys Felix Rechuuld in Palau and Benjamin Lajipun in the Marshalls passed away as elder and respected members of their communities. Victor Hermann, who accompanied Ellis from Kusaie to Koror, lived a productive life in America after his career in Micronesia, passing away in California in the 1970s. Joseph Tellei, the Palauan policeman who was assigned to keep Ellis under surveillance, became an important person in Palau and helped the Americans get established there after World War II. He passed away in Koror in 1989. Henry Fleming, the German-Marshallese businessman who met Ellis in Yap in 1922, passed away in the 1970s at Tinian in the Marianas. Brother Gregorio and Kilili Sablan, who also knew Ellis at Saipan, survived the American invasion during the war but have also died.

Katharine Dunlap, who most likely introduced Ellis to Elizabeth Allen Rogers, wrote an undated memoir sometime after learning of their friend's untimely death. Although the intent of the charming recollection has been lost to history, it serves to provide historians with an intimate portrait of one of the Marine Corps's most enigmatic characters. She described him as "tall, rangey [*sic*] and quiet-spoken . . . with steady, grey eyes and mouse-colored hair, close-cropped. He walked along—a little aloof, as a measure of self-protection to his shyness. For his sensitiveness could have made him vulnerable and he would never have acknowledged that!"

To Katharine Dunlap, Ellis proclaimed himself a "loner." However, she proclaimed that "to the few—the very few—who knew him well he was a devoted friend, generous and completely loyal." The Dunlaps' friendship with Ellis dated from a tour at the Naval War College almost a decade before, and Katharine Dunlap recalled that "to Pete, being a Marine was a full-time job. He studied deeply the potentialities and possibilities of his Corps and the most efficient use for it in any future war. He foresaw, to an almost uncanny degree, how and where that war would be fought and what the Marines' part would be in it." She remembered listening to discussions on amphibious warfare between her husband and Ellis in Newport: "pros and cons being analyzed, estimates of the situation being formed, missions being developed and Pete's voice, seldom raised, trying to make his point with quiet persistence: 'No, Hal, no; it's like this . . .'"

Katharine Dunlap harbored a recollection of Pete Ellis as someone who "was the soul of honor and set a high standard for himself. All along, as I look back on it now, it seems to me that he was the sort destined to sacrifice himself to a self-imposed duty." Although she admitted, like others who knew Ellis, that alcohol had taken over his life, she claimed that she "never saw him when he gave evidence of it." Excusing his dipsomania, Katharine Dunlap could not believe that Ellis's "drinking was an integral part of his character. Rather it was a temporary refuge which he sought during periods of inactivity in the loneliness and peril of the work he had undertaken by choice. His undaunted courage needed no bolstering," she concluded.

Reflecting on the news of Ellis's death, Katharine Dunlap believed that "when word came to us, in China, of his mysterious death in the islands it almost seemed as though we had known it must happen that way, but we had a sense of irreparable loss." She added what many Marines of his era, and since, have concluded: "The Marine Corps had lost a most brilliant and unique officer, whose vision was to be justified by the events of the coming war. And we had lost a friend."[7]

It is difficult to speculate on Ellis's future had he not succumbed to the poison of alcohol. While many of his contemporaries drank more than was advisable, and it did not seem to hinder their careers, others became so disabled from the toxicity of their excesses as to be superannuated before reaching mandatory retirement age. By the mid-1920s, both Lejeune and Butler had become teetotalers, and the latter a militant prohibitionist. Neville's ill health precluded any over-indulgence in alcohol on his part. Logically, had Ellis continued his fondness for binge-drinking and frequency of hospitalization for neurasthenia, even devoted friends such as Lejeune and Neville would have likely ordered his premature retirement.

Assuming, however, that Ellis had succeeded in curbing his passion for alcoholic spirits, sobriety and professional acumen would not necessarily have resulted in increased rank and responsibility. Lacking a political sponsor, Ellis's friendship with Lejeune and Neville would have most likely seen his elevation to general officer status during the latter's tenure as Commandant of the Marine Corps. But that tenure was short-lived, and Neville's successor, Ben Fuller, had not served with Ellis. Once both Feland and Butler slipped into retirement, the new Commandant demonstrated a proclivity to surround himself with general officers who were fellow graduates of the Naval Academy. Fuller's handpicked successor, John Russell, another graduate of the Naval Academy, had not served with Ellis either.[8]

Given Ellis's talents and professional reputation, it is likely that by the time of Thomas Holcomb's nomination to the commandancy in 1936, Ellis would have received a second star—just before reaching retirement age in 1942. Holcomb served until the end of 1943, advancing in rank to lieutenant general, and died on 28 May 1965.

Ellis's contemporary and fellow aide-de-camp to the Major General Commandant from 1915 until 1917 was commissioned on 4 April 1900, barely two years before Ellis's name appeared on the lineal list of officers. It was left for Holcomb to head the Marine Corps throughout the preparation and conduct of the greatest amphibious campaign in the history of the modern world—much of which Ellis had predicted decades before.

8 ~ The Legacy of Pete Ellis

ELLIS'S TENURE IN THE MARINE CORPS, slightly more than two decades, encompassed an important era of transition for the smaller of the naval services. For the first century of its service to the Republic, Marines performed duties characteristic for the age of sail. Armed soldiers of the sea helped generations of Navy officers maintain strict discipline and order in the ships of the fleet, provided security at stations ashore, and, on occasion, manned the backbone of landing parties. By the time Ellis entered the Marine Corps in those halcyon days following the Spanish-American War, this mission appeared increasingly anachronistic. After a hundred years of treating the Navy's enlisted force as a mutinous rabble, recruited mostly from the immigrant populations of seacoast cities, many senior officers concluded that a wall of Marine bayonets was no longer required to keep the enlisted force in check. Heady with the teachings of Capt. Alfred Thayer Mahan, the prominent naval theorist of the era, luminaries within the Department of the Navy argued with increasing passion that the time had come for the Marine

Corps to abandon its traditional role aboard ship and become a source of expeditionary forces for the fleet. When Ellis took the oath of office as a second lieutenant in 1902, the initiatives and imperatives of these reformist ideas were reaching fruition.[1]

By fits and spurts, the Corps lurched into the twentieth century, and Ellis sailed with it. While Navy reformers pursued institutional changes, the exigencies of America's new era of neocolonialism held sway. Increasingly, requirements emerged for deployment of armed bodies of men sent ashore in a variety of neocolonial enterprises. Former European colonies, both in East Asia and in the Caribbean, appeared more and more likely to achieve a heavy dose of American imperialism clothed in Yankee altruistic rhetoric. For much of Ellis's first decade in uniform, service in the Philippines embodied the new-found belief in the idealism of the American Century. Yet by the completion of even his first tour in the Western Pacific, Ellis had grown callous and displayed harsh racist and ethnic biases. The lethargy associated with tedious duty in the tropics was replaced by a chance assignment involving duties with an advanced-base outfit.

By the end of his second tour in the Philippines, Ellis appeared to have found his niche within the Marine Corps. After he had spent almost a decade in uniform, his record reveals increasingly outstanding marks and evaluations. Yet he had not displayed that flash or brilliance likely to attract the attention of his superiors; worse, he failed to perceive the requirement to obtain a sponsor—political or naval—with which to propel his career along. Participation with the advanced-base construction on an island in the mouth of Subic Bay appears to have been a watershed in Ellis's career; much of the second decade of his service involved refinement of and participation in what an increasing number of luminaries viewed as the Marine Corps's new and most important mission.

Careers for Marine Corps officers of Ellis's era turned on two diametrically opposite factors: chance assignments, in which the incumbent performed superlatively and earned praise and recognition; and important connections, through which professional patronage might be established. Ironically, Ellis's career was affected by both ingredients. Because he was the only officer available from among the staff at the Naval War College for deployment with the first exercise of the advanced-base force, Ellis gained immeasurable professional stature as a result of the short stint in the Caribbean. At the same time, his further association with two of the Marine Corps's rising stars, John A. Lejeune and George Barnett, meant that he had achieved quasi-sponsorship for career aggrandizement of sorts. On the eve of America's reluctant entry into World War I, Ellis served at the seat of power for the Marine Corps and had garnered the sponsorship of both Lejeune and Barnett.

Duty during World War I provided Ellis with an interesting and worthwhile interlude from traditional naval duties; not all of his contemporaries were so fortunate. Some officers served not in France, but in traditional assignments at naval stations or in the ships of the fleet; others manned expeditionary forces in neocolonial duties. Lejeune's sponsorship of Ellis was paramount after the two of them arrived in France in 1918; Ellis could have easily been siphoned off into the manpower pool of officers and spent the waning days of the war serving in the Services of Supply, just like a disgusted Smedley D. Butler. Ellis's role in bringing the staff functioning of the 4th Brigade (Marine), AEF, to the apogee of efficiency and professionalism is well documented. But the myths surrounding his contribution serve to obfuscate the legend. Hard evidence fails to support allegations that he provided Lejeune with the daring scheme of a maneuver for the assault on Blanc Mont; had Ellis done so, the mercurial adjutant for the 4th Brigade shares some of the blame for a flawed maneuver resulting in horrendous and excessive casualties.[2]

Institutionally, service in France provided professional succor for the Marine Corps for a generation or more. The Corps's sometimes tired recruiting slogan, "First to Fight," retained its substance even though senior Army officers attempted to keep the Marines out of

France. Although the token Marine Corps force performed gallantly at Belleau Wood, Soissons, St. Mihiel, Blanc Mont, and in the Meuse-Argonne offensive, typical leatherneck swagger and élan rubbed Army sensibilities raw. For a generation, senior Army officers viewed Marines as interlopers. Worse, lecturers at the Army War College and the Army Command and General Staff College argued that opposed amphibious operations had proven impossible, citing the British debacle in the Dardanelles during the war to support their thesis; unopposed amphibious operations, on the other hand, remained simply a matter of administrative detail and were easily accomplished by army forces. Proponents of this line of reasoning swung easily into discussions questioning the need for a separate naval service with expertise in amphibious warfare.

In the postwar era, the Department of the Navy expected the Marine Corps to return to its traditional duties: security of naval stations at home and abroad, detachments with the ships of the fleet, and the manning of advanced bases to support deployment overseas. While the first two missions required no refinement—the world war had not altered them in any significant fashion—the third function of the smaller of the naval services began increasingly to appear as the Corps's raison d'être. Indeed, at the turn of the twentieth century, most Western nations supported some sort of marine force, even in a limited fashion, and some countries, notably Great Britain, boasted that its marines constituted a combined-arms force. But by the end of the wartime era almost all of the marine forces in the Western world had disappeared; even the British Royal Marines had lost their combined-arms capability and begun to draw supporting arms and service support from Royal Army units. American Marines appeared as no stranger to the retrenchment and critical examination of the 1920s, and Commandant Lejeune recognized the fragile existence of his beloved corps.

Ellis's ill-conceived and ill-fated mission reflects both personal initiative and the imperatives of service politics. From the jaded perspective of the mercurial Ellis, it must have appeared in 1921 that his once promising career had stalled. Although no evidence exists suggesting that he attempted to gain a combat command in France during the war, the luminaries and icons in forest green for the next decade and more had all amassed significant combat time in command. A return to colonial infantry duties appeared not to dissuade him from his calling, just as a return to routine garrison duties did not hold his attention for long. Thus the "escape" to Micronesia may well be viewed as a desperate cry for help in the quest to rescue a career gone awry. Ellis possessed sufficient intelligence to realize that the sickness of alcoholism had taken over his life, limited his professionalism as an officer in the naval services considerably, and probably meant dismissal and early retirement once he had lost favor with the hierarchy of the Marine Corps. While in his first "White Letter" as Commandant, Lejeune trumpeted that "I want each of you to feel that the Commandant of the Marine Corps is your friend," at the same time he emphasized the requirement for a "high standard of conduct" on the part of all Marines.[3]

It would be fatuous to conclude that Ellis concocted the mission to Micronesia in isolation. More likely, he hoped that a personal reconnaissance might refine some of the geographical and hydrographical theses in his study. Once the plan took root, it only follows that the Department of the Navy seized on the junket as a means to answer nagging questions about the mandates that had lingered for almost a decade. Japanese seizure of German-held islands in Micronesia during the opening months of World War I had ended on a seemingly duplicitous note. Although Japan's occupation of German centers in the Marshalls, Marianas, and Carolines was completed by the end of October 1914, Imperial Naval Headquarters announced only the seizure of Jaluit Atoll in the Marshalls. While Americans viewed the occupation as a potential threat to their supply lines to the Philippines, senior British officials looked askance at the sudden, swift advance of Japanese naval units into the region. Great Britain had only requested that Tokyo, a signatory to a 1905 agreement with London, assist in keeping the peace in East Asia and search out and destroy any German ships in the region.

Ellis's tour in Guam coincided with American concerns for the vulnerability of the tiny outpost. His study of the island's suscepti- bility, and his recommendations for the immediate construction of fortifications, coincided with increased naval activity in the region. Near the end of 1914 the German warship *Cormoran* steamed into Apra Harbor with Japanese gunboats hot on its trail. Subsequently, foreign merchants who normally operated throughout Micronesia with impunity found to their dismay that Japanese authorities had taken several administrative measures to impede their access and trade.

While Japan's muscle-flexing in the region might have alarmed keen observers, reports from repatriated German nationals fueled speculation that Japan intended to expand its new holdings in Micronesia; worse, exaggerated tales of a military and naval buildup appeared in interrogation reports of Germans who passed through Peking, Shanghai, Tokyo, and Honolulu following their expulsion from the islands. The Office of Naval Intelligence (ONI) ordered the governor of Guam (a Navy officer) to report on Japanese activities. Subsequently, information on Japan's intrusion in the Central Pacific was obtained from missionaries, businessmen, travelers, scientists, special agents, and the islanders themselves.[4]

Although none of the reports gleaned from this variety of sources supported claims of Japanese fortifications appearing in the islands— except in a minor, cursory, and unsubstantiated fashion—other Jap- anese activities, such as mail censorship, the installation of commu- nication sites, and a brief denial of trading rights to firms operating routinely in the region, stimulated the continuance of surveillance and even widened the scope of the intelligence-gathering agenda. Although Great Britain and the United States sputtered discontent- edly at Japan's claim for outright annexation following the war, nei- ther power appeared willing to challenge Japan's legal basis for the

occupation and outright suzerainty in Micronesia. Even though the
main signatories to the peace agreement signed at Versailles decided
against any attempt to thwart Japan's expansion into the Central
Pacific, a coalition of interested nations (Great Britain, Australia,
New Zealand, and the United States) succeeded in getting Japan to
join the League of Nations and administer the islands through a
mandate. By the time of Ellis's mission, Japan had acquiesced to the
curtailment in naval tonnage below that of either Great Britain or
the United States. While the signatories agreed not to fortify holdings in the Pacific, the treaty provided for no on-site inspections.[5]

Ellis's plea to visit Micronesia and the speedy concurrence by his
superiors within the Department of the Navy underscored the concern that existed in naval circles with regard to Japan's machinations
in the islands. While generations of historians and journalists have
suggested foul play on the part of the Japanese in Ellis's death, no evidence exists to support such claims. Perhaps the injudicious delivery
of two bottles of whiskey to the suffering alcoholic, with full knowledge that the afflicted dipsomaniac would consume them immediately, could be construed as prima facie evidence that the Japanese
poisoned Ellis. In truth, however, the entire affair served to embarrass everyone concerned. By 1923, Japan had undertaken no construction of fortifications in the islands and sought to defray Western
concerns to the contrary. That another signatory to the agreements
of the Washington Naval Arms Limitation Treaties thought otherwise contributed to ill will between the Empire of Japan and the
United States.

As a result of Ellis's demise and the subsequent disclosure of his
amateurish intelligence-gathering mission, ONI found it increasingly
difficult to obtain information or to inject agents into the islands.
Hans G. Hornbostel, Ellis's friend from his tour on Guam, became
an informant for ONI through his position with the Bishop Museum
in Honolulu. Following Ellis's death, Hornbostel visited the islands
but found the Japanese authorities increasingly secretive and obstruc-

tionist. Officials even attempted to entrap the amateur sleuth in a variety of potentially embarrassing situations so as to discourage further intelligence-gathering ventures by the West.[6]

While careful shielding of any complicity beyond that of Ellis's immediate superiors in the venture has succeeded, ample evidence exists to implicate a variety of officials beyond the Division of Operations, Headquarters Marine Corps (HQMC). Although Ellis left Lejeune with an undated letter of resignation, the Commandant chose not to use it. Then, in a confusing scenario, Lejeune protected both himself and the Marine Corps by declaring that Ellis had absented himself without leave from the naval hospital in Yokohama. Lejeune's complicity in the genesis of the mission appears in any number of documents, including the correspondence of those close to the Commandant.[7]

Comdr. Luke McNamee, the Director of ONI, sounded the first warning that the ill-fated mission involved officials other than those at HQMC. Even before the report of Ellis's death reached Washington, concerns for the unpredictable intelligence-gatherer had made their way throughout the Department of the Navy. McNamee sent a query to the Commandant, Twelfth Naval District, requesting that he ask the First National Bank of San Francisco if funds from Ellis's account had been withdrawn. In the correspondence, McNamee revealed that the monthly stipend was five hundred dollars and that "the above subject has been on a special trip for sometimes [sic], the expenses of which are being paid by this office."[8]

The complicity of both the Secretary of the Navy and the Chief of Naval Operations (CNO) is revealed through a second letter prepared by McNamee. After the announcement of Ellis's death, the Director of ONI prepared a memorandum for the CNO that outlined the steps he thought would defuse the potentially embarrassing situation: notify the next of kin, and publish the fact of Ellis's death with an acknowledgment that he was on extended leave with official permission to go abroad; direct the naval attaché, Tokyo, to request that the Imperial Japanese Government assist in obtaining Ellis's remains and effects for shipment to the naval hospital in Yokohama for identification and further disposition; and finally, have ONI assist in the identification of Ellis. Copies of this correspondence exist in a variety of repositories, but one copy in the ONI files contains two significant annotations at the bottom of the page: "approved," with the signatures of Edwin H. Denby and Robert E. Coontz. Thus, any disavowment by the Secretary of the Navy, the CNO, and the Director of ONI is groundless and indeed fatuous.[9]

The real worth of Ellis's contribution lay in his articulate writing and war-planning efforts. In an organization once cited by a frequent critic for its "vacuity of intellect," his prophetic studies ranged far beyond the positions he held as a field-grade officer. Whatever notes and studies he prepared while in Micronesia failed to survive. Indeed, the chance interview of an officer who served at ONI in the 1920s disclosed that Ellis's confidant and supporter, missionary Jesse Hoppin, turned the amateur sleuth's possessions over to the Japanese police.

In the decade following Ellis's death, much of what he either predicted or recommended came to fruition. While arguably Lejeune seized on preparation for the Marine Corps in the implementation of War Plan Orange as the vehicle to protect the existence of the smaller of the naval services, some of his senior officers recognized a new mission for the Marine Corps. Many of the notables of Ellis's era, such as Joseph H. Pendleton, Smedley D. Butler, Logan Feland, and Frederick M. Wise, found solace in leatherneck missions of the past. Even as Congress sought to disengage from neocolonial endeavors, and the colonial infantry duties that accompanied them, many senior Marine Corps officers continued to believe that naval forces constituted the best contribution to American altruism in the Caribbean or East Asia. Other influential officers visualized an expeditionary force in support of the fleet. In a significant departure from accepted doctrine, by the early 1920s a new mission appeared increasingly important—amphibious assault.

The fleet maneuvers of 1922, held between January and April at Guantánamo Bay and Culebra, appeared as a watershed in the evolution of amphibious warfare. In a scenario differing little from the maneuvers of 1913 and 1914—in which Ellis played a significant role—bluejackets ferried leathernecks to the beach to wrestle huge naval guns ashore and construct emplacements for their protection. Mostly, however, the exercise consisted of determining whether a Marine company could put ashore field artillery pieces (155mm and 75mm calibers) with their accompanying five-ton tractors. The evolution differed little from what Ellis experienced the decade before in Guam. Only one infantry company and one artillery company participated.[10]

During the fleet maneuvers of 1923, held in the Caribbean between December 1923 and February 1924, the role of the Marine Corps in amphibious exercises increased markedly. The entire East Coast Expeditionary Force from Quantico, more than thirty-three hundred Marines, participated. Brig. Gen. Eli K. Cole and Col. Dion Williams led the leatherneck contingent, and both officers represented a class of officers—like Ellis—with foresight and intellect. Clearly, Ellis's studies and recommendations could be seen in the scenario. But the landings in the Caribbean continued to underscore major problems for the practitioners of amphibious warfare. Observers and senior commanders witnessed the landing of forces on the wrong beaches, sporadic and inadequate naval gunfire support, improper loading and unloading of supplies, and the employment of unsuitable landing craft. Lejeune appeared determined to improve, as did Cole and Williams. By then Ellis's study of Marine Corps participation in support of War Plan Orange had become known to the senior officers of the Marine Corps.[11]

By the time of the fleet maneuvers in 1925, Ellis's sibylline studies had influenced the amphibious play significantly. More than twenty-five hundred Marines, gleaned from stations on both coasts, participated in the exercise to form a constructive force of two divisions. Army units from Oahu played the role of defenders in the Hawaiian Islands, while the Marines actually conducted an amphibious assault. For the first time, the Navy provided adequate naval gunfire support, which included eleven battleships. In an innovative move, one that would have warmed Ellis, Col. Robert H. Dunlap used the staff and students from Quantico as an ad hoc staff during the exercise.[12]

Unfortunately, increasing commitments and congressional retrenchment precluded the conduct of significant amphibious exercises for the remainder of the 1920s. What remained, however, were not more rehearsals but the codification of doctrine and the assignment of the amphibious assault mission to the Marine Corps. As a result of Marine Corps participation in fleet exercises during the 1920s, senior officers directed indoctrination throughout the schools at Quantico. Extensive staff development and direction appeared at HQMC. The Joint Army-Navy Board specified in *Joint Action of the Army and Navy* in 1927 that naval forces were to "seize, establish, and defend until relieved by Army forces, advanced naval bases and to conduct such related auxiliary land operations as necessary to the prosecution of the naval campaign."[13]

The retrenchment of the interwar years subsided with the election of Franklin D. Roosevelt as President in 1932. The year before, the General Board of the Navy had intermittently studied the role of the Marine Corps in support of the fleet. While acknowledging the mission of both defending and seizing advanced bases, the board noted that subsequent operations ashore must pass to Army forces. Planners envisioned a further continuance of any naval campaign and the requirement for Marines as part of the amphibious force. Knowing of the board's deliberations, the Commandant of the Marine Corps, Maj. Gen. Ben H. Fuller, invited its attention to an important study, "History of Advanced Base Training in the Marine Corps." By 1932,

Fuller and his staff had taken a firm position against the Navy's predilection to use shipboard detachments as part of a ready amphibious force. At about the same time, Fuller informed the Director,
War Plans Division, General Board of the Navy, that he intended to
conform solely to the requirements resulting from Naval War College
Advanced Base Problem No. One; in addition, his staff intended to
undertake a study of the organization of the advanced-base force to
support the major strategic plan—obviously, War Plan Orange.[14]

Fuller's final step, and one that Ellis would have applauded wholeheartedly, was to alter the operating forces of the Marine Corps sub-
stantially. HQMC ordered the dissolution of the expeditionary forces
and their replacement by fleet Marine forces under direct control of
fleet commanders. The Commandant criticized the lack of suitable
doctrine, as evidenced by the gyrations of the General Board of the
Navy. Then, in a far-reaching and vatic order that would have pleased
Ellis no end, Fuller ordered the Commandant, Marine Corps Schools,
to "proceed as expeditiously as practicable to prepare for publication
a manual for landing operations." The Commandant directed Quantico to begin work no later than 15 November 1933 and authorized
the suspension of classes to use the staff and students to work on it.[15]

The studies and prophetic analyses of Earl H. "Pete" Ellis are evi-
dent in the events of the 1920s and early 1930s. The Marine Corps's
seizure of the amphibious assault mission in support of the fleet,
accompanied by a cogent doctrine, appeared as everything Ellis
would have wanted. That he recommended such measures more
than a decade before, and then failed to see them reach fruitions
because of his personal misconduct, remains a tragedy buried in the
history of the Marine Corps that he served so faithfully.

✍ Notes

ABBREVIATIONS

AEF   American Expeditionary Forces
ANJ   *Army-Navy Journal*
CMC   Commandant of the Marine Corps
CNO   Chief of Naval Operations
FRC   Federal Records Center, Suitland, Maryland
HQMC   Headquarters Marine Corps, Washington, D.C.
MARC   Micronesian Area Research Center, University of Guam
MCHC   Marine Corps Historical Center, Washington Navy Yard
MD-LC   Manuscripts Division, Library of Congress, Washington, D.C.
NARA   National Archives and Records Administration, Washington, D.C.
ONI   Office of Naval Intelligence
RG   Record Group
SecNav   Secretary of the Navy

INTRODUCTION

1. Ellis file, Records of the ONI, Entry 78, Records of the Office of the CNO, RG 38, NARA. See also Reber, "Pete Ellis," 54.

2. City Directories, Washington, D.C.: 1923, p. 1349; 1924, p. 1229; and 1925, p. 1256, Library of Congress. See also Rogers's correspondence with Ellis, Ellis MSS, MCHC.

3. Press release, Ellis biographical file, reference section, MCHC. See also oral history, Gen. Lemuel C. Shepherd, Jr., 1967, MCHC. Shepherd was one of Lejeune's aides-de-camp.

4. Zimmerman, "The Marines' First Spy."

5. John A. Lejeune to the Paymaster, 11 September 1923, General Correspondence, Entry 18, Records of the U.S. Marine Corps, RG 127, NARA.

6. Lt. Garnet Hulings, Assistant Naval Attaché, U.S. Embassy, Tokyo, to Capt. H. Fujita, Minister of Marine, 26 May 1923, copy in Ellis file, Entry 78a, ONI Records, Records of the CNO, RG 38, NARA.

7. Captain Cotten's report to the Director of Naval Intelligence, 30 August 1923, Ellis file, Entry 78a, RG 38, NARA.

8. George Barnett to the CMC, 25 May 1923, Entry 18, RG 127, NARA.

9. John A. Lejeune to Ralph Ellis, 14 November 1923, folder 16, container 3, Ellis MSS, MCHC.

10. CMC to the Judge Advocate General of the Navy, 2 April 1924, file 0260-1 over ACC-84-njw, Entry 18, RG 127, NARA.

11. Cf. Ellis M. Zacharias, *Secret Missions: The Story of an Intelligence Officer* (New York: Putnam, 1946), with *Nihon to no Himitsu Sensō* (Tokyo: Roudou-Tuushinsha, 1958).

12. Heinl, *Soldiers of the Sea,* 257; Moskin, *The U.S. Marine Corps Story,* 460; Millett, *Semper Fidelis,* 326; and Edward Miller, *War Plan Orange,* 174.

13. Resident Naval Officer, South Sea Islands, to Aide for Navy Minister and Aide for Chief of General Staff, 31 May 1923, Taishō 12 nen Kobun biko [Japanese Navy Official Document File 1923], vol. 152, quoted in Hirama, "Death of LCOL. Earl H. Ellis," (27)–73.

14. Resident Naval Officer, South Sea Islands, to Aide for Navy Minister and Aide to Chief of General Staff, 29 July 1923, Taishō 12 nen Kobun biko, vol. 152, quoted in Hirama, "Death of LCOL. Earl H. Ellis," (27)–72 (emphasis added).

15. *Emporia (Kansas) Gazette,* 28 April 1942, 1. See also Zimmerman, "The Marines' First Spy," 2–3, 19–20; and *National Enquirer,* 10 December 1972, 12.

16. Central Liaison and Coordination Office, Tokyo, to the General Headquarters of the Supreme Commander of the Allied Forces, 14 September

and 5 October 1948, files C.I.C.O. no. 3230 and C.I.C.O. no. 3462, copies in Ellis's official record.

17. Ballendorf, "The Micronesian Ellis Mystery"; see also Ballendorf, "Earl Hancock Ellis."

18. See, for example, Montross, "The Mystery of Pete Ellis," and Pierce, "The Unsolved Mystery."

19. "Dedicate Marine Hall," *ANJ,* 25 October 1952, 222.

CHAPTER 1. GROWING UP, 1880–1901

1. Diary entry, 27 August 1900, container 1, Ellis MSS, MCHC.

2. Gray, *Pioneers, Saints, and Sinners,* 44–46.

3. Dorothy Ellis Gatz to John Reber, 17 December 1977, Ellis MSS, MARC; and 1880 Census, Kansas, vol. 16, ED 320, Sheet 27, Line 7.

4. "Centennial Edition," *Colfax (Washington) Gazette-Commoner,* 13 July 1972, 57.

5. *The Trail Guide,* vol. 9 (Topeka: Kansas State Historical Society, 1964); Certificate 3043, RG 49, NARA. See also "Centennial Edition," *Colfax (Washington) Gazette-Commoner,* 13 July 1972.

6. "Centennial Edition," *Colfax (Washington) Gazette-Commoner,* 13 July 1972, 54–56.

7. Dorothy Ellis Gatz to John Reber, 17 December 1977, Ellis MSS, MARC; *Pratt (Kansas) Daily Tribune,* 19 December 1923; and 1900 Census, Kansas, vol. 42, ED 175, Sheet 3, Line 42.

8. Pratt High School transcript, Ellis file, reference section, MCHC.

9. "Status of Marine Corps," *ANJ,* 25 December 1886, 428.

10. *ANJ,* 6 September 1890, 23, and 20 September 1890, 58. Between 1800 and 1861, 19 percent of all courts-martial involved Marines, and 30 percent of all death sentences awarded went to Marines; Valle, *Rocks and Shoals,* 22–23.

11. Shulimson, "The Transitional Commandancy," 70–73.

12. Ellis diary, 4 September 1900, container 1, Ellis MSS, MCHC; see also Alphabetical Card List of Enlisted Men of the Marine Corps, Entry 75, Records of the U.S. Marine Corps, RG 127, NARA.

13. Muster rolls, Entry 101, RG 127, NARA.

14. James Forney to the CMC, 7 October 1881, Entry 10, Letters Received (1819–1903), RG 127, NARA.

15. Shulimson, *The Marine Corps' Search,* 28.

16. Journal of the Academic Board, 28 May and 28 June 1883, Entry 201, Records of the Naval Academy, RG 405, NARA, Nimitz Library, Annapolis. Of the total of eighty-six graduates, twenty-three received commissions, two refused them, and one was found to be infected with secondary syphilis. See also *Register of Alumni,* 180–81.

17. *ANJ,* 20 May 1905, 10; the fitness reports of the eleven graduates of the Naval Academy, Class of 1881, who entered the Marine Corps can be found in Records of Boards of Examination, Entry 62, Records of the Judge Adjutant General of the Navy, RG 125, FRC. For a sample of Lincoln Karmany's marital problems see John Weeks to Edwin H. Denby, 30 June 1921, Denby MSS, Burton Collection, Detroit Public Library; and Cronin, *Cabinet Diaries of Josephus Daniels,* 83.

18. Karsten, "Armed Progressives" and Bartlett, "Annapolis Marines," 90–95.

19. *Annual Report of the Secretary of the Navy,* 1900 (Washington, D.C.: GPO, 1900), 1254–59; and 1902 (Washington, D.C.: GPO, 1902), 999–1000.

20. Entry 84, Registers of Promotions of Noncommissioned Officers, RG 127, NARA.

21. *New York Times,* 13 November 1889, 5; and *ANJ,* 7 December 1889, 2967.

22. Ellis to his father, 25 February 1901, folder 2, container 1, Ellis MSS, MCHC. See also Charles I. Long to the SecNav, 9 April 1901, file 3917-707, Correspondence to and from the SecNav, 1897–1915, RG 80, NARA; and Charles Heywood to John D. Long, 9 April 1901, Registers of Communications Sent, Entry 1, RG 127, NARA. See also letter files L 86 12, L 92 700, L 93 651-2, and S 11 467 in the same entry; and files 3917-707 and 26260-3918 in RG 80. For a discussion of the selection and examination system, see Shulimson, *The Marine Corps' Search,* 198–99. Indication that Ellis called on Congressman Long is found in Ellis to his mother, 2 October 1902, folder 10, container 2, Ellis MSS, MCHC.

23. Charles Heywood to Earl H. Ellis, 21 December 1901 and 10 January 1902, Entry 5, Press Copies of Letters Sent, RG 127, NARA. See also *Register of Commissioned and Warrant Officers of the Navy and Marine Corps* (Washington, D.C.: GPO, 1903–22); Ellis's lineal precedent is in the *Register* for 1903, 144–45.

24. Earl H. Ellis to John W. Ellis, 21 April 1901, folder 2, container 1, Ellis MSS, MCHC (emphasis in the original).

25. History of Advanced Base Training in the Marine Corps, 28 August 1931, General Board Study 432, Records of the General Board, RG 80, NARA.

26. George Barnett to the CMC, 11 November 1897, Entry 10, Letters Received, RG 127, NARA; and William F. Fullam to the SecNav, 1 May 1913, and CMC to the SecNav, 23 June 1913, General Board Study 432, RG 80, NARA.

27. *Boston Sunday Transcript,* 15 January 1882, Entry 46, Scrapbooks of Clippings (1880–1901, 1908–9), RG 127, NARA. See also "Promotion in the Marine Corps," *ANJ,* 24 October 1891, 148; and Shulimson, *The Marine Corps' Search,* 202–10.

CHAPTER 2. THE JUNIOR OFFICER, 1902–1911

1. CMC to Ellis, 1 March 1902, Press Copies of Letters Sent, Entry 5, Records of the Marine Corps, RG 127, NARA; see also "Our Marines in China," *ANJ,* 30 November 1901, 310. In Ellis's first fitness report as an officer, 11 January–2 March 1902, Colonel Pope marked him "good" in every category; Ellis's fitness report file, Records of Marine Corps Examining Boards, Entry 62, Records of the Judge-Advocate General of the Navy, RG 125, FRC.

2. Shulimson, "Daniel Pratt Mannix," 469–85; and Shulimson, *The Marine Corps' Search,* 102–3, 112–16, 122–26, 151–52, and 205–6.

3. Ellis to Tad, 20 March 1902, folder 3, container 1, Ellis MSS, MCHC; and *Annual Report of the Secretary of the Navy,* 1902 (Washington, D.C.: GPO, 1902), 967–75.

4. Brian Linn, "Marines in Philippines," unpublished essay; Dion Williams, "Thirty Years Ago," *Marine Corps Gazette* 13 (March 1928): 3–24 and (April 1928): 99–111; Braisted, *United States Navy in the Pacific,* 126, 144; "Marines to Cavité," *ANJ,* 18 March 1899, 673–74; and *Annual Report of the Secretary of the Navy,* 1902 (Washington, D.C.: GPO, 1902), 967–75.

5. Ellis to his mother, 24 August 1902, folder 8, container 1, Ellis MSS, MCHC; for other glimpses of Ellis's view of garrison life in the Philippines and his worldview, see Ellis to Tad, 18 April 1902, folder 4, container 1, Ellis to his sister, 18 August 1902, and Ellis to his mother, 20 August 1902, all in folder 8, container 1, Ellis MSS, MCHC.

6. "Social Life in Manila," *ANJ,* 21 March 1903, 716.

7. Ellis to his mother, 21 May and 29 June 1902, folder 6, container 1, Ellis MSS, MCHC (emphasis in the original). For additional vintage Ellis commentary on the Samar incident, see Ellis to his mother, 30 July 1902, folder 6, and Ellis to his father, 8 August 1902, folder 7, both in container 1, Ellis

MSS, MCHC. On Waller and Samar see Gates, *Schoolbooks and Krags,* 254–55. See also the commentary in *ANJ,* 23 November 1901, 239; 28 December 1901, 414; 25 January 1902, 625; and 22 May 1902, 727.

8. "Report of the Marine Corps," *ANJ,* 2 November 1902, 219; and "Brilliant Work of Marines," *ANJ,* 23 November 1902, 289.

9. Ellis to his mother, 3 June 1902, folder 6, container 1, Ellis MSS, MCHC.

10. Ellis's fitness reports for 16 March–30 June 1902; his report for 1 July–31 December 1902 was also marked "excellent"; Ellis's fitness report file, Entry 62, RG 125, FRC. See also Ellis to Tad, 18 April 1902, folder 4, container 1, Ellis MSS, MCHC. For a sample of Ellis's leisure activities, see Ellis to Katharine, 17 October 1902, and Ellis to his mother, 27 October 1902, folder 2, container 1, Ellis MSS, MCHC.

11. Ellis to his mother, 13 June, 6 and 15 July 1902, folder 6, and Ellis to Tad, 22 September 1902, folder 19, all in container 1, Ellis MSS, MCHC.

12. "Lament of a Marine," Timothy Buckley MS, U.S. Army Military History Institute, Carlisle Barracks, Pennsylvania, quoted in Millett, *Semper Fidelis,* 155.

13. *ANJ,* 21 March 1903, 716.

14. Ellis to Dorothy Ellis, 27 May 1902, folder 5, container 1, Ellis MSS, MCHC. See also Ellis to his father, 8 and 28 August 1902, folder 10, container 1, Ellis MSS, MCHC; and "Conditions in the Philippines," *ANJ,* 8 August 1903, 1238.

15. Ellis to Ralph Ellis, 20 September 1902, folder 10; Ellis to his mother, 3 June 1902, folder 6; and Ellis to his father, 28 October 1902, folder 2, all in container 1, Ellis MSS, MCHC.

16. Record of a board of examination, Cavite, 25 June 1904, Ellis file, Entry 62, RG 125, FRC.

17. Ellis to his mother, 19 and 27 January 1903, folder 11, and 7 February 1903, folder 12, container 1, Ellis MSS, MCHC; Ellis to the CMC, 21 January 1903, Letters Received, Entry 10, Records of the U.S. Marine Corps, RG 127, NARA; Log of the *Kentucky,* RG 24, NARA; Ellis to the CMC, 21 January 1903, Entry 5, Letters Received, RG 127, NARA; and Register of Officers' Sea Duty, Entry 72, RG 127, NARA. Ellis's fitness reports for 21 January–16 March 1903, 1 June–25 May 1903, 16 May–30 June 1903, and 1 July–31 December 1903 are in Entry 62, RG 125, FRC.

18. Ellis file, Entry 62, RG 125, FRC; see also the files on Hughes, McAllister, and Perkins in the same collection. McAllister committed suicide on 30 June 1906. After Hughes got into a fistfight with a second lieutenant in Panama

in 1912, Smedley D. Butler cabled in vain for his recall; see Butler to the CMC, 24 May 1912, in Hughes's fitness report file, Entry 62, RG 125, FRC.

19. Ellis to Tad, 22 September 1902, folder 19, container 1, Ellis MSS, MCHC; the account of the formal dinner in the mess may be found in Ellis to his mother, 2 May 1902, folder 4, container 1, in the same repository.

20. John A. Lejeune to the SecNav, n.d. [1935], reel 6, Lejeune MSS, MD-LC; Hilary A. Herbert to President Roosevelt, 2 June 1903, and Mark A. Hanna to President Roosevelt, 22 September 1903, vol. 7, p. 1202, and vol. 9, p. 1530, William H. Moody MSS, MD-LC. See also Cressman, "Maj. Gen. Elliott's 40 yr's Record," *New York Times,* 22 April 1928, part 3, p. 1.

21. Ellis to his mother, 9 March 1903, folder 13, container 1, Ellis MSS, MCHC.

22. Ellis to Ralph Ellis, 29 August 1902, folder 8, container 1, Ellis MSS, MCHC; Ellis's adventures and observations while serving in the *Kentucky* may be found in Ellis to his father, 21 April 1903, and to his mother, 1 and 26 April 1903, folders 12 and 13, container 1, Ellis MSS, MCHC.

23. Ellis to his father, 10 May 1903, folder 12, container 2, Ellis MSS, MCHC. See also Log of the *Kentucky,* RG 27, NARA; Ellis to Tad, 15 and 22 February 1903, and Ellis to his mother, 11 February, 9, 14, 21, and 26 March, 5 April, 1 May, and 7 and 17 June, all in folder 12, container 1, Ellis MSS, MCHC.

24. Entry 68, Press Copies of Military Histories of Service of Marine Corps Officers, 1904–11, and Entry 72, Register of Officers' Sea Duty, RG 127, NARA; see also George Barnett, "Soldier and Sailor Too," unpublished memoir, Barnett MSS, MCHC; Log of the *Kentucky,* RG 24, NARA; and George F. Elliott to the Adjutant and Inspector, 11 March 1904, Entry 16, Synopsis Cards for Correspondence, 1904–12, RG 127, NARA.

25. Ellis's fitness reports: 1–30 June and 1 July–2 October 1905; 2 May–30 June and 1 July–18 October 1907, Entry 62, RG 125, FRC. See also Ellis to the CMC, 25 May and 13 June 1904, Entry 16, Synopsis Cards for Letters Sent and Received, and Barnett to the CMC, 22 July 1903, Entry 10, Letters Received, both in RG 127, NARA.

26. "The Marine Corps," *ANJ,* 21 January 1905, 551; and "Fair Play for the Marines," *ANJ,* 25 May 1905, 807.

27. Ellis's fitness reports: 31 July–31 December 1906 and 1 January–19 April 1907, Entry 62, RG 125, FRC; see also Entry 68, Press Copies of Military Histories of Services of Marine Corps Officers, RG 127, NARA.

28. "Passage of Naval Appropriations Bill," *ANJ,* 16 May 1908, 1009; see also Barnett's file in Entry 68, RG 127, NARA. Barnett joined the admiral's staff on 29 July 1903 and was detached on 19 March 1904.

29. Ellis's fitness report, 11 February–30 June 1908, Entry 62, RG 125, FRC.

30. Theodore Roosevelt to the Joint Board, 20 October 1907, files 305 and 308, microfilm series 1421, Records of the Joint Army-Navy Board, RG 225, NARA.

31. Ellis's fitness reports: 1 July–30 September, 1 October–7 November, 12 November–4 December, and 5–31 December 1908, Entry 62, RG 125, FRC.

32. Report of a board of examination, Cavite, 21–22 October 1908, Entry 62, RG 125, FRC; see also CMC to Ellis, 8 December 1908, Entry 16, RG 127, NARA.

33. Ellis's fitness report file, Entry 62, RG 125, FRC; and Zimmerman, "The Marines' First Spy," 97.

34. Ellis's fitness reports: 1 March–30 June 1910 and 1 October 1910–12 January 1911, Entry 62, RG 125, FRC.

35. Ellis to the CMC, 22 March 1911, Entry 17, Letters and Endorsements Received, RG 127, NARA.

CHAPTER 3. INCREASING RESPONSIBILITIES, 1911–1916

1. Ellis to the CMC, 22 May 1911, copy in container 2, folder 5, Ellis MSS, MCHC; see also *Register of Commissioned and Warrant Officers of the Navy and of the Marine Corps* (Washington, D.C.: GPO, 1911), 188–91.

2. "Representative Hull Suggests Marines Be Put Under Jurisdiction of U.S. Army," *New York Times,* 23 November 1908, 5; William F. Fullam to [Edward L.] Beach, 21 November 1908, and William S. Sims to Fullam, 31 October 1908, container 3, Fullam MSS, MD-LC.

3. Shulimson and Cosmas, "Teddy Roosevelt," and John Miller, "Fullam's War." See also John A. Lejeune to Augustine Lejeune, 27 November and 10 December 1908, 2 March 1909, reel 1, Lejeune MSS, MD-LC, for a dismal view of career prospects should the transfer take effect.

4. John A. Lejeune to Augustine Lejeune, 28 July 1910, reel 1, Lejeune MSS, MD-LC.

5. Wiegand, "The Lauchheimer Controversy"; a copy of the investigative report is contained in Elliott's military record, and copies of the adminis-

trative punishments meted out to the other participants may be found in
their respective promotion files, Entry 62, Records of Marine Corps Examining Boards, RG 125, Records of the Judge Advocate General of the Navy,
FRC. See also *ANJ*, 11 June 1910, 1189, and 16 July 1910, 1379.

6. Linn, "William Phillips Biddle." See also John A. Lejeune to John H. Russell,
n.d. [1935], reel 6, Lejeune MSS, MD-LC; Wiegand, "Patrician in the Progressive Era," 110–15; and "The Marine Corps," *ANJ*, 1 October 1910, 171.

7. Ellis's fitness reports: 22–31 March and 1 April–27 May 1911, Entry 62,
RG 125, FRC.

8. Knight and Pulleston, "History of the Naval War College," 2–3; see also
Spector, *Professors of War.*

9. Ellis's fitness reports: 1 October 1912–31 March 1913 and 1 April–13
October 1913, Entry 62, RG 125, FRC. Ellis's seminar papers are in RG
8, Naval War College archives.

10. William C. Biddle to Ellis, 14 August 1911, Ellis file, Entry 62, RG 125,
FRC; see also Rodgers to Eli K. Cole, 23 September 1913, Ellis biographical file, MCHC.

11. "History of Advanced Base Training in the Marine Corps," General Board
Study 408, 1 May, 15 May, and 29 September 1913, RG 80, NARA; General Board Study 432, 28 August 1931, General Records of the Department of the Navy, RG 80, NARA. See especially SecNav to the CMC, 24
March 1910, in the same file, and George Barnett to the SecNav, file
1975.10, General Correspondence, Entry 18, Records of the U.S. Marine
Corps, RG 127, NARA; see also Biddle to Daniels, 10 April 1913, file 408-
1913, Records of the General Board, RG 80, NARA, and General Board
Study 408, recommendations concerning advanced-base outfits and their
location, 5 February 1913, RG 80, NARA.

12. General Board Study 408, studies dated 15 May and 29 September 1913,
Records of the General Board of the Navy, RG 80, NARA. See also
William F. Fullam to Daniels, 1 May 1913, file 408-1913, Records of the
General Board, RG 80, NARA; Biddle to Daniels, 17 May 1913, Entry 18,
General Correspondence, RG 127, NARA; Fullam to Daniels, 27 June
1913, container 3, Fullam MSS, MD-LC; and General Board Study 432,
drill of expeditionary force of Marines with advanced-base outfit in the
West Indies, 3 May 1913, file 10190-5, entry 17, RG 127, NARA.

13. William F. Fullam to the SecNav, 1 May and 29 September 1913, General
Board Study 408, RG 80, NARA.

14. General Board of the Navy to the SecNav, 8 March and 21 July 1913, General Board Study 432, RG 80, NARA.

15. George Dewey to William F. Fullam, 14 June 1909, and Fullam to Daniels, 23 June, 16 and 18 October 1913, container 3, Fullam MSS, MD-LC.

16. "Marine Corps Notes," *ANJ*, 15 November 1913, 337; a roster of the Advanced Base Force is located in container 7, Franklin D. Roosevelt MSS, Roosevelt Presidential Library, Hyde Park, New York. See also Biddle to Daniels, 16 September, 18 December 1913, 30 January, and 24 February 1914, Entry 18, RG 127, NARA.

17. "Marine Corps Advanced Brigade," *ANJ*, 13 December 1913, 472. Reports prepared by Lejeune and Ellis are in file 1975-80-20, Entry 18, RG 127, NARA.

18. File 1975-80-20, General Correspondence, Entry 18, RG 127, NARA.

19. William F. Fullam to the SecNav, 1 May 1913, General Board Study 432, RG 80, NARA.

20. Shulimson and Cosmas, "The Culebra Maneuver," 293–308; and Ellis's fitness report, 20 October 1913–3 January 1914, Entry 62, RG 125, FRC. See also "Marine Corps Advanced Brigade," *ANJ*, 13 December 1913, 472, and 7 February 1914, 724; William J. Sims to George Barnett, 23 January 1914, reel 3, Lejeune MSS, MD-LC; and Sims to Commander in Chief, Atlantic Fleet, 3 February 1914, folder 6, container 2, Barnett MSS, MCHC.

21. John A. Lejeune to John H. Russell, n.d. [1935], reel 6, Lejeune MSS, MD-LC; *Register of the Commissioned and Warrant Officers of the United States Navy and Marine Corps* (Washington, D.C.: GPO, 1913); Cronin, *Cabinet Diaries of Josephus Daniels*, 83; Josephus Daniels, *The Wilson Years: Years of Peace, 1910–1917* (Chapel Hill: University of North Carolina Press, 1944), 322–23; and Barnett, "Soldier and Sailor Too," chapter 23 in unpublished autobiography, Barnett MSS, MCHC. Cf. the fitness reports of the major contenders for the commandancy in 1913–14, which reveal that Barnett had the superior record; Entry 62, RG 125, FRC. See also the commentary in *ANJ* from November 1913 to February 1914.

22. Ellis's fitness report, 1 April–30 September 1914, Entry 62, RG 120, FRC.

23. Earl H. Ellis, "Report of a Military Reconnaissance of the Island of Guam, 1914–1915," *Guam Recorder* 3 (July–September 1973): 12–15; the original report, dated 25 September 1915, is in RG 38, NARA.

24. Excerpt from Ellis's medical record, Ellis's fitness report file, Entry 62, RG 125, FRC.

25. Ellis's fitness report, 1 April–29 September 1915, Entry 62, RG 120, FRC; and Ellis's medical record, copy in the Ellis biographical file, MCHC.

26. John A. Lejeune, "The Mobile Defense of the Advance Base," *Marine Corps Gazette* 1 (March 1916): 1–18; and John H. Russell, "A Plea for Mission and Doctrine," *Marine Corps Gazette* 1 (June 1916): 109–22.

27. Press release, 22 April 1914, George Barnett's officer qualification record, HQMC. See also William F. Biddle to the SecNav, 24 February 1914, file 1240-30; Victor Blue to [SecNav], [?] March 1914, file 1240-35; and Bradley A. Fiske to the SecNav, 5 March 1914, all in Entry 18, RG 127, NARA.

28. Shulimson, "First to Fight"; see also *Annual Report of the Secretary of the Navy, 1913* (Washington, D.C.: GPO, 1913), 527–28; *1914* (Washington, D.C.: GPO, 1914), 457–59; and *1915* (Washington, D.C.: GPO, 1915), 755–75.

29. Marine Corps Personnel Board to the SecNav, 3 February 1916, file 9236, Entry 18, RG 127, NARA.

30. George Barnett to Joseph H. Pendleton, 25 June 1916, folder 13, Pendleton MSS, MCHC.

31. Barnett's testimony before the House Naval Affairs Committee, 28–29 February 1916, U.S. Congress, House, Committee on Naval Affairs, *Hearings on Estimates by the Secretary of the Navy, 1916,* 64th Cong., 1st sess., 29 February 1916.

32. Smedley D. Butler to Mrs. Thomas S. Butler, 21 February 1916, Butler MSS, Newtown Square, Pennsylvania (privately held).

33. *ANJ,* 25 April 1914, 1079; see also Charles H. Lauchheimer to Joseph H. Pendleton, 4 February, 21 March, and 17 April 1916, folder 13, Pendleton MSS, MCHC.

34. George Barnett to Franklin D. Roosevelt, 9 May 1916, folder 7, Roosevelt MSS.

35. Ellis to his mother, 22 June 1916, file 6, container 2, Ellis MSS, MCHC.

36. Merrill L. Bartlett interview, Lelia Gordon Lucas, 7 June 1979, Huntly, Virginia. See also Lelia Montague Barnett, "Command Performances" and "Washington Dinner Disasters," unpublished memoirs, Barnett MSS, MCHC; and Bartlett, "Mrs. George Barnett," 8–9.

37. Ellis's medical record and fitness reports, 1 April–24 October 1916, 13 December 1915–31 March 1916, Entry 62, RG 125, FRC.

38. George Barnett to the Judge Advocate General of the Navy, 3 November 1916, Ellis file, Entry 62, RG 125, FRC.

CHAPTER 4. WORLD WAR I, 1917–1918

1. U.S. Congress, House, House Naval Affairs Committee, *Hearings on Estimates Submitted by the Secretary of the Navy, 1917,* 67th Cong., 1st sess., 1917; George Barnett to William S. Benson, 17 March 1917, container 3, Benson MSS, MD-LC; and General Board of the Navy to the SecNav, 26 June 1917, General Board Study 432, General Records of the Department of the Navy, RG 80, NARA. See also Shulimson, "First to Fight."
2. Josephus Daniels, *The Wilson Years: Years of War and After, 1917–1923* (Chapel Hill: University of North Carolina Press, 1947), 150; see also Barnett, "Soldier and Sailor Too," chapter 25, Barnett MSS, and Secretary of War to the SecNav, 16 May 1917, Table of Organization subject file, both in MCHC.
3. Smedley D. Butler to Thomas S. Butler, 16 May 1917, Butler MSS, Newtown Square, Pennsylvania. Apparently Lejeune, not Barnett, made the initial personnel assignments for the 5th Marines; see also Frederick W. Wise with Megs O. Frost, *A Marine Tells It to You* (New York: Sears, 1929), 157.
4. Ellis to his sister, n.d. [1918], folder 7, container 2, Ellis MSS, MCHC. See also George Barnett to Josephus Daniels, 2 March 1918, George Barnett file, container 64, Daniels MSS, MD-LC; and Surgeon J. D. Dennis to the CMC, 22 June 1917, file 6, container 2, Ellis MSS, MCHC.
5. Pershing to the Adjutant General, War Department, 31 August 1917, no. 133-S, and Adjutant General to Pershing, 17 September 1917, Records of the Commander in Chief, Entry 6, Records of the AEF, RG 120, NARA.
6. Smythe, *Pershing,* 54; Coffman, *War to End All Wars,* 141–42, 249–50; and Vandiver, *Blackjack,* 2:562, 838.
7. Oral history, Thomas Holcomb, MCHC; James G. Harbord, *Leaves from a War Diary* (New York: Dodd, Mead, 1925), 278; "Organization of the Marine Corps League," *New York Times,* 15 May 1923, 1; Harbord to Lejeune, 12 July 1918, reel 3, Lejeune MSS, MD-LC; and Harbord to Franklin D. Roosevelt, 14 November 1918, container 94, Daniels MSS, MD-LC.
8. Frederick C. Wheeler to Lejeune, 29 March 1919, reel 3, Lejeune MSS, MD-LC; and Gibbons, "Hottest Four Hours," 34–35, 143–48. See also William S. Sims to Wendell C. Neville, 6 August 1918, folder 4, Neville MSS, MCHC.

9. Pershing to the Secretary of War, 18 June 1918, AEF 1322-S, and Peyton
   C. March to Pershing, 1561-R, cablegrams sent and received, Entry 269,
   RG 120, NARA. See also John A. Lejeune, *Reminiscences of a Marine*
   (Philadelphia: Dorrance, 1930), 260; John J. Pershing, *My Experiences in
   the World War,* 2 vols. (New York: Stokes, 1931) 2:97, and diary entry, 17
   June 1918, Pershing MSS, MD-LC; and Palmer, *Newton D. Baker,* 1:148.
   For additional commentary on the issue of commonality, see H. I. Cone
   to William S. Benson, 26 June 1918, 25–27 June 1918 file, container 8,
   Benson MSS, MD-LC.
10. William S. Sims to William S. Benson, 10 July 1918, 7–12 July 1918 file,
    container 8, Benson MSS, MD-LC.
11. Diary entries, 4 and 9 June 1918, Pershing MSS, MD-LC; Lejeune to
    Daniels, 5 August 1918, and Daniels to Lejeune, 12 September 1918,
    Lejeune 1913–19 file, container 88, Daniels MSS, MD-LC; and Pershing
    to James C. McAndrew, 9 July 1918, Commander in Chief file, Entry 16,
    Memoranda from and to the Chief of Staff, RG 120, NARA. Ellis's orders
    are in AEF no. 180, 29 June 1918, directing him specifically to the 32nd
    Division as adjutant in whatever brigade Lejeune commands; folder 7, con-
    tainer 2, Ellis MSS, MCHC. Additional orders with regard to Lejeune and
    Ellis from AEF Headquarters are in special orders 169 and 180, copies in
    the Lejeune biographical file, MCHC.
12. Harbord, *Leaves from a War Diary,* 339; Harbord to Pershing, 25 October
    1918, container 87, Pershing MSS, MD-LC; diary entry, 4 September
    1918, Harbord MSS, MD-LC; diary entry, 26 and 27 July 1918, Pershing
    MSS, MD-LC; Newton D. Baker to Woodrow Wilson, 8 June 1918, in
    Arthur S. Link, ed., *The Papers of Woodrow Wilson* (Princeton: Princeton
    University Press, 1966), 48:265–68; and Peyton March, *The Nation at War*
    (New York: Doubleday, Dolan, 1932), 193–97.
13. Littleton W. T. Waller to William S. Benson, 26 March 1918, and John
    Gribbel to Benson, 10 April 1918, 17–20 April 1918 file, container 7,
    Benson MSS, MD-LC. Cf. Daniels to Lejeune, 12 September 1918,
    Lejeune 1913–19 folder, container 88, Daniels MSS, MD-LC, with
    Daniels to Lejeune, 5 March 1941, reel 9, Lejeune MSS, MD-LC.
14. Frederick G. Wheeler to Lejeune, 29 March 1919, reel 3, Lejeune MSS,
    MD-LC; and Richard Derby, *Wade in Sanitary* (New York: Putnam, 1919),
    98–99. See also Paul G. Malone to Harbord, 13 June 1919, Records of the
    Chief of Staff, Entry 15, RG 120, NARA; André Brewster to Pershing, 12

July 1918, file 712-1, Entry 588, General Correspondence, RG 120, NARA; and James G. Harbord, *The American Army in France* (Boston: Houghton Mifflin, 1936), 290–91.

15. Scrapbook clipping, container 5, Harbord MSS, MD-LC.

16. Hunter Liggett, *Commanding an American Army: Recollections of the World War* (Boston: Houghton Mifflin, 1925), 63–65; Liggett, *Ten Years Ago in France* (New York: Dodd, Mead, 1928), 134; Commanding General, 2nd Division, to Commanding General, I Corps, report of operations, 12–16 September 1918, in *Records of the Second Division (Regular)*, 6 vols. (Washington and Fort Sam Houston, Texas: Second Division Association, 1930–32), 6; and Summary of the St. Mihiel Offensive and Journal of Operations, 2nd Division, AEF, Entry 271, Journals of Operations, RG 120, NARA.

17. McClellan, "The St. Mihiel Salient."

18. Thomason, *Fix Bayonets and Other Stories*, 97.

19. Lejeune to Harbord, 29 June 1934, reel 6, Lejeune MSS, MD-LC.

20. Cf. Zimmerman, "The Marines' First Spy," 97, with Lejeune, *Reminiscences of a Marine*, 338–43.

21. Quoted in Shubert, "Critical Analysis," 58; see also "Blanc Mont," monograph no. 9 (Historical Branch, War Plans Division, Army General Staff, June 1921).

22. Quoted in Shubert, "Critical Analysis," 58; cf. Clark, *The Marine Brigade at Blanc Mont*, 32–33, with Thomason, "Marines at Blanc Mont." The 2nd Division surgeon recalled that not only did the French divisions fail to maintain pace on the flanks, but they often withdrew under enemy fire only to renew their assault; the result was a whipsaw effect on the battlefield; Derby, *Wade in Sanitary*, 134–35.

23. Shubert, "Critical Analysis," 56–58, 111–13.

24. Lejeune to Charles G. Long, 19 October 1918, reel 3, Lejeune MSS, MD-LC. See also 2nd Division, AEF, situation report, 15 September–9 October 1918, reel 11, Lejeune MSS, MD-LC; and John A. Lejeune, "Resumé of the Operations of the Second Division in Champagne, from October 2 to 9, 1918," *Marine Corps Gazette* 27 (September 1942): 17.

25. "The 2nd Division with the IV French Army in Champagne," file 1034, folder 1144, Entry 268, Secret General Correspondence, RG 120, NARA; the German perspective may be found in Otto, "The Battle at Blanc Mont," 95.

26. Brewster, "The Crossing of the Meuse River," 22–23, 51–53.

27. Harbord to Franklin D. Roosevelt, 14 November 1918, container 94, reel 59, Daniels MSS, MD-LC; see also McClellan, "A Brief History of the Fourth Brigade." The 2nd Division, AEF, suffered 5,150 killed and another 18,066 wounded, more casualties than either the veteran 1st or 3rd Divisions; *A Guide to American Battlefields in Europe* (Washington, D.C.: GPO, 1927), 268.

28. Pershing to the Adjutant General of the Army, 8 April 1919, Entry 6, General Correspondence of the Commander in Chief, AEF, RG 120, NARA; see also Franklin D. Roosevelt to Daniels, 13 August 1918, reel 59, Daniels MSS, MD-LC.

29. Earl H. Ellis, "Liaison in the World War," *Marine Corps Gazette* 5 (June 1920): 135–41.

CHAPTER 5. TRANSITION TO PEACETIME, 1919–1920

1. AEF general order no. 203, 12 November 1918; Harbord-Pershing correspondence, Harbord MSS, MD-LC.

2. Malin Craig to the Commanding General, III Corps, 22 November 1918, reel 3, Lejeune MSS, MD-LC; see also Derby, *Wade in Sanitary*, 189–92, for the most detailed account of the march to the Rhine.

3. Derby, *Wade in Sanitary*, 197; and Edwin M. McClellan, *The United States Marine Corps in the World War* (Washington, D.C.: Headquarters Marine Corps, 1920), 56–57.

4. Smedley D. Butler to Thomas S. Butler, 20 March 1919, Butler MSS, Newtown Square, Pennsylvania; see also Butler to his parents, 5 October 1918, in the same repository.

5. Assistant Secretary of the Navy to Ellis, 6 September 1919, file 28578-664, Correspondence to and from the SecNav, RG 80, NARA; and *Register of Commissioned Officers of the Navy and of the Marine Corps* (Washington, D.C.: GPO, 1921), 298.

6. CMC to Ellis, 15 August 1919, Ellis's officer qualification record, HQMC.

7. CMC to Ellis, 2 December 1919, Ellis's officer qualification record, HQMC.

8. Lejeune's version of the ouster is found in Lejeune to the CMC, n.d. [1935], reel 6, Lejeune MSS, MD-LC; cf. with Daniels, *The Wilson Years: Years of Peace*, 322–23, and *The Wilson Years: Years of War and After*, 155.

9. A handwritten copy of the letter of dismissal is in the Barnett 1920 file, container 64, Daniels MSS, MD-LC; a typed copy appears in the Denby MSS, Burton Collection, Detroit Public Library. The original typed order, dated 20 June 1920 and with Daniels's signature, is in Barnett's officer qualification record, HQMC.

10. Barnett, "Soldier and Sailor Too," chapter 30; Lelia Montague Barnett, "Command Performances" and "Washington Dinner Disasters," unpublished memoirs, all in Barnett MSS, MCHC.

11. Thomas S. Butler to Lejeune, 6 July 1920, reel 13, Lejeune MSS, MD-LC; cf. William S. Benson to Lejeune, 20 August 1920, reel 13, Lejeune MSS, MD-LC, with Benson to Barnett, 27 August 1920, container 15, Benson MSS, MD-LC.

12. Oral histories by Benis M. Frank, MCHC: Gen. Clifton B. Cates, 1967; Maj. Gen. Ray A. Robinson, 1968; and Maj. Gen. William A. Worton, 1967; and interview by Merrill L. Bartlett: Lelia Gordon Lucas, 1979.

13. George Barnett's death certificate, Barnett's officer qualification record, HQMC; and interviews by Merrill L. Bartlett in 1979: Brig. Gen. Lester A. Dessez, Lt. Col. R. Frederick Roy, and Vice Adm. Lloyd M. Mustin.

14. Logan Feland to the CMC, 25 October 1920. See also Fuller and Cosmas, *Marines in the Dominican Republic,* 31–40 passim; and Log of the *Kittary,* RG 24, NARA. The transport departed Charleston on 27 April 1920.

15. Ellis to the CMC, 9 April 1921, folder 10, container 2, Ellis MSS, MCHC; and Wendell C. Neville to Director, ONI, 2 September 1920, copy in folder 9, container 2, Ellis MSS, MCHC. See also CMC to the SecNav, and SecNav to the CMC, 4 May 1921, both copies in the Ellis biographical file, MCHC.

16. Lejeune to the CNO, 16 August 1920, file 11112-1644, General Records of the Department of the Navy, RG 80, NARA; and Conduit, Johnstone, and Nargile, *A Brief History of Headquarters Marine Corps,* 2–4.

17. Robert H. Williams, "Those Controversial Boards," 92. Secretary of the Navy Daniels involved himself directly in the reduction of the brigadier generals, insisting that rewards in the form of promotion go to "those who have been at the cannon's mouth." Josephus Daniels to Josephus Daniels, Jr., 1 August 1919, container 23, Daniels MSS, MD-LC.

18. William Veazie Pratt, unpublished memoir, chapter 17, Pratt MSS, Naval Historical Center; diary of Theodore Roosevelt, Jr., Theodore Roosevelt, Jr., MSS, MD-LC; and Robert E. Coontz, *From the Mississippi to the Sea* (Philadelphia: Dorrance, 1930), 414.

19. Quoted in Hagan, *This People's Navy,* 266; see also Clifford, *Progress and Purpose,* 25–26, for the Marine Corps's response to the treaties. For a sample of the Navy's view, see Potter, *Sea Power,* 233–34, 581; and Rosen, "The Treaty Navy."

20. Robert E. Coontz to the CMC, "Function of Marine Corps in War Plans," 28 January 1920 and 28 June 1920, file 221-2, SecNav/CNO Confidential Correspondence, RG 80, NARA; and Col. Ben H. Fuller to the CMC, 1 August 1923, "Advanced Bases," file 2515, Entry 18, General Correspondence, RG 127, NARA.

21. Lejeune, "Future Policy of the Marine Corps as Influenced by the Conference on Limitation of Armaments," 11 February 1922, Records of the General Board of the Navy, RG 80, NARA; see also Robert H. Dunlap, "Lessons for Marines from the Gallipoli Campaign," *Marine Corps Gazette* 6 (September 1921): 237–52.

22. *National Cyclopaedia of American Biography,* 24:172; Census, 1900, New York, vol. 154, sheet 17, R. D. 547, line 45; City Directories, Washington, D.C.: 1923, p. 1349, 1924, p. 1924, and 1925, p. 1256, Library of Congress; and fitness report file, Henry Sheldon Green, Entry 62, RG 125, FRC.

23. SecNav to Ellis, 19 February 1920, file 19585-2120, microfilm series M1052, RG 80, NARA.

24. Ellis, "Bush Brigades," *Marine Corps Gazette* 6 (March 1921): 1–15. The reference to Butler in Nicaragua is found in Schmidt, *Maverick Marine,* 54. Permission for the publication of Ellis's polemic is in SecNav to Ellis, 9 February 1920, file 19585-2120, RG 80, NARA.

25. Seligman, "The Conquest of Haiti"; see also Heinl and Heinl, *Written in Blood,* 465.

26. George Barnett to John H. Russell, 2 October 1919, container 2, Barnett MSS, MCHC; and Cronin, *Cabinet Diaries of Josephus Daniels,* 553–58. See also "Guard Is Gradually Being Withdrawn from Haiti," *New York Times,* 31 March 1923. Barnett's version may be found in container 3, Denby MSS, Burton Collection, Detroit Public Library, and in chapters 30–31 of "Soldier and Sailor Too," Barnett MSS, MCHC. The official report is in "Haiti and Dominican Republic Military Occupation and Administration by the U.S.," U.S. Congress, Senate, 66th Cong., 3rd sess., 1920, documents 204-0-A and 204-0-B.

27. SecNav to Ellis, 22 January 1921, file 19585-2098, microfilm series 1052, RG 80, NARA.

28. Advanced Base Operations in Micronesia, Operation Plan 712J (secret), approved on 23 July 1921. Copies of this study are in the Ellis biographical file, MCHC, and in the Research Center, Marine Corps University, Quantico.

29. Lt. Gen. Thomas Holcomb to Adm. Harold R. Stark, 7 June 1942, folder 10, Holcomb MSS, MCHC. The oral history of Gen. Lemuel C. Shepherd, Jr., one of Lejeune's aides-de-camp at the time, is silent on the subject; Benis M. Frank, oral history, 1967, MCHC.

CHAPTER 6. MISSION TO THE CENTRAL PACIFIC, 1921–1923

Note: Geographical and historical descriptions of the islands in the Central Pacific are taken from Wuerch and Ballendorf, *Historical Dictionary of Guam and Micronesia*, and Karolle, *Atlas of Micronesia*.

1. Ellis to the CMC, 9 April 1921, folder 10, container 2, Ellis MSS, MCHC; see also CMC to the SecNav, 4 May 1921, and SecNav to the CMC, 4 May 1921, in the same folder.

2. The Denby MSS, Burton Collection, Detroit Public Library, and the Theodore Roosevelt, Jr., MSS, MD-LC, contain no mention of Ellis or his mission. The diary of William Veazie Pratt, Naval Historical Center, Washington, D.C., is also silent on the subject. But given the classified nature of the undertaking, it hardly seems likely that any of the repositories would.

3. Wheeler, "Edwin H. Denby," 585–86. See also Wilds, "How Japan Fortified the Mandates," 401; and Burns, "Inspection of the Mandates," 445.

4. Ellis to the CMC, 19 April 1921, container 2, Ellis MSS, MCHC.

5. Ellis's medical record, Ellis file, reference, MCHC.

6. Ellis was promoted to temporary lieutenant colonel on 28 August 1918, but reverted to major on 20 August 1919 because of postwar retrenchment. He was later promoted to lieutenant colonel again, with a date of rank of 25 July 1921. The passing of the undated letter of resignation is revealed in Zimmerman, "The Marines' First Spy," 98–100. Lejeune acknowledges such a letter in Lejeune to Ralph Ellis, 14 November 1923, folder 16, container 3, Ellis MSS, MCHC; the oral history of one of Lejeune's aides-de-camp, Lemuel C. Shepherd, Jr., is silent on the subject, however.

7. R. C. Bannerman, Chief Special Agent, Department of State, to ONI, 23 May 1923, Entry 78A, RG 38, NARA; and Ralph Ellis to Lynn G. Turner, 14 September 1923, folder 15, container 3, Ellis MSS, MCHC. Turner was apparently a family confidant and the attorney who settled Ellis's estate.

8. Ballendorf interview, Gertrude Hornbostel, Singapore, 19 November 1969. See also the correspondence after Ellis's death between Director, ONI, and the Commandant of the 12th Naval District, and Ellis's memo report no. 7 (n.d.) in Entry 78A, RG 38, NARA; and Ellis to his mother, 18 June 1921, folder 10, container 2, Ellis MSS, MCHC.
9. Ellis to his mother, 24 June 1922, folder 9, container 3, Ellis MSS, MCHC.
10. Ellis to Robert H. Dunlap, 28 June 1922, Entry 78A, RG 38, NARA; and Ellis to John Ellis, 23 June 1923, folder 14, container 3, Ellis MSS, MCHC (emphasis in the original).
11. George Barnett to the CMC, 25 May 1923, Entry 18, General Correspondence, RG 127, Records of the U.S. Marine Corps, NARA. Ellis to Logan Feland, 19 June 1922, Entry 18, RG 127, NARA; copy in Ellis biographical file, MCHC. Cf. with Ellis to John Ellis, 28 April 1922, folder 8, container 3, Ellis MSS, MCHC.
12. Betty Allen Rogers to Ellis, 1 December 1921, 28 and 29 January 1922, 2 February 1922, and 15 March 1922, folders 4–7, container 3, Ellis MSS, MCHC; see also Betty Allen Rogers to John Ellis, 7 December 1921, folder 3, container 3, Ellis MSS, MCHC.
13. Betty Allen Rogers to John Ellis, 7 December 1921, folder 3, and Robert H. Dunlap to Earl H. Ellis, folder 7, both in container 3, Ellis MSS, MCHC.
14. Commander, Naval Station, Cavite, to the CMC, 19 June 1922 (Ellis to Feland), Ellis biographical file, MCHC; Ellis to John Ellis, 28 April 1922, folder 8, container 3, Ellis MSS, MCHC.
15. Ellis's medical report, 12 August 1922, Yokohama Naval Hospital, file 20996-3313, Entry 70A, RG 38, NARA; see also Capt. Lyman A. Cotten to Director, ONI, 26 December 1922, in the same file.
16. Ulysses S. Webb to the SecNav, 7 October 1922, Ellis biographical file, MCHC.
17. Director, ONI, to Naval Attaché, Tokyo, 26 December 1922, and Naval Attaché, Tokyo, to Director, ONI, 30 December 1922, file 20996-3313, entry 70A, RG 38, NARA.
18. Commandant, Twelfth Naval District, San Francisco, to Director, ONI, 20 November 1922 and 8 January 1923, file 20996-3313, Entry 70A, RG 38, NARA.
19. Ballendorf interview, Brother Gregorio, Colonia, Yap, 10 April 1968.
20. Ballendorf interview, Henry G. Fleming, Tinian, 8 August 1967.
21. Ballendorf interviews: Henry G. Fleming, Tinian, 8 August 1967; and Charles Gibbons, Koror, 24 May 1967.

22. Cf. Ballendorf interview, Victor Hermann, San Francisco, 3 August 1968, with Commandant, Twelfth Naval District, San Francisco, to ONI, 16 June 1923, file 20996-3313, Entry 70A, RG 38, NARA.

23. Jesse Hoppin to Tanaka Shoji, 24 July 1923, and Hoppin to Rev. James L. Barton, 24 July 1923, American Board of Commissioners for Foreign Missions Archives (hereafter ABCFM), Houghton Library, Cambridge, Mass.

24. Darley Downs, ed., *Newsbulletin* (Japan Mission of the American Board) 24 (February 1930): 6, ABCFM.

25. Jesse Hoppin to James L. Barton, ABCFM; copy in Ellis MSS (p. 27 in the index), MARC. When Ellis's sisters interviewed Mother Hoppin, they learned nothing from the circumspect missionary; when approached by a Marine Corps officer, she refused to be interviewed.

26. Ballendorf interview, Hilton Philip Millander, Majuro, 20 February 1968.

27. Ballendorf interview, Benjamin Lajipun, Majuro, 17 July 1967 and 19 February 1968.

28. Ballendorf interview, Felix Rechuuld, Koror, 8 May 1967.

29. Ballendorf interviews on Koror: Metauie, 10 May 1967; Felix Rechuuld, 8 May 1967; Antonio Ngirakelau, 22 June 1967; and Charles Gibbons, 24 May 1967.

30. Logan Feland to John Ellis, 11 May 1923, container 2, Ellis MSS, MCHC; Lejeune to Mrs. Ellis, 25 May 1923, Ellis biographical file, MCHC; and Ballendorf interview, Laurence F. Safford, Washington, D.C., 3 April 1971.

Chapter 7. Epilogue

1. John A. Lejeune, "Resumé of the Operations of the Second Division in Champagne, from October 2 to 9, 1918," *Marine Corps Gazette* 27 (September 1942): 17; and Lejeune to the CMC, 22 October 1940, Lejeune's officer qualification record, HQMC.

2. Smedley D. Butler to Lejeune, 26 January 1925, reel 3, Lejeune MSS, MD-LC.

3. Candidates for Commandant file, 1929, container 36, Hoover MSS, Hoover Presidential Library, West Branch, Iowa; Lejeune to the CMC, n.d. [1936], reel 6, Lejeune MSS, MD-LC; and Feland-Harbord and Lejeune-Harbord correspondence, 1929, Harbord MSS, New York Historical Society.

4. Candidates for Commandant file, 1930, container 36, Hoover MSS, Hoover Presidential Library, West Branch, Iowa; see also chapters 2 and 3 of John Richard Meridith Wilson, "Herbert Hoover and the Armed Forces: A Study of Presidential Attitudes and Policy" (Ph.D. diss., Northwestern University, 1971).

5. Bartlett, "Old Gimlet Eye"; Asprey, "The Court-Martial of Smedley Butler"; Schmidt, *Maverick Marine,* 202–13; and Donald F. Bitner, "Conflict under the Dome: Senator Hugo Black, General Smedley Butler, and the Challenged Appointment of John Russell as Commandant of the Marine Corps," a paper presented at the Annual Meeting of the American Historical Association, Chicago, 28 December 1984. For vintage Butler outrage see "To Hell with the Admirals! Why I Retired at Fifty," *Liberty,* 5 December 1931, 14–16, 18, and 22–23, and Butler to Franklin D. Roosevelt, 17 July 1933, file 18E, Franklin D. Roosevelt MSS, Roosevelt Presidential Library, Hyde Park, New York.

6. City Directories for Washington, D.C., 1922–29, Library of Congress; and *National Cyclopaedia of American Biography,* 24:172.

7. Katharine Dunlap, "Pete," n.d., Robert H. Dunlap MSS, MCHC.

8. Bartlett, "The Road to 'Eighth and Eye,'" 73–80.

CHAPTER 8. THE LEGACY OF PETE ELLIS

1. This thesis is articulated best in Shulimson, *The Marine Corps' Search.*

2. Cf. Zimmerman, "The Marine Corps' First Spy," with Clark, *The Marine Brigade at Blanc Mont.*

3. White Letter no. 1, 19 September 1922, Lejeune's biographical file, MCHC.

4. Director, ONI, to the Governor of Guam, 15 September 1917, file 21067-3, Records of the CNO, RG 38, NARA.

5. Burns, "Inspection of the Mandates."

6. Chief of Military Intelligence, Fort Shafter, Hawaii, "Interview with Mr. Hornbostel Relative to his Visit to the Marianne [*sic*] Islands," 22 October 1926, file K-5A, RG 38, NARA.

7. Lejeune to Ralph Ellis, 14 November 1923, folder 16, container 3, Ellis MSS, MCHC.

8. Luke McNamee to the Commandant, Twelfth Naval District, 28 November 1922, file 20996-3313, Entry 78A, RG 80, NARA.

184 ~ *Notes to Pages 159–62*

9. Director, ONI, to the CNO, 23 May 1923, file 20996-3313, Entry 78A, RG 80, NARA.

10. Clifford, *Progress and Purpose,* 31; see also "Records Relating to United States Fleet Problems I to XXII, 1923–1941," microfilm series M964, NARA.

11. Dion Williams, "The Fall Exercises of 1924"; and file 62A-2059, Entry 18, General Correspondence, Records of the U.S. Marine Corps, RG 127, FRC.

12. Dion Williams, "Blue Marine Corps Expeditionary Force"; see also "Records Relating to United States Fleet Problems I to XXII, 1923–1941," microfilm series M964, NARA.

13. *Joint Action of the Army and Navy* (Washington, D.C.: GPO, 1927), sections IV and VII.

14. Director, War Plans Division, General Board of the Navy, to the General Board, 10 August 1931, and CNO to the CMC, 20 April 1931, file KA-KV (secret), RG 80, NARA; General Board Study 432, 28 August 1931, RG 80, NARA; CMC to the CNO, 3 November 1932, SecNav/CNO secret files, RG 80, NARA; CMC to Director, Division of Operations and Training, HQMC, and Commandant, Marine Corps Schools, Quantico, and Director, War Plans Division, General Board of the Navy, 29 November 1932, SecNav confidential files, RG 80, NARA; and CNO to the SecNav with the comments of the CMC, 2 March 1933, and CMC to the SecNav, 11 April 1933, file 1240-30, Entry 18, General Correspondence, RG 127, NARA.

15. Ben H. Fuller to Commandant, Marine Corps Schools, Quantico, 28 October 1933, file 1520-30-120, Entry 18, RG 127, NARA. John Russell, Fuller's successor, lays claim to initiating this change; see Russell, "The Birth of the Fleet Marine Force."

∽ Bibliography

Primary Sources

At the Marine Corps Historical Center (MCHC) in the Washington Navy Yard, researchers interested in Earl H. "Pete" Ellis's life and times will find a plethora of interesting materials. Correspondence from Ellis to his family in Kansas is located in the personal papers collection. While gaps in the material exist, sufficient commentary is available for historians to grasp Ellis's worldview and professional acumen. Related correspondence may be found in the personal papers of George Barnett (which include materials from Leila Montague Barnett), John A. Lejeune, James G. Harbord, Thomas Holcomb, Joseph H. Pendleton, Smedley D. Butler, and Wendell C. Neville. In the reference section, the voluminous file kept on Ellis will keep any researcher gainfully occupied. While these materials present a scattershot approach, some documents offer exciting clues for further inquiry. Nearby, the materials in the Naval Historical Center may prove useful, and include the diary of William Veazie Pratt and biographical materials on the Navy officers who played a role in Ellis's ill-fated mission. Access to Ellis's official record is obtained through the reference section, MCHC.

Ellis's fitness reports may be found in Entry 62, Records of Marine Corps Examining Boards, RG 125, Records of the Judge Advocate-General of the Navy, National Archives and Records Administration, Federal Records Center, Suitland, Maryland. Similar files on Ellis's contemporaries are located in the same repository. While such reports were usually hagiographic and rarely contained critical commentary, Ellis's file reveals him to be a superior officer throughout his more than two decades in uniform. Significantly, no reporting senior demonstrated the professional fortitude to note his increasing dependence on alcohol. In downtown Washington, additional record groups of the National Archives contain information germane to any study of Ellis: RG 24 (Records of the Bureau of Personnel [ship logs]); RG 38 (Records of the Office of the Chief of Naval Operations); RG 45 (Naval Records Collection of the Office of Naval Records and Library); RG 120 (Records of the American Expeditionary Forces); RG 127 (Records of the U.S. Marine Corps); and RG 225 (Records of the Joint Army-Navy Board). In the Manuscript Division, Library of Congress, researchers might find the following personal papers useful: John A. Lejeune, Woodrow Wilson, Josephus Daniels, John G. Pershing, James G. Harbord, William F. Fullam, William S. Benson, and Theodore Roosevelt, Jr.

A number of volumes published by the Government Printing Office proved helpful to the authors: the annual reports of the Commandant of the Marine Corps, appearing as part of the annual reports of the Secretary of the Navy, provide a yearly summary of significant events; the registers of commissioned officers of the Navy and Marine Corps, also appearing annually, contain important items such as lineal precedence and dates of rank and assignment. Finally, the MCHC has sponsored the publication of useful registers of personal papers of value to researchers interested in the professional era of Earl H. Ellis: George Barnett, Thomas Holcomb, John A. Lejeune, and Joseph H. Pendleton.

Outside the Washington area, materials germane to Ellis's life and times may be found in the following repositories: James G. Harbord, in the New York Historical Society; Franklin D. Roosevelt, Roosevelt Presidential Library, Hyde Park, New York; Herbert Hoover, Hoover Presidential Library, West Branch, Iowa; Edwin Denby, Burton Collection, Detroit Public Library; Smedley D. Butler, Newtown, Pennsylvania (privately held); and the Marine Corps Research Center, Marine Corps University, Quantico, Virginia. The Micronesian Area Research Center at the University of Guam contains a voluminous collection of materials collected by the late John H. Reber and by Dirk Anthony Ballendorf. Included in this valuable repository are copies of correspondence to and from potential witnesses or participants to the Ellis saga, as well as transcripts of oral histories taken by Ballendorf. Correspondence from Jesse Hoppin, with references to Ellis's mission to Micronesia, is located in the American Board of Commissioners for Foreign Missions Archives, Houghton Library, Cambridge, Massachusetts. Archival materials on Ellis's contemporaries who graduated from the U.S. Naval Academy, held in conjunction with the National Archives, are retained in Annapolis. Testimonies by the various Commandants of the Marine Corps during the more than two decades of Ellis's service, as well as that of senior members of the staff before congressional naval affairs committees, serve to provide researchers with an understanding of the often tenuous role of the smaller of the naval services as it competed for both mission and appropriations on Capitol Hill.

Published memoirs helpful to an understanding of Ellis and his era include John A. Lejeune, *Reminiscences of a Marine* (Philadelphia: Dorrance, 1930); Josephus Daniels, *The Wilson Years: Years of Peace, 1910–1917* (Chapel Hill: University of North Carolina Press, 1944) and *The Wilson Years: Years of War and After* (Chapel Hill: University of North Carolina Press, 1947); Frederick W. Wise with Megs O. Frost, *A Marine Tells It to You* (New York: Sears, 1929); and Smedley D. Butler with Lowell Thomas, *Old Gimlet Eye: The Adventures of Smedley D. Butler* (New York: Farrar and Rinehart, 1933).

Memoirs peculiar to World War I that are useful in placing Ellis's role as adjutant of a brigade of infantry into prospective include John J. Pershing, *My Experiences in the World War,* 2 vols. (New York: Stokes, 1931); James G. Harbord, *Leaves from a War Diary* (New York: Dodd, Mead, 1925) and *The American Army in France* (Boston: Houghton Mifflin, 1936); Richard Derby, *Wade in Sanitary* (New York: Putnam, 1919); Hunter Liggett, *Commanding an American Army: Recollections of the World War* (Boston: Houghton Mifflin, 1925) and *Ten Years Ago in France* (New York: Dodd, Mead, 1928); and John W. Thomason, *Fix Bayonets and Other Stories* (New York: Scribner, 1925).

The service magazine of Ellis's era, the *Army-Navy Journal,* provides a handy and indispensable reference for semiofficial commentary on a variety of topics. Although ostensibly unofficial, this weekly often reflected official policy. Both the U.S. Naval Institute *Proceedings* and the *Marine Corps Gazette* offered an outlet for professional commentary and, at times, frustrations. The *New York Times* also contained useful materials germane to the history of the naval services.

All primary sources are cited fully at first mention in the endnotes; for the complete citation of secondary sources, interested readers must refer to the following compilation of materials.

SECONDARY SOURCES

Asprey, Robert. "The Court-Martial of Smedley Butler." *Marine Corps Gazette* 43 (December 1959): 28–33.

Ballendorf, Dirk Anthony. "Earl Hancock Ellis: A Final Assessment." *Marine Corps Gazette* 74 (November 1990): 78–87.

———. "The Micronesian Ellis Mystery." *Guam Recorder,* 2nd ser., 5, no. 1 (1975): 34–48.

———. "Secrets without Substance." *Journal of Pacific History* 19 (April 1984): 83–99.

Bartlett, Merrill L. "Annapolis Marines." U.S. Naval Institute *Proceedings* 118 (April 1992): 90–95.

———. "The Inside Track to Commandant." U.S. Naval Institute *Proceedings* 121 (January 1995): 58–63.

———. "Josephus Daniels and the Marine Corps, 1913–1921." In *New Interpretations in Naval History: Selected Papers from the Eighth Naval History Symposium,* edited by William B. Cogar, 190–208. Annapolis, Md.: Naval Institute Press, 1989.

———. "Leathernecks, Doughboys, and the Press." *Naval History* 7 (September–October 1993): 46–53.

———. *Lejeune: A Marine's Life, 1867–1942.* Columbia: University of South Carolina Press, 1991. Reprint. Annapolis, Md.: Naval Institute Press, 1996.

———. "Mrs. George Barnett: Mother of Marines." *Fortitudine* 9 (Winter 1979–80): 8–9.

———. "Old Gimlet Eye." U.S. Naval Institute *Proceedings* 117 (November 1986): 65–72.

———. "Ouster of a Commandant." U.S. Naval Institute *Proceedings* 106 (November 1980): 60–65.

Beede, Benjamin R., ed. *The War of 1898 and U.S. Interventions, 1898–1934.* Hamden, Conn.: Garland, 1995.

Braisted, William R. *The United States Navy in the Pacific, 1897–1907.* Austin: University of Texas Press, 1958.

Brewster, D. L. S. "The Crossing of the Meuse River by Second Division A.E.F. on 10–11 November 1918." *Marine Corps Gazette* 26 (March 1941): 22–23, 51–53.

Burns, Richard D. "Inspection of the Mandates, 1919–1941." *Pacific Historical Review* 37 (November 1968): 445–62.

Clark, George B. *The Marine Brigade at Blanc Mont.* Pike, N.H.: The Brass Hat, 1994.

Clifford, Kenneth J. *Progress and Purpose: A Developmental History of the Marine Corps, 1900–1920.* Washington, D.C.: GPO, 1973.

Coffman, Edward M. *The War to End All Wars: The American Military Experience in World War I.* New York: Oxford University Press, 1968.

Conduit, Kenneth W., John H. Johnstone, and Ella W. Nargile. *A Brief History of Headquarters Marine Corps.* Washington, D.C.: Headquarters Marine Corps, 1970.

Cronin, David, ed. *The Cabinet Diaries of Josephus Daniels, 1913–1921.* Lincoln: University of Nebraska Press, 1963.

Fuller, Stephen M., and Graham A. Cosmas. *Marines in the Dominican Republic, 1916–1924.* Washington, D.C.: GPO, 1974.

Gates, John Morgan. *Schoolbooks and Krags: The United States Army in the Philippines, 1898–1902.* Westport, Conn.: Greenwood, 1973.

Gibbons, Floyd. "The Hottest Four Hours I Ever Went Through." *American Magazine* 87 (March 1919): 34, 143–48.

Gray, Rufus. *Pioneers, Saints, and Sinners.* Pratt, Kans.: Rotary Club, 1968.

Hagan, Kenneth J. *This People's Navy: The Making of American Sea Power.* New York: Macmillan, 1991.

Harrod, Frederick S. *Manning the New Navy: The Development of a Modern Naval Enlisted Force, 1899–1940.* Westport, Conn.: Greenwood, 1978.

Heinl, Robert D., Jr. *Soldiers of the Sea: The United States Marine Corps, 1775–1962.* Annapolis, Md.: Naval Institute Press, 1962; rpt., Baltimore: Nautical and Aviation Publishing Company of America, 1991.

Heinl, Robert D., Jr., and Nancy Heinl. *Written in Blood.* Boston: Houghton Mifflin, 1978.

Hirama, Yoichi. "The Death of LCOL. Earl H. Ellis, U.S. Marine Corps—Why Was the Japanese Navy Suspected of Poisoning Him?" *Journal of the Pacific Society* 11 (July 1988): (27)–74.

Karolle, Bruce G. *Atlas of Micronesia.* 2nd ed. Honolulu: Beas, n.d.

Karsten, Peter. "Armed Progressives: The Military Reorganizes for the American Century." In *The American Military in America from the Colonial Era to the Present,* edited by Peter Karsten, 229–271. New York: Macmillan, 1980.

Knight, Austin M., and William D. Pulleston. "History of the United States Naval War College." N.p., 1916.

Linn, Brian McAllister. "William Phillips Biddle, 1911–1914." In *Commandants of the Marine Corps,* edited by Allan R. Millett. Annapolis, Md.: Naval Institute Press, forthcoming 1998.

McClellan, Edwin M. "The Battle of Mont Blanc Ridge." *Marine Corps Gazette* 7 (March 1922): 1–21.

———. "A Brief History of the Fourth Brigade." *Marine Corps Gazette* 4 (December 1919): 342–68.

———. "In the Marbache Sector." *Marine Corps Gazette* 6 (September 1921): 253–68.

———. "The St. Mihiel Salient." *Marine Corps Gazette* 6 (December 1921): 375–96.

———. *The United States Marines in the World War.* Rev. ed. Washington, D.C.: Headquarters Marine Corps, 1968.

Miller, Edward S. *War Plan Orange: The U.S. Strategy to Defeat Japan, 1897–1945.* Annapolis, Md.: Naval Institute Press, 1991.

Miller, John G. "William Freeland Fullam's War with the Corps." U.S. Naval Institute *Proceedings* 105 (November 1975): 38–45.

Millett, Allan R. *The General: Robert L. Bullard; and Officership in the United States Army, 1881–1925.* Westport, Conn.: Greenwood, 1975.

———. *In Many a Strife: General Gerald C. Thomas and the U.S. Marine Corps, 1917–1956.* Annapolis, Md.: Naval Institute Press, 1993.

———. *Semper Fidelis: The History of the United States Marine Corps.* New York: Macmillan, 1980.

Montross, Lynn. "The Mystery of Pete Ellis." *Marine Corps Gazette* 38 (July 1954): 30–33.

Moskin, Robert J. *The U.S. Marine Corps Story.* New York: McGraw-Hill, 1977.

Nalty, Bernard C. *A Brief History of U.S. Marine Corps Officer Procurement.* Washington, D.C.: Headquarters Marine Corps, 1970.

Otto, Ernst. "The Battle at Blanc Mont." U.S. Naval Institute *Proceedings* 56 (January 1930): 1–27; (February 1930): 89–112; (March 1930): 177–99; and (April 1930): 304–16.

Palmer, Frederick. *Newton D. Baker: America at War.* 2 vols. New York: Dodd, Mead, 1931.

Pierce, P. "The Unsolved Mystery of Pete Ellis." *Marine Corps Gazette* 56 (February 1962): 35–40.

Pomerly, Earl S. *American Strategy in Guam and Micronesia.* Stanford: Stanford University Press, 1951.

Potter, E. B. *Sea Power: A Naval History.* 2nd ed. Annapolis, Md.: Naval Institute Press, 1981.

Reber, John J. "Pete Ellis: Amphibious Warfare Prophet." U.S. Naval Institute *Proceedings* 103 (November 1977): 53–64.

Register of Alumni. Annapolis, Md.: Naval Academy Alumni Association, 1982.

Rosen, Philip T. "The Treaty Navy, 1919–1937." In *In Peace and War: Interpretations of American Naval History, 1775–1978,* edited by Kenneth J. Hagan, 221–36. Westport, Conn.: Greenwood, 1978.

Russell, John. "The Birth of the Fleet Marine Force." U.S. Naval Institute *Proceedings* 72 (October 1936): 49–51.

Schmidt, Hans. *Maverick Marine: General Smedley D. Butler and the Contradictions of American Military History.* Lexington: University Press of Kentucky, 1987.

Seligman, Herbert J. "The Conquest of Haiti." *Nation,* 10 July 1920, 35–36.

Shubert, R. H. "A Critical Analysis of Flank Protection, Second Division (AEF, France) 3 October to 9 October 1918." *Marine Corps Gazette* 26 (November 1941): 56–58, 111–13.

Shulimson, Jack. "Daniel Pratt Mannix and the Establishment of the Marine Corps School of Application, 1889–1994." *Journal of Military History* 55 (October 1991): 469–85.

———. "First to Fight: Marine Corps Expansion, 1914–1919." *Prologue* 8 (Spring 1976): 5–16.

———. *The Marine Corps' Search for a Mission: 1880–1898.* Manhattan: University Press of Kansas, 1993.

———. "The Transitional Commandancy: Colonel Charles G. McCawley and Uneven Reform." *Marine Corps Gazette* 72 (October 1988): 70–77.

Shulimson, Jack, and Graham A. Cosmas. "The Culebra Maneuver and the Formation of the U.S. Marine Corps' Advance Base Force." In *Changing Interpretations and New Sources in Naval History,* edited by Robert W. Love, Jr., 293–308. New York: Garland, 1980.

———. "Teddy Roosevelt and the Corps' Sea-Going Mission." *Marine Corps Gazette* 65 (November 1981): 54–61.

Smythe, Donald. *Pershing: General of the Armies.* Bloomington: University of Indiana Press, 1986.

Spector, Ronald. *Professors of War: The Naval War College and the Development of the Naval Profession.* Newport, R.I.: Naval War College Press, 1977.

Thomason, John W. *Fix Bayonets and Other Stories.* New York: Scribner, 1925; rpt., Quantico, Va.: Marine Corps Association, 1973.

———. "Marines at Blanc Mont." *Scribner's,* September 1925, 227–31.

Valle, James E. *Rocks and Shoals: Order and Discipline in the Old Navy.* Annapolis, Md.: Naval Institute Press, 1980.

Vandiver, Frank. *Blackjack: The Life and Times of John J. Pershing.* 2 vols. College Station: University of Texas A&M Press, 1977.

Venzon, Anne Cipriano, ed. *General Smedley Darlington Butler: The Letters of a Leatherneck, 1898–1931.* New York: Praeger, 1992.

———. *The United States in the First World War.* Hamden, Conn.: Garland, 1995.

Wheeler, Gerald E. "Edwin H. Denby." In *American Secretaries of the Navy,* 2 vols., edited by Paolo E. Coletta, 2:585–586. Annapolis, Md.: Naval Institute Press, 1980.

Wiegand, Wayne A. "The Lauchheimer Controversy: A Case of Group Political Pressure during the Taft Administration." *Military Affairs* 40 (April 1976): 54–59.

———. "Patrician in the Progressive Era: A Biography of George von Lengerke Meyer." Ph.D. dissertation, Southern Illinois University, 1975.

Wilds, Thomas. "How Japan Fortified the Mandates." U.S. Naval Institute *Proceedings* 81 (April 1955): 401.

Williams, Dion. "Blue Marine Corps Expeditionary Force." *Marine Corps Gazette* 10 (September 1925): 76–88.

———. "The Fall Exercises of 1924." *Marine Corps Gazette* 10 (June 1925): 30–35.

Williams, Robert H. "Those Controversial Boards." *Marine Corps Gazette* 66 (November 1982): 91–96.

Wuerch, William L., and Dirk Anthony Ballendorf. *Historical Dictionary of Guam and Micronesia.* Metuchen, N.J.: Scarecrow, 1994.

Zimmerman, John L. "The Marines' First Spy." *Saturday Evening Post,* 23 November 1946, 19, 97–98, 100.

～ Index

Adams, Charles Francis, 145
Advanced Base Force: genesis of,
    54–55; criticism of by William F.
    Fullam, 56–57; first exercise at
    Culebra, 58–59
"Advanced Base Operations in
    Micronesia," 119–22
Apra Harbor, Guam, 64
Arizona, USS, 59
Army-Navy Club, Manila, 32
Axline, Andrew (paternal grandfather),
    14–15

Baker, Newton D., 75
Barnett, George: reports conversation
    with Victor Hermann, 7; criticizes
    role and mission of Marine Corps,
    25; and School of Application, 29;
    as fleet Marine officer, Asiatic Fleet,
    with Ellis, 42; as candidate for com-
    mandant, 52; commands barracks
    in Philadelphia, 55, 57; and
    Culebra maneuvers, 58–59; selected

as commandant, 60–61; selects
    Ellis as an aide-de-camp, 65; and
    Council of Aides, 67; and personnel
    shortages, 68; Congressional testi-
    mony of, 69–70; and promotion
    of colonels to brigadier generals,
    70; and expansion of Marine Corps,
    74; and employment of a division
    in France, 81–82; and promotion of
    Lejeune to major general, 84; orders
    Ellis to Galveston and Mexico,
    101–2; ousted as commandant,
    103–7
Barnett, Lelia Montague: prominence
    of in Washington society, 71; fury
    of over her husband's ouster,
    104–5; refuses to join husband in
    "exile," 106
Bearss, Hiram I.: commands 2d
    Regiment at Olongapo, 43–44
Belleau Wood: battle of, 80; journalism
    on, 81; Marine Corps animosity
    with the Army over, 82

March, Peyton C., 82

Marine Corps Gazette, 66

"Marinettes," 109

Matsuyama Maru: Ellis takes from Saipan to the Carolines and Marshalls, 132

Maxwell, William J.: heads special study group to Guam, 61; erratic behavior of, 61–62; Ellis earns wrath of, 62; prepares fitness reports on Ellis, 64–65, 72–73

McAlister, Arthur: commissioned with Ellis, 25; reports to Marine Barracks, Boston, with Ellis, 28; receives poor fitness report in Philippines, 39

McCawley, Charles G.: reform efforts of as commandant, 18–19; and improvements in officer procurement, 21; and poor quality of enlistees, 24; and School of Application, 29

McNamee, Luke: and news of Ellis's death 3; and ONI involvement in Ellis mission, 129

mess nights, 39

Metauie (Ellis's Palauan wife), 140, 147

Meyer, George von Lengerke: and the Lauchheimer controversy, 51

Millander, Hilton Phillip, 139

Millander, Johann V., 139

Miller, Edward S.: author of study of War Plan Orange, 9

Millett, Allan R., 9

Moses, Franklin J., 35

Moskin, Robert J., 9

Murray, Charles I.: witnesses formal relief of Barnett, 105

Naulin, André: commands French XXIX Corps at Blanc Mont, 88

Naval Academy, U.S.: and Marine Corps accessions, 22

Nelson, Claude, 137

Nelson, Myra Heine, 137

Neville, Wendell C., 107; complains of

berthing in the transport *Prairie,* 59; commands 4th Brigade (Marine), AEF, 89; lauds Ellis's performance as adjutant, 4th Brigade (Marine), AEF, 95; as assistant to the commandant, 109; chairs "plucking board" to reduce officer strength, 110; involvement in Ellis's prophet study questioned, 122; admires Ellis, 123; in Ellis's chain of command, 129; acknowledges receipt of cablegram from the U.S. naval attaché in Tokyo, 131; succeeds Lejeune as commandant, 145

Ngerdoko (wife of William Gibbons of Koror), 147

Ngiraklau, Antonio: purchases liquor for Ellis in Palau, 140

Noa, Walter A.: commissioned with Ellis, 25; assigned to Marine Barracks, Boston, 28

Orote Peninsula, Guam: Ellis proposes as site for Advanced Base Force, 64

Parker, William H.: relieves Ellis on *Kentucky,* 41

Pendleton, Joseph H.: commands 2d Regiment at Olongapo, 46; Barnett informs of possible promotions to brigadier general, 68; supports Barnett, 105

Penrose, Boies, 52

Perkins, Con Marrast, 39

Pershing, John J.: punitive expedition to Mexico, 70; and initial contingent to France in 1917, 75; employs Marines in rear-echelon duties, 78; moves to end deployment of Marines to France, 78; on physical condition of senior officers, 79; Lejeune and Ellis dine with at Chaumont, 81; worries over potential combat losses for Marine Corps, 82; learns that the Department of

～ About the Authors

Dirk Anthony Ballendorf teaches history and Micronesian studies at the University of Guam's Micronesian Area Research Center, and has been resident in the islands for over thirty years. He was educated at Pennsylvania State College at West Chester, Howard University, and Harvard. Dr. Ballendorf is married to Francesca Remengesau of Palau; they have four children between them.

Merrill Lewis Bartlett is a retired Marine Corps lieutenant colonel. In 1977–1982 he taught history at the U.S. Naval Academy, Annapolis, where he received the William P. Clements Award as the outstanding military educator (1979–1980). The editor, and author, of several books, he has twice won the Robert D. Heinl, Jr. Award for the outstanding essay on Marine Corps history (1980, 1987). He lives and writes on Vashon Island, Washington.

The **Naval Institute Press** is the book-publishing arm of the U.S. Naval Institute, a private, nonprofit, membership society for sea service professionals and others who share an interest in naval and maritime affairs. Established in 1873 at the U.S. Naval Academy in Annapolis, Maryland, where its offices remain today, the Naval Institute has members worldwide.

Members of the Naval Institute support the education programs of the society and receive the influential monthly magazine *Proceedings* and discounts on fine nautical prints and on ship and aircraft photos. They also have access to the transcripts of the Institute's Oral History Program and get discounted admission to any of the Institute sponsored seminars offered around the country.

The Naval Institute also publishes *Naval History* magazine. This colorful bimonthly is filled with entertaining and thought-provoking articles, first-person reminiscences, and dramatic art and photography. Members receive a discount on *Naval History* subscriptions.

The Naval Institute's book-publishing program, begun in 1898 with basic guides to naval practices, has broadened its scope in recent years to include books of more general interest. Now the Naval Institute Press publishes about 100 titles each year, ranging from how-to books on boating and navigation to battle histories, biographies, ship and aircraft guides, and novels. Institute members receive discounts of 20 to 50 percent on the Press's nearly 600 books in print.

Full-time students are eligible for special half-price membership rates. Life memberships are also available.

For a free catalog describing Naval Institute Press books currently available, and for further information about subscribing to *Naval History* magazine or about joining the U.S. Naval Institute, please write to:

Membership Department
U.S. Naval Institute
118 Maryland Avenue
Annapolis, MD 21402-5035
Telephone: (800) 233-8764
Fax: (410) 269-7940
Web address: www.usni.org